QUEER ART CAMP SUPERSTAR

THE SUNY SERIES

HORIZONS OF CINEMA

MURRAY POMERANCE | EDITOR

Also in the series

William Rothman, editor, *Cavell on Film*
J. David Slocum, editor, *Rebel Without a Cause*
Joe McElhaney, *The Death of Classical Cinema*
Kirsten Moana Thompson, *Apocalyptic Dread*
Frances Gateward, editor, *Seoul Searching*
Michael Atkinson, editor, *Exile Cinema*
Paul S. Moore, *Now Playing*
Robin L. Murray and Joseph K. Heumann, *Ecology and Popular Film*
William Rothman, editor, *Three Documentary Filmmakers*
Sean Griffin, editor, *Hetero*
Jean-Michel Frodon, editor, *Cinema and the Shoah*
Carolyn Jess-Cooke and Constantine Verevis, editors, *Second Takes*
Matthew Solomon, editor, *Fantastic Voyages of the Cinematic Imagination*
R. Barton Palmer and David Boyd, editors, *Hitchcock at the Source*
William Rothman, *Hitchcock: The Murderous Gaze, Second Edition*
Joanna Hearne, *Native Recognition*
Marc Raymond, *Hollywood's New Yorker*
Steven Rybin and Will Scheibel, editors, *Lonely Places, Dangerous Ground*
Claire Perkins and Constantine Verevis, editors, *B Is for Bad Cinema*
Dominic Lennard, *Bad Seeds and Holy Terrors*
Rosie Thomas, *Bombay before Bollywood*
Scott M. MacDonald, *Binghamton Babylon*
Sudhir Mahadevan, *A Very Old Machine*
David Greven, *Ghost Faces*
James S. Williams, *Encounters with Godard*
William H. Epstein and R. Barton Palmer, editors, *Invented Lives, Imagined Communities*
Lee Carruthers, *Doing Time*
Rebecca Meyers, William Rothman, and Charles Warren, editors, *Looking with Robert Gardner*
Belinda Smaill, *Regarding Life*
Douglas McFarland and Wesley King, editors, *John Huston as Adaptor*
R. Barton Palmer, Homer B. Pettey, and Steven M. Sanders, editors, *Hitchcock's Moral Gaze*
Neenad Jovanovic, *Brechtian Cinemas*
Will Scheibel, *American Stranger*
Amy Rust, *Passionate Detachments*
Steven Rybin, *Gestures of Love*
Seth Friedman, *Are You Watching Closely?*
Roger Rawlings, *Ripping England!*
Michael DeAngelis, *Rx Hollywood*

QUEER ART CAMP SUPERSTAR

Decoding the CINEMATIC CYBERWORLD of Ryan Trecartin

RICARDO E. ZULUETA

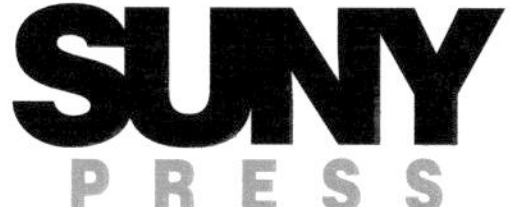

Cover art design: Kirk Warren Studio

Published by State University of New York Press, Albany

Printed in the United States of America

For information, contact State University of New York Press
Albany, NY
www.sunypress.edu

Library of Congress Cataloging-in-Publication Data

Names: Zulueta, Ricardo Estanislao, author.
Title: Queer art camp superstar : decoding the cinematic cyberworld of Ryan Trecartin / Ricardo E. Zulueta.
Description: Albany, NY : State University of New York Press, 2018. | Series: SUNY series, Horizons of cinema | Includes bibliographical references and index.
Identifiers: LCCN 2017018230 (print) | LCCN 2017019162 (ebook) | ISBN 9781438468952 (e-book) | ISBN 9781438468938 (hardcover : alk. paper) | ISBN 9781438468945 (paperback : alk. paper)
Subjects: LCSH: Trecartin, Ryan, 1981-—Criticism and interpretation. | Video art—United States—History and criticism.
Classification: LCC N6537.T665 (ebook) | LCC N6537.T665 Z85 2018 (print) | DDC 777.0973—dc23
LC record available at https://lccn.loc.gov/2017018230

10 9 8 7 6 5 4 3 2 1

Contents

Illustrations

Acknowledgments

I AM GRATEFUL TO William Rothman for his friendship, insightful comments on drafts of this manuscript, and continued unwavering support of my work. I also wish to thank Murray Pomerance, the Horizons of Cinema series editor, for his enthusiasm for the project. Much gratitude goes to James Peltz, Rafael Chaiken, Beth Bouloukos, Jenn Bennett, and Michael Campochiaro at SUNY Press for their diligent attention and assistance in navigating the publication process. Additionally, the quality of this book was undoubtedly improved with the careful reading and productive comments of the anonymous peer reviewers.

I extend my sincere appreciation to Damian Young, Tom Roach, and Michael McGandy for their willingness to engage in conversation concerning this book project. Gratitude is also due to Walter Van Beirendonck, Nick Cave, Dan and Corina Lecca, and Bernhard Willhelm. I would like to acknowledge members of my doctoral dissertation committee, Grace Barnes, Steve Butterman, Christina Lane, and William Rothman, as well as former University of Miami faculty, John Renaud and the late Paula Harper for their invaluable advice. Thanks also go to my students at the University of Miami who inspired and challenged me with dynamic discussions regarding art, film and media, and technology.

I owe much gratitude to my mother, Guillermina Riaño, whose unconditional love and encouragement has sustained me in achieving many of my aspirations. Finally, I could not have completed this book without the love and support of my spouse, Jonathan Choukroun, to whom this book is dedicated.

Introduction

I WAS INTRODUCED TO Ryan Trecartin's videos on YouTube in 2008 and later experienced his work offline while attending his first major solo museum exhibition, *Any Ever*, at the Museum of Contemporary Art, North Miami in 2011 (simultaneously exhibited at MoMA PS1). I recall meandering from one immersive cinematic installation to another, attempting to absorb the expulsion of color and special effects gushing out of multiple huge screens that comprised the exhibition. Watching Trecartin's videos was something of an endurance exercise, as each shot succinctly unfolded at a vertiginous speed reminiscent of viral pop-ups ejected onto computer screens. While lying on a queen-size bed facing an overwhelming projection of genderqueer characters prancing around Miami's Design District, I realized that this work's impact did not merely reside in its apparent shock value but in its intrinsic ability to materialize the anxiety and excitement of a timely cultural revolution.

According to Peter Schjeldahl, head art critic for the *New Yorker*, Ryan Trecartin is "the most consequential artist to have emerged since the nineteen-eighties,"[1] while Roberta Smith from the *New York Times* declared the artist to be an "immense" talent who was "bound for greatness" and whose work was "game-changing."[2] She goes on to make the claim that Trecartin "shreds the false dichotomies and mutually demonizing oppositions that have plagued the art world for decades—between the political and the aesthetic, the conceptual and the formal, high and low, art and entertainment, outsider and insider, irony and sincerity, gay and straight."[3] What is at the heart of Trecartin's worldview, Smith concludes, is "an aspirational faith in the potential of uninhibited self-expression, both individual and collective, as an active agent against the mounting materialism of everyday life [. . .] What he has unleashed is larger than himself, which is why both his sudden appearance and continuing evolution are such cause for hope."[4]

Ryan Trecartin has produced a substantial body of work that spans from his early, pre-YouTube era video series *Early Baggage* (2001–03) to *Temple Time* (2016). Despite the recognition Trecartin has continued to receive among art critics, however, there exists to date no comprehensive study of this prolific artist's work. Typically, the articles and blogs that celebrate his videos—he prefers to call them "movies"—have been written by critics, mostly untrained in cinematic analysis, who forgo close readings of his dense narratives, and with few exceptions, limit themselves to brief summaries. Regrettably, the field of film studies itself has all but completely ignored these significant and timely works, even though, as the chapters that follow demonstrate, they are profoundly relevant to many of the field's concerns. The lack of close examination of Trecartin's movies is no doubt due, at least in part, to the sheer difficulty of rigorously describing and interpreting these challenging, complex, multifaceted artworks. They unfold so quickly that almost every shot lasts a brief fraction of a second and are rife with semiotic instability. However, for all their obscurities, ambiguities, and ironies, these cinematic narratives are nonetheless intelligible and can be read.

Queer Art Camp Superstar: Decoding the Cinematic Cyberworld of Ryan Trecartin compensates for this absence of critical analyses of this timely work by looking closely at a selection of his most significant movies in order to discern their essential qualities while foregrounding their cultural currency. It constitutes the first book-length study of Trecartin's artistic genealogy, evolving aesthetics, radical approach to digital and internet culture, and impact on contemporary art, film, and media. Precisely chosen screen captures extracted directly from the videos demonstrate the serious attention paid to camera angles, mise-en-scène and shot transitions, thus revealing and reflecting on the concepts that underwrite and are underwritten in these narratives.

The artist's complex codes, motifs, and symbols cannot be described or contained within singular categories, as each individual video is packed with numerous interconnected concepts. Trecartin's network of layered references to the grotesque and abject, carnivalesque and ludic, and camp imagery is given careful attention in order to illustrate and explain how the artist takes on reality television, technology, fashion, consumption, and cyberspace. The chapters that follow adhere to a faithful chronological order, thereby inviting readers to witness the ways thematic and formal concerns have evolved from Trecartin's earliest movies to his most recent multimedia cinematic installations.

Ryan Trecartin was born in Webster, Texas, in 1981, the beginning of a decade that has proved to be an important historical juncture. The growth of the art market reflected the period's heightened consumerism when the commercialization of art was fueled by the proliferation of Wall Street's nouveaux riches and the implementation of aggressive marketing strategies by auction houses such as Sotheby's and Christie's. In this thriving market, many artists became overnight celebrities whose paintings and sculptures fetched millions of dollars. In addition, a surge in political activism through public art and performances, particularly within the LGBTQ community, erupted as a response to the AIDS crisis. The mid- to late 1980s also marked the advent of personal computers and digital video cameras, the widespread use of compact disc players, and the development of hypertext-writing systems.

The assimilation of digital technology has since transformed the long-established practices of painting, sculpture, and drawing, while also generating new categories, including internet and new media art. From the beginning of the new millennium, new media art has received increasingly productive critical attention and found its position within the art market. This increased interest is also apparent in the proliferation of organizations such as Rhizome, Eyebeam, Electronic Arts Intermix, and more recently New, Inc. founded to exhibit, curate, and/or commission new media projects. In addition, the Museum of Modern Art in New York City, for example, has established the Digital Art Vault collection to collect and preserve digital and electronic art.

Trecartin belongs to the first generation of artists introduced to computers at an early age. He began to create work at the beginning of the new millennium that acutely reflects the ways we interface, communicate, and relate to others. This is significant as Trecartin's critical and commercial acclaim is due in large part to his art's ability to further our understanding of new technology and its ramifications on our virtually mediated existence. In his essay "The Post-Reality Show," Jeffrey Deitch asks the question, "Could Ryan Trecartin be the first twenty-first century artist?,"[5] and follows by declaring, "He is one of the first artists whose work looks and feels like life today."[6] But how does it feel to live in today's world? And, what is a twenty-first century artist? As a member of the Millennial Generation, he has been immersed in digital culture from an early age, and its deep impact is inseparable from the formation of his art. This in turn has played a crucial role in the development of his distinctive visual and verbal language that resonates not only with his own generation, but also with a broad cross-section of intergenerational hyperconnected cultural consumers who possess computers, smartphones, iPads, and iPods.

Individuals, regardless of their age, race, gender, and sexuality, rely on technological devices every day and have developed (sub)cultures around this digital sphere. In cyberspace, web surfers can create virtual communities and engage in multiplayer games allowing them to play out extraordinary scenarios in imaginary worlds and build polygonal avatars of varying physical appearance. The propagation of social networks such as Facebook, Twitter, Snapchat, and Instagram, has redefined human interaction. Thus, Web 2.0 provides both a space and an opportunity to perform in front of a global audience.

As a result of this phenomenon, contemporary art has expanded beyond early examples of internet-based projects. Constant technological innovations, globalization, and the impact of the omnipresence of the net, have not only shaped the content of art but also changed the way it is exhibited. Art is no longer exclusively experienced at museums, galleries, and art fairs, but also on mobile devices, for example. Contemporary artists do not have to wait to be "picked up" by a gallery or featured in a museum show to achieve visibility; they can simply post their work directly online in the hope of gaining mass exposure. In fact, Ryan Trecartin became an internet sensation before finding major gallery representation.[7]

While he is obviously not opposed to the commercial sale of his art (as is evidenced by a history of gallery representation including Elizabeth Dee Gallery and Andrea Rosen Gallery in New York City, Regen Projects in Los Angeles, and Sprüth Magers in Berlin), he posts and shares for free the majority of his videos online, thereby creating a hybrid model for exhibition and distribution. As we will discuss later on in chapter 3, his use of online sharing platforms as vehicles of dissemination and circulation informs his populist, do-it-yourself aesthetic.

The artist has established and sustained a viable relationship with web-based spectators. His exhibitionistic jam-packed videos comprised of a hodgepodge of pop culture references fit right in amid webcam-recorded YouTube confessionals. Each movie is perfectly formatted for phones, tablets, and computer screens in order to broaden his reach for distribution and collaboration.

With their incessant jump cuts and frenetic flow of information, Trecartin's films hyperbolize high-speed communication as is exemplified in (*Tommy-Chat Just E-mailed Me.*) (2006). In this work, which the artist describes as a "narrative video short that takes place inside and outside of an e-mail,"[8] characters are depicted as projected combinations of stereotypes that reflect Trecartin's and his contemporaries' response to our media-saturated culture. His aim in designing these characterizations is not to define each character as representing a single identity. To Trecartin, the self is capable of having multiple identities (virtual avatar, social network identity, public work identity, various genders, etc.) that can be programmed, updated, and even deleted at will.

The opening scene introduces us to one of the protagonists, Tammy 1 (Ryan Trecartin) by means of a split screen. Tammy 1 occupies a small portion of the bottom right of the frame, surrounded by overwhelming close-ups of a laptop and printer that appear to suffocate her. An array of electronic gadget and ringing telephone sounds relegate Tammy's high-pitched shriek to the sonic background. The protagonist and her roommate Beth (Lizzie Fitch) suddenly receive an e-mail from their friend Tommy inviting them to "go out." They both proceed to address the camera as if communicating with other friends via cam, urging them to join them on their outing. The camera moves from character to character as the narrative is propelled at a manic pace following the protagonists' frenzied electronic interactions. Scenes depicting online mediation are crosscut to overlap each other; images constantly fade in and out; and special effects appear and disappear haphazardly without any apparent logical connection. Viewers are meant to feel like they are surfing through web pages.

As in most of his movies, Trecartin performs the role of several characters simultaneously: Tammy 1, Tammy 2, Tommy Chat, High/Low Tommy Video Voice, and Tommy Video Girl. Costume and makeup help create characters distinct from one another, but Ryan Trecartin's voice, face, and body undeniably emanate from each. By not casting other actors to play the above-named characters, but rather playing all these parts himself, he communicates his understanding of the self as a multiplicity of identities in constant flux.

When asked about the place his physical self takes within his work, Trecartin replied that he ultimately wishes for bodies to dissolve or mutate into nonphysical forms of expression.[9] During postproduction, he is able to animate his body (via filtering and three-dimensional modulation) in ways live performance cannot achieve. This practice enables him to enact the performance beyond the physical limitations of corporeal existence. The artist seeks to break away from previous essentialist notions of identity by creating characters that are able to switch and merge genders and sexual orientation. For the artist, the body is simply a vehicle that helps him translate his ever-shifting multiple "personalities."[10]

Although watching Trecartin's videos may feel like entering an overwhelming technological cosmos, they are not at all alienating. On the contrary, the artist's work clearly reflects the world we live in. Cybernated cultural landscapes and new media have become integral to our everyday lives. Like internauts who proclaim that, "if you are not online, you don't exist," characters chat in web slang ad absurdum. We might perceive them as overidentifying with digital culture. Yet, as foreign as they may seem, they do not appear unfamiliar. Curator Chris Wiley suggests that they act, "in a manner that you might if you accepted every aspect of contemporary culture at face value."[11]

Historical Context

Ryan Trecartin's work can be placed within a lineage of experimental cinema, performance, and video art. Avant-garde aesthetics, experimental editing, and televisual style are detectable in his subversive approach. The disruptive and anarchic spirit expressed in Trecartin's movies can be traced back to Dada's provocative performances and readings at the Cabaret Voltaire, which often ended in mayhem. Self-proclaimed nihilists, members of the Dada movement protested against the bourgeoisie, capitalism, and the art establishment, opting instead to embrace irrationality and disorder in a rebellious attempt to condemn social practices and the atrocities of World War I.

Dadaists did not aspire to craft elegant objects, opting instead to challenge artistic norms by creating conceptual works unconcerned with visual appeal. For example, Raoul Hausmann's photomontages—cutouts of random photographs, newspapers, and advertising—initiated an approach that can be detected in Trecartin's visual mash-ups of found internet footage. And, while Hausmann's experimental two-dimensional photographic collages appear static, they do succeed in transmitting a sense of chaos and disorder that Trecartin's disjointed cinematic montages successfully convey. The popularity of Trecartin's work is clearly not due, in fact, to refined aesthetics or high production values. It is precisely because it appears unpolished that the work draws so much attention. His highly processed and layered digital alterations at first give the impression that they are solely a wild and random collision of signs and symbols. However, on closer inspection, it becomes apparent that his movies are scripted and carefully crafted. He celebrates the spirit of anarchy and freedom, but under the direction of a carefully orchestrated revolution.

Dadaism's proclivity for irrationality and disorder is well illustrated in poetic "word salads," such as Tristan Tzara's "Cinema Calendar of the Abstract Heart–09" (1920), in which mixtures of random words and phrases are reassembled in the most ludicrous fashion as a way to shock audiences. Ryan Trecartin composes all of his scripts with a distinctive vocabulary utilizing computer language, symbols, and internet jargon.

> "IT is not |You|,,, IT IS WE!" […] "IT is not |em| and>/ Will not matter as Such." […] "The New Look for This Company, IS re-Thinking the Word |Humanity| as an Object with a (Goal)."[12]

The artist's experimentation with language disrupts syntax and grammar, opening itself to misinterpretation and misreading. *P.opular S.ky* (section ish) (2009), for instance, opens with the word "REMEMBER" in enormous bold type only to meld a few seconds later into a cryptic message that reads "R3N.3ND3R." This might seem to amount to nothing more than a non sequitur, but it is a way for Trecartin to comment on the fragile and sometimes failing logic of technology and telecommunications. While Roberta Smith contends that the artist idealizes technology, I view him as maintaining a critical distance from it by acknowledging its shortcomings.[13] Yet, the artist does not treat computer glitches and corrupted strings of programming code simply as limitations, but as opportunities to find alternative modes of expression that escape the predictable, the norm, the orderly. Language, manipulated at will, functions in tandem with his ever-shifting, open-ended, fast-paced visuals.

Dada filmic experimentation that helped pave the path to the emergence of avant-garde cinema featured animated rayographs in Man Ray's *Retour à la Raison* (1923), whirling Rotoreliefs in Marcel Duchamp's *Anémic Cinéma* (1926), and stop-motion animation in Hans Richter's *Ghosts before Breakfast* (1928). Later filmmakers such as Stan Brakhage, Jonas Mekas, and Kenneth Anger sought to explore the potential and challenge the limitations of the medium by playing with a variety of techniques that included painting directly onto film, scratching the celluloid surface, and superimposing multiple exposures. Trecartin's labor intensive, postproduction process, infused with the application of a broad range of digital effects similarly creates spectacular digital collages that showcase his experimental style. Lev Manovich writes, "The avant-garde [has become] materialized in a computer."[14] In an interview for CreativePlanetNetwork.com, Trecartin discussed the new technological freedom available to him.

> When you break down the hierarchy of [traditional] editing, you have people doing a rough cut, then a final cut, then they work on sound and visual effects. But in After Effects you can do all these things at the same time if you want to, and that helps me massage the work and bring out nuances.[15]

Although he applies visual effects to alter digital footage, much as avant-garde filmmakers manipulated the film medium, Trecartin is not primarily interested in exploring the medium for form's sake but rather to express his view of contemporary culture in which social constructs and labels are disrupted and erased. As he points out,

> At the moment in time I was born, it was natural not to recognize boundaries between artistic mediums—as well as ideas, genders, races, and all sorts of nuances that are historically shoved into and understood in terms of categorical containers. I grew up alongside computer adolescence.I think lots of people born at

> the same time, or anytime after the birth of the home computer, see "-isms" as applications rather than truths and see definitions as filters rather than containers. It's an exciting privilege to be chucked into the culture flow after so many people have made it possible to be fluid in practice, instead of merely in theory.[16]

By creating a feeling of total digital immersion, Trecartin's movies serve as allegories of our dual mode of existence, at once inside and outside the realm of digital technology and devoid of rigid categorizations.

Avant-garde films have been positioned against the dominant mode embodied by the Hollywood film industry. Yet, filmmakers like Jack Smith, "King of the Underground,"[17] have celebrated aspects of mainstream Hollywood, especially its camp qualities. Smith developed an experimental style consisting of a mélange of camp aesthetics, Hollywood orientalism, and kitsch. Working outside the mainstream, the filmmaker enjoyed a creative freedom that allowed him to push the boundaries by challenging standards of "good taste." His eccentric narratives often featured transvestites, androgynous actors, vampires, and monsters all taking part in orgiastic debauchery. *Flaming Creatures* (1963), his most notorious film, consists of a series of black-and-white sequences juxtaposed in a nonlinear fashion. In it, Smith employed off-center shots, in-and-out-of-focus cinematography, and extreme close-ups of various body parts in order to blur the distinction between intertwined seminude male and female bodies. Although Trecartin's videos are not overtly sexual, they also feature bizarre characters with ambiguous sexualities and gender(s). Trecartin's butch queens, vogue femmes, girlfags, guydykes, and other genderqueer[18] characters all partake in his delirious narratives, dancing, sashaying, and convulsing in mythical and ritualistic performances reminiscent of *Flaming Creatures*. His low-tech aesthetic, like Smith's, is identifiable: handheld cameras, handmade sets, fragmented shots and twisted camera angles, and complete disregard for continuity editing.

After his last feature *No President* (1967–70), Smith ceased exhibiting his films in art house cinemas and opted instead to project re-edited excerpts of them. His decision to recut his films for each of his live performances was primarily motivated by the fact that he rejected the commodification of his work.[19] As Julia Stoscheck writes in *Collection Number Six*:

Flaming Creatures, "Smith vehemently resisted being swallowed up by pop culture."[20] Conversely, Trecartin embraces everything there is about popular culture—indeed, he has been swallowed up by it.

In this regard, Trecartin's approach shares a connection with that of Andy Warhol, whose keen interest in mass consumerism led him to recontextualize, glamorize, and immortalize Coca-Cola bottles and cans of Campbell's soup as symbols of 1960s Americana by transplanting such pop culture iconography into museums, traditionally the realm of high art. Richard Dyer comments that what drew media attention to Warhol's work was not the skillful artistry required to produce it but the audacity of glorifying such objects of "mass culture trash."[21] Trecartin's preoccupation with consumer culture reveals itself through the abundance of mass-produced objects he incorporates in his sets and costumes. The artist often names protagonists after commercial software companies such as Adobe or Cedar and inscribes corporate logos onto their skin. Smartphones, computers, tablets, clothing, and jewelry surround and at times appear almost to smother the protagonists. Objects are simultaneously fetishized and rendered disposable—much like tech gadgets, initially marketed as collector's items, only to be constantly rendered obsolete when an updated and repackaged version of the "toy" is introduced into the marketplace.

Warhol became familiar with the films of Stan Brakhage, Kenneth Anger, and Jack Smith, not to imitate them but rather to break away and develop a new and quite distinct cinematic aesthetic. Unlike the avant-garde lyrical, dreamlike, highly processed films, Warhol "simply turned the camera on and walked away."[22] Contrary to Trecartin, who bombards viewers with imagery at the speed of creative thought, Warhol suspends you in real-time minimalist contemplation. Trecartin's proclivity for in-your-face visual stimulus is associated with earlier avant-garde formal practices rather than Warhol's prestructuralist fixed-frame cinematography of continuous long takes. Thus, Trecartin's work clearly intersects with Warhol's in terms of content, rather than form.

The connections between the work of Ryan Trecartin and avant-garde filmmakers are undeniable, although their respective mediums and access to technology fundamentally differed. Historically, individual mediums remained generally distinct from one another. While avant-garde filmmakers sought to challenge the codes and conventions of classical American cinema (often neglecting to recognize its underlying affinities with them), video art, as it emerged in the United States, was initially preoccupied with critiquing commercial television. Trecartin celebrates both and extends the discourse to examine the liberating potential of the internet. His approach takes into account the net's relatively recent history while understanding its impact as an infinite network.

The initial wave of pioneer video artists such as Nam June Paik and Wolf Vostell was responding to the commercialization and control of traditional news and the influence of mass media. In his piece *TV Dé-coll/age* (1961), Vostell altered the image of several TV sets by interfering with the television receivers of a department store in Paris.[23] In 1963, Nam June Paik also distorted TV images electronically with the help of an engineer who reconfigured TV circuits for his exhibition, *Exposition of Music-Electronic Television*.[24] With the advent of the Portapak videotape analog recording system by Sony in 1967, artists finally found a device that could directly record and playback their footage.[25] Despite the low-contrast grainy black-and-white quality of the video recorder and its very limited capabilities, the new technology attracted many artists precisely because of its newness. As Chris Meigh-Andrews notes, "video had no tradition [. . .] it had no formal burdens at all."[26] It is worth mentioning that initially Paik and Vostell primarily employed video sculpturally as both single and multimonitor installations playing prerecorded content.

By the mid-1960s, many feminist artists eager for self-representation, such as Yoko Ono, Marina Abramović, and Ana Mendieta, began to use video as a recording device to document their live performances. The 1960s and 1970s were indeed organically linked with the rise of second-wave feminism, opening up the debate to issues such as abortion rights and equality in the workplace. These female artists explored social and sexual boundaries in provocative and personal performances. In *Cut Piece* (1965), Yoko Ono kneeled in a traditional Japanese woman's submissive pose and invited the audience to approach her onstage and cut off pieces of her clothes with scissors she had placed on the floor in front of her. In her endurance performance, *Rhythm 0* (1974), Marina Abramović placed seventy-two objects, some of which could administer pleasure while others delivered pain, on a table in front of the audience, allowing them to use them on her body while she stood still naked. In *Untitled* (*Body Tracks*) (1974), Ana Mendieta dipped her hands into animal blood and utilized her body as a paintbrush to leave vertical tracks from top to bottom on long sheets of paper, while Cuban drumming played in the background. This performance refers to the objectification of the female subject by the male gaze throughout the history of painting. Regarding such early performances, Amelia Jones comments, "The often shocking enactment of these taboos allowed the artist to experience a personal transformation through the event, and the audience was also affected, expected to undergo a mass sense of release."[27]

The performative aspects of Trecartin's work do not lie in the embodied physicality of his characters but rather reside primarily in his editing process. As he explains in his interview with Cindy Sherman, "The performance is not live; everything is performed for the edit—performed to become live through mediation. Editing is itself a part of articulating the character, and so I see it as a performative gesture."[28] Although the artist's edited performances do not take place in real time, they nevertheless trigger powerful and visceral responses from viewers, thanks in part to the mediated immediacy of their enveloping multisensory stimulation. The early feminist performance artists mentioned above recorded live performances employing their fixed bodies, whereas Trecartin transforms and mutates bodies, gender, and race via the endless options available through editing and software.

Chris Burden also sought to push the limits of the body through ritualistic time-based performances. In *Shoot* (1971), Burden asked a friend to shoot him with a .22 rifle from a distance of fifteen feet, which resulted in the bullet going through his left arm. With his explosive tendencies and penchant for the outrageous, Burden became a harbinger of the emerging punk sensibility. The punk movement rebelled against conservative politics, capitalist consumerism, and mainstream culture, beginning in the mid-1970s. Its subculture created defiant and sometimes violent forms of expression. This energy was expressed in part through punk music spearheaded by bands such as the Ramones in New York City, the Sex Pistols in London, and Black Flag in Los Angeles, among many others. Their live concerts were orchestrated as aggressive stage performances meant to shock the public—smashing guitars into pieces, playing with blood, stage diving, and insulting audience members were all part of the program. The eruptive emergence of slam dancing reflected the movement's forceful vitality through direct confrontational body contact, including tackling, shoving, and stomping.

This sense of punk anarchist expression is palpable in Trecartin's "Let's fuck shit up"[29] attitude—the leitmotif of *Priority Infield's Junior War* (2013), a 24-minute short composed of footage of Trecartin's high school friends drinking, smoking, and smashing mailboxes and television sets with sledge hammers. The artist has expressed in several interviews that his goal while making it was to document belligerent escapades with his friends. The result is a decoupage of randomly edited grainy video shots filmed in night-vision mode. The seven movies that comprise *Any Ever* (2009–10) further emphasize a defiant subtext, as each one also culminates with characters destroying and shattering personal possessions—perhaps as a way to rebel against consumption, or as a way to start anew and consume again.

Album covers designed by Jamie Reid arguably constitute the most powerful remnants of punk's iconography. In one of his most renowned creations, a poster for the Sex Pistols' album *God Save the Queen* (1977), Reid altered a Cecile Beaton photograph of Queen Elizabeth II by inserting a large safety pin through her nose. This irreverent gesture echoes Marcel Duchamp's iconoclastic bold move of drawing a moustache and goatee on a reproduction of Leonardo DaVinci's *Mona Lisa*.

Although the punk movement emerged roughly sixty years after Dadaism, Dada's original mission to disrupt the dominant system constituted a cultural intervention that resonated with the one undertaken by punk youth decades later. Like the Dadaists, punks rejected refined aesthetics, choosing instead to appropriate, reuse, and/or recontextualize mundane items in unlikely ways. This practice mirrored Marcel Duchamp's philosophy behind his "readymades." In *Bicycle Wheel* (1913), for example, Duchamp mounted a bicycle fork with its front wheel upside-down onto a wooden stool, turning it into a kinetic sculpture. Similarly, punks repurposed found objects and transformed them into art and accessories as a form of rebellion.

Punk style became instrumental in conveying a sense of individualism and opposition to popular culture. Punks repurposed razor blades, trash bags, or tampons in a do-it-yourself spirit while originating unisex looks. Designers Vivienne Westwood and Zandra Rhodes also created androgynous fashions featuring bondage pants, studded motorcycle jackets, cropped blazers, and tattered or ripped separates. Looks were personalized with loose neckties or dog collars worn over shredded T-shirts, often paired with Dr. Martens boots. Men and women applied makeup, shaved their heads military style, or fashioned Mohawk crests of hair.

Trecartin's protagonists' outfits rival and pay homage to punk subversion in their disregard for social customs, order, and gender norms. A red brick may be converted into a purse, an iPad with a ponytail glued to its back stands in as a handheld mirror, watches are hung together on a chain to form a necklace, a Wite-Out bottle is converted into an earring, and an image of an automobile dashboard is imprinted across a character's forehead. Punk-inspired protagonists like Shin in *A Family Finds Entertainment* (2004) and Pasta in *I-BE Area* (2007) sport gender fluid garments with garish makeup and wigs, making it difficult—if not impossible—to determine their gender from an established binary model.

The DIY and cut-and-paste aesthetic of punk went hand-in-hand with video's ability to mediate a sense of rawness and immediacy. In the mid-1970s, the San Francisco-based art collective, Target Video, founded by Joseph Rees, began taping punk performances and activist happenings with a video camera. The art collective's video works consisted of a bricolage of performance footage, two-dimensional graphics, found footage, and special effects.[30] Target Video anticipated the potential of videotape as an artistic medium beyond that of a recording device.

Indeed, video as an art medium engendering its own language would not emerge until the mid- to late-1970s, a decade following Paik's and Vostell's early experimentations, when artists began to subvert televisual tropes to challenge the conservative ideologies and images promulgated by mainstream broadcasting. This shift occurred, in part, thanks to new editing equipment becoming available for home use. In her video, *Semiotics of the Kitchen* (1975), for instance, Martha Rosler poses as the host of a TV cooking program in which she catalogs kitchen utensils in alphabetical order, and then proceeds to demonstrate their use in strange and sometimes violent ways. In this parody of televised food shows, Rosler plays with televisual conventions. The static camera frames Rosler in direct address with a supposed audience and suggests that she is not only confined inside her small cramped kitchen but also trapped within the square television box.

Trecartin incorporates a televisual style of structuring devices such as immediacy, seriality, fragmentation, fluidity, and direct address not to undermine the institution of television but as a means to pay homage to TV he grew up watching. A sense of immediacy is evoked consistently through his intense rapid cutting. Many of his movies do not provide any sense of closure or resolution. Rather, they end in a "to be continued..." manner, leaving the viewer wondering what will happen next. This sense of seriality is further explored in Trecartin's later series, *Any Ever*, in which recurring characters take part in several completely unrelated ongoing narratives. Fragmentation and fluidity are also tropes to be considered when reflecting on *Wayne's World* (2003), for instance, whereby a TV-viewing experience is simulated by segmenting the plot, switching back and forth from commercial breaks to talk show, and from talk show to daytime soap opera. The notion of fluidity or flow, as articulated by John Fiske, takes television to be "a continuous succession of images which follows no laws of logic or cause and effect, but which constitutes the cultural experience of 'watching television.'"[31] Trecartin achieves this illusion primarily by linking fragmented and unrelated scenes or sequences through a continuous soundtrack. Busy signal tones and computer sound-bites intersperse his audio tracks, pointing to the very connectivity of the technology(ies) commercially available to him and his intended audience. In fact, the director often addresses his spectators as if they were communicating with each other online. For instance, *Roamie View: History Enhancement* (2009–10) opens with a high-angle shot of JJ Check (Trecartin) in his bedroom/art studio. The character breaks the fourth wall by explaining the conceptual framework of the art surrounding him while directly addressing the audience. This direct mode of address is in line with the artist's goal to augment viewer engagement.

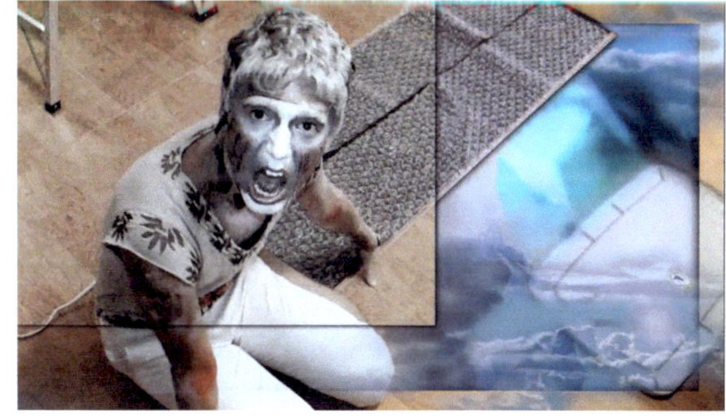

Figure I.1 *Roamie View: History Enhancement (Re'Search Wait'S)* (2010)

Ryan Trecartin's cinematic installations with their interactive mise-en-scène go further in breaking down the barrier between art and audience, an integral component of the original mission of performance art. As RoseLee Goldberg writes, "The history of performance art in the twentieth century is the history of a permissive, open-ended medium with endless variables, executed by artists impatient with the limitations of more established art forms, and determined to take their art directly to the public. For this reason its base has always been anarchic."[32]

Queer performance artists in the 1980s, such as Holly Hughes and Tim Miller (members of the NEA Four denied their federal artist grants), took action toward reclaiming their human rights, LGBTQ identity, and even marriage equality. Felix Gonzalez-Torres also turned to performance in his piece *Untitled* (*Go-Go Dancing Platform*) (1991) in which a gay male go-go dancer danced on top of a stripper platform box encased in light bulbs. Although seemingly playful at first sight, the performance provided a cross-section of viewers a peek into a gay subculture, with its allusion to discos, saunas, and sex clubs. More recently, Ron Athey and Franko B, known for their extreme bloody ritualistic performances involving aspects of sadomasochism, often scar and mutilate their own bodies to challenge preconceived notions about AIDS, masculinity, and/or organized religion.

While the humorous and colorful world of Ryan Trecartin appears to deviate from confrontational and sometimes painful performances, his subversive work engages with socially charged themes, including the emergence of virtual algorithms as tools of surveillance, queer visibility, and the homogenizing force of global corporate culture. Trecartin understands and acknowledges the relevance of past contributions made by his predecessors. However, he has digested the past and now elects to move beyond it.

Postmodernism and Queer Theory

Although some art and film critics, as well as bloggers, have contextualized Trecartin's videos within postmodernism, I argue that, because his art cannot be identified solely through reductive classifications such as identity politics, his work in fact challenges postmodernism's restrictive value system. Postmodernism has been and still remains a point of contention among scholars. While many believe postmodernism is dead, others believe it never took place, and some think we are in fact still in its midst. The various (and often contradictory) perspectives revolving around the notion of postmodernism and what postmodernism is often diverge.

In comparing Jack Halberstam's understanding of the concept of postmodernism to Terry Smith and Nicolas Bourriaud's, it appears that the term, as it pertains to queer theory according to Halberstam, is indeed closely related to its art historical meaning. In his pivotal book, *In a Queer Time and Place: Transgender Bodies, Subcultural Lives*, he claims that "queer/queerness" is intimately connected to postmodernism as he explains, "'queer time' is a term for those specific models of temporality that emerge within postmodernism."[33] The author, however, does not provide a clear time frame for what he considers to be "postmodernism"; rather, he writes,

> I see postmodernism as simultaneously a crisis and an opportunity—a crisis in the stability of form and meaning, and opportunity to rethink the practice of cultural production, its hierarchies and power dynamics, its tendency to resist or capitulate.[34]

This definition implies that postmodernism is a period of transition since it is both a "crisis and an opportunity." But a transition between what time frame? In his book *What Is Contemporary Art?*, Terry Smith argues that postmodernism is "the moment of transition between these two eras [modernism and contemporary art], an anachronism from the 1970s and 1980s."[35] Smith attempts to answer the seemingly simple yet extremely complex question, "What is contemporary art?" For Smith, contemporary art is "much more than a mindless embrace of the present."[36] Smith claims that at the turn of the millennium, the direction of contemporary art has shifted. According to him, "contemporaneity" has several meanings and thus cannot be contained within one singular definition. In its ordinary usage, the term refers to the quality or state of being in the *now*, in the present.[37] In relation to art, however, "contemporaneity manifests itself not just in the unprecedented proliferation of art, or only in its seemingly infinite variegation, but above all in the emergence of, and contestation between, quite different ways of making art and communicating through it to others."[38]

Ryan Trecartin's mixed-media approach to art-making explores today's cultural momentum in ways that could not have been possible before the mass popularization of the internet. As Trecartin notes, "Because of the way people read, share, and merge information now, the way something is contained and framed is just as valuable as the content inside."[39] The implications of this perspective of understanding what constitutes a work of art are very much anchored in contemporaneity. How artists maintain a relationship to their work in an interactive context and, in turn, the role identity fluidity plays when exhibited through open access technological platforms are questions Trecartin's highly provocative interventions in contemporary art raise and address.

In *Altermodern*, Nicolas Bourriaud refers to postmodernism as "the philosophy of mourning, a long melancholic episode in our cultural life"—which started roughly around the early 1970s.[40] Interestingly, Halberstam argues that "queer time" came to consciousness within the LGBT community at the end of the twentieth century with the AIDS crisis, around the same time Smith and Bourriaud date postmodernism. Such accounts of queer life under AIDS are problematic as they perpetuate the pathologization of queer mourning in their linking of nonheteronormative time to loss and grief. In *Time Binds*: *Queer Temporalities*, *Queer Histories*, Elizabeth Freeman comments on queer scholars' tendency to situate queerness in such a gloomy historical context.

> Queer theory, then, pays attention to gaps and losses that are both structural and visceral: the all-too-real limits presented by the stigmatization of AIDS, by violence against lesbians and gays, by the unbearable heaviness of the gender binary. [. . .] Within this paradigm, queer becoming-collective-across-time and even the concept of futurity itself are predicated upon injury—separations, injuries, spatial displacements, preclusions, and other negative and negating forms of bodily experience.[41]

Freeman finds more productive ways to historicize queerness by suggesting that queer time "emerged beyond this heterosexually gendered double-time of stasis and progress" as ludic, deconstructed, and asynchronous.[42] Her conception of queer time is closer to Bourriaud's notion of altermodernism, a moment in time "when it became possible for us to produce something that made sense starting from an assumed heterochrony, that is, from a vision of human history as constituted of multiple temporalities."[43] As such, altermodernism challenges postmodernism as a restrictive and linear system. Bourriaud argues that during postmodernism, artists and art critics found meaning in a work of art by examining the social background of its production, asking questions such as "Where does the artist come from?" In the postmodern era, identification with gender, ethnicity, and sexual orientation became a system of allotting meaning and reducing individuals' identity to their origins.[44] According to his proclamation titled "Altermodern Manifesto: Postmodernism Is Dead," the postmodern has been replaced. Thus, the term *postmodern* does not define a specific style but rather a tool that seeks to categorize, compartmentalize, and standardize identity. Much like Halberstam, I believe that this historical moment presented both an "opportunity" and a "crisis"—an opportunity for minorities to gain more visibility in the art world, but a crisis in which artworks were labeled according to identity categories such as race, gender, sexuality, or nationality, thus setting up these artworks for their incorporation into the hegemonic capitalist system.

Cultural producers today are international and global. No longer is the art market controlled exclusively by Western artists, dealers, critics, collectors, and institutions, nor is a discussion primarily surrounding multiculturalism essential in this globalized market as it was at the end of the twentieth century. While Trecartin may cast Asian, Black, Hispanic, and/or White actors in his work, he destabilizes the very concept of racial identity by cross-accessorizing their looks with unexpected nontraditional hair and skin choices manifested for example through blue wigs, ghostly white faces, or stripes of makeup of varying skin tones. Trecartin commented on the styling of his personae and said, "We might try to interpret a car commercial as a hairdo, an ideology as a designer skin tone, a banking situation as a cheekbone, copyright issues as a jaw line, or maybe an application as a facial agenda."[45] His protagonists no longer represent human beings, but rather embody our commodifying culture in which time, space, and identity are no longer necessarily straightforward, linear, quantifiable, and/or classifiable. As such, this work aligns itself with the concept of open-endedness articulated in queer theory.

In an interview for the *Economist*, Ryan Trecartin was asked to comment on the lack of distinction regarding his characters' gender. He replied,

> I see it less as a lack of distinction in binary terms and more as an exploration of territories within infinite gender creation, individualization and specificity. I imagine this as a type of multiplex space. I'm often interested in realities where gender takes a back-seat to personality articulation [. . .] and the thing I love about personality is that it can be added to, changed or re-worked at will, while not being classified or grouped very easily. [. . .] I see my characters exploring a technologically driven yet non-gender-centric psychologically complex transitional world which is inherently positive and energetic as opposed to neutral and formulaic.[46]

While the artist does not explicitly refer to his artwork as queer, preferring instead to describe his movies as "realities where gender [and sexuality] take[s] a back-seat," I will argue, however, that queerness is a central concept in Trecartin's work. In order to better comprehend how queerness operates in his work, it is necessary to clarify how the term will be employed.

According to Halberstam, queer time and space exist "in opposition to the institutions of family, heterosexuality, and reproduction."[47] The author analyzes the narrative of Kimberly Peirce's *Boys Don't Cry* (1999) to illustrate the concept of a queer place, pointing to the fact that when the film premiered, some film reviewers, queer and nonqueer alike, wondered why the transgender protagonist remained in a closed-minded rural environment instead of moving to the city where she would be accepted.[48] It seems then that spectators' expectations concur with the understanding that queer subcultures can only thrive in urban areas.[49]

While Halberstam's theory may apply to some queer narratives, his concept does not entirely pertain to Ryan Trecartin's work, as neither its production nor its content is restricted to a specific city locale. Trecartin's studio can take on different formats (art space, video green screen, editing room, computer, etc.) and be located anywhere; in fact, he often creates work in the suburbs or rural areas. For instance, the series *Any Ever* (2009–10), produced while in residency in Miami, was mainly shot in suburban settings. As Bourriaud notes, "In a world every inch of which is under satellite surveillance, territory takes the form of a construction or a journey."[50] Therefore, trying to categorize specific geographic sites as queer or straight loses its political appeal after we erase the imaginary frontiers of our global world. In addition to being freely distributed online, Trecartin's art has been exhibited internationally in venues such as the National Gallery of Victoria in Melbourne (2015), Kunst-Werke Institute of Contemporary Art in Berlin (2014), Zabludowicz Collection in London (2014), Musée d'Art Moderne de la Ville de Paris (2011), and at contemporary art biennials, including the Venice Biennale (2013), Singapore Biennial (2011), and Gwangju Biennial (2010), making his art widely accessible. By inviting audiences to interact with the work on and offline, the artist provides an opportunity to experience his movies in diverse settings. Furthermore, his narratives function outside heteronormative constraints, in a parallel universe where transgender, genderless, and hybrid characters coexist regardless of the environments in which they situate themselves.

Halberstam's monolithic concept of queer time and place seems problematic, for it suggests that queer subcultures exist primarily outside heteronormativity. Thus, a queer identity is one, according to him, that counteridentifies with the dominant ideology. However, other academics have proposed alternate strategies to counteridentification. Borrowing from Michel Pêcheux's theory of disidentification, José Muñoz, in his book *Disidentifications: Queers of Color and the Performance of Politics*, describes the three modes through which queer minorities shape their identity in relation to the dominant culture.[51] Muñoz distinguishes between identification (or assimilation), which he says means to embrace, take on, and willingly reenact what the dominant ideology dictates, and counteridentification, which he explains as rejecting, refusing, and denying the dominant ideology. He writes that disidentification is a third mode of dealing with dominant ideology, "one that neither opts to assimilate within such a structure nor strictly opposes it; rather, disidentification is a strategy that works on and against dominant ideology. [. . .] this 'working on and against' is a strategy that tries to transform a cultural logic from within, always laboring to enact permanent structural change while at the same time valuing the importance of local or everyday struggles of resistance."[52] As he explains, "these subjects' [queers of color] different identity components occupy adjacent spaces and are not comfortably situated in any one discourse of minority subjectivity.[53] These hybridized identificatory positions are always in transit, shuttling between different identity vectors."[54] According to Muñoz, these "identity vectors" refer to sexuality and race. To illustrate this concept, he investigates the works of various artists (and queers of color), such as Carmelita Tropicana, Vaginal Crème Davis, and Felix Gonzalez-Torres, who negotiate their double minority identities by creating their own queer worlds through their art. They acknowledge social injustice, are concerned about it, and aware of its problematic history. Yet, they react to it by being playful, humorous, and mildly sarcastic as a form of disidentification.

Although Muñoz applies his concept of disidentification strictly to queers of color, I would argue that any queer subject can disidentify. In his book's final chapter, Muñoz proposes a recontextualization of the term.

> Disidentification is about cultural, material, and psychic survival. It is a response to state and global power apparatuses that employ systems of racial, sexual, and national subjugation. [. . .] Disidentification is about managing and negotiating historical trauma and systemic violence.[55]

I assert that this broad definition may apply to any queer individual of any race or ethnicity. However, when speaking exclusively in regards to queers of color, it becomes evident that varying disidentification strategies exist. This is illustrated in the selection of artists Muñoz includes in his study. While Carmelita Tropicana and Vaginal Crème Davis both create work that clearly deals with their sexual and racial minority status, Felix Gonzalez-Torres "actively rebelled against any reductive understanding of how his identity affects his cultural production."[56] Indeed, Felix Gonzalez-Torres, completely rejected restrictive definitions of identity. Thus, Muñoz's decision to include him in his pivotal book points to the fact that there are multiple philosophical approaches from which to disidentify. In the case of Gonzalez-Torres, his disidentificatory strategy consists of implementing a neominimalist vernacular as a method for both dispelling individual identity labels and addressing larger societal issues relating to sexuality. Trecartin does not merely disidentify by doing away with fixed identity categories but by redefining the concept of identity as a set of interchangeable traits. As Trecartin states,

> Ten or twenty years ago, identity politics was essential to creating a space for diversity. We are heirs to the potential consequences of those battles and many now assume that we can simply declare—or behave as—who and what we are in more mutable ways, without a need to always state these things in opposition to some prevailing norm. You no longer need to create dichotomies to catalyze progress or be the embodiment of a movement. There is more room to simply utilize a movement as an application or instigate contextual innovation.[57]

Both Halberstam and Muñoz use *queer* to mean *gay* or any nonstraight way(s) of being. While their definitions of queer provide a starting point, they fail to account for the complex and sometimes contradictory ways the term is deployed in scholarly writings. For a more comprehensive definition of the term, I turn to Alexander Doty's *Flaming Classics: Queering the Film Canon.*

According to Doty, "queer/queerness" has historically been synonymous with gay, lesbian, or bisexual orientation.[58] "Queer" has also been used as an umbrella term that takes into account any nonstraight position. The term has also been applied to describe nonheteronormative modes of spectatorship that allow for different readings of texts regardless of the sexuality of the person who originally produced the text. Queer/queerness may refer to nonnormative or in-between genders not easily categorized within the binary paradigms male/female.[59] Among the various definitions Doty proposes, his sixth and last is the one I find most useful for its inclusivity. He frames the term as follows, "To describe those aspects of spectatorship, cultural readership, production, and textual coding that seem to establish spaces not described by, or contained within, straight, gay, lesbian, bisexual, transsexual, or transgendered understandings and categorizations of gender and sexuality."[60] I believe this final definition accurately reflects how Ryan Trecartin incorporates a sense of queerness in his work. He creates narratives that are not strictly linked to sexuality(ies) and often blurs external signifiers such as gender, which allows him to develop new identity categories that cannot be solely described as straight, gay, lesbian, bisexual, transsexual, or transgendered. Indeed, the artist's characters are always situated at the edge of these boundaries. They can generally be considered genderfuck, which, as Jodie Taylor puts it in *Playing It Queer*, "deliberately mixes gender cues in an attempt to subvert the logic of the sex/gender/sexuality paradigm by exposing the false dualities that lie at the heart of heteronormativity."[61] Trecartin's work reflects Doty's understanding that anyone can be queer regardless of their sexual orientation. Therefore, the term *queer* will be used interchangeably throughout this book to specifically denote both nonstraight sexualities, as well as nonheteronormative and nonfixed positions. The concept of nonfixity plays a particularly significant role in the artist's work, as queerness is not affixed to a singular body.

As he states in an interview for the *Economist*, Trecartin uses the body as a blank canvas onto which personalities are projected, negotiated, and articulated—the body is thus open-ended.[62] Interestingly, it is precisely this idea of liminality in relation to the body and identity that places Mikhail Bakhtin's writing about the body of carnival at the intersection between the grotesque and queer.

The Grotesque, Abject, and Carnivalesque

In *Rabelais and His World*, Bakhtin defines the grotesque body as an open, unsealed body that is always in the process of becoming and engendering another body. He writes,

> The grotesque body [. . .] is a body in the act of becoming. It is never finished, never completed; it is continually built, created, and builds and creates another body. [. . .] Thus the artistic logic of the grotesque image ignores the closed, smooth, and impenetrable surface of the body and retains only its excrescences (sprouts, buds) and orifices, only that which leads beyond the body's limited space or into the body's depths.[63]

For Bakhtin, the grotesque challenges identity, system, and order. It transgresses and merges bodily limits and can be best described as in-between and ambiguous. He emphasizes specific characteristics of the grotesque body, namely its openness, its penetrative aspect, and the "lower stratum." Indeed, the grotesque body is aware of its own orifices (mouth, anus, vagina, etc.). He explains, "all these convexities and orifices have a common characteristic; it is within them that the confines between bodies and between the body and the world are overcome: there is an interchange and an interorientation."[64] The author contrasts the open-ended body of carnival as the grotesque body par excellence from the "classical body of official culture," which, as he explains, is "an entirely finished, completed, strictly limited body, which is shown from the outside as something individual."[65] The carnival is a collective phenomenon—it unifies the individuals taking part in it. As the author notes, "[. . .] the carnival celebrated temporary liberation from the prevailing truth and from the established order; it marked the suspension of all hierarchical rank, privileges, norms, and prohibitions."[66] Thus, members of carnival no longer see themselves as individuals but as belonging to a broader whole, as being part of a community. During these festivities, social hierarchies are suspended and emphasis is placed on the body and its connection to the life of the community. The grotesque quality of Trecartin's work is often attributed to the eccentric appearance of his protagonists. However, Trecartin's cinematographic formal elements and editing techniques also need to be examined in order to expose the evident link between Bakhtin's theory and the artist's montage. All of Trecartin's movies involve anarchic festivities shot through multiple camera angles, extreme close-ups, long shots, partial views, high and low angle shots, all crosscut in a disjointed yet unifying manner, thereby confounding bodies into one giant fluid mass. The same way participants undergo a transformative process by donning costumes and masks during carnival, the grotesque body is also in a perpetual state of in-betweenness. The grotesque body is thus also a queer body according to Doty's sixth rendering of queerness.

Scholars have often employed the concepts of the grotesque and the abject alongside one another without differentiating them. While these two terms are in fact closely related, they are nevertheless distinct. In her book *Powers of Horror*, Julia Kristeva defines the abject as "something rejected from which one does not part, from which one does not protect oneself as from an object. Imaginary uncanniness and real threat, it beckons to us and ends up engulfing us."[67] She then clarifies that what causes abjection is "what disturbs identity, system, order. What does not respect borders, positions, rules. The in-between, the ambiguous, the composite."[68] Thus, like the grotesque, the abject disturbs notions of fixed identity by occupying the state of in-betweenness and ambiguity. However, unlike Bakhtin's conception of the grotesque, which is characterized by the carnivalesque and ludic, the abject is traumatic and threatening.

The utopian and playful aspect of Bakhtin's writing on carnival relates to Trecartin's jubilant digital universe. When problematizing the ludic aspect of the artist's work, there may seem at first to be a disconnection between the carnivalesque playfulness inherent in it and its subversiveness. However, the two are not mutually exclusive, as Victor Turner writes in his essay "Carnival in Rio: Dionysian Drama in an Industrialized Society."

> The play frame, where events are scrutinized in the leisure time of the social process, has to some extent inherited the function of the ritual frame. The message it delivers are often serious beneath the outward trappings of absurdity, fantasy, and ribaldry, as contemporary stage plays, some movies and some TV shows illustrate. Clearly, carnival is a form of play.[69]

Turner makes an argument similar to Bakhtin's when he writes that during the carnival festivities, society is in "its mood of fantasizing, its playful mood."[70] According to Turner, playfulness can be serious and even subversive. The transgressiveness of Trecartin's art lies in its ability to address time-sensitive issues in a nonthreatening, playful, humorous, and even mischievous way. Indeed, underneath the artifice of Trecartin's carnivalesque sonic and visual explosions are very serious thematic undercurrents.

Furthermore, Turner points to the fact that although the ludic can seem chaotic, void of structure or rules, the carnival, in all its fantasy and apparent eccentricity, actually demands great technical control, synchronization of dance and music, and a lot of preparation in the design of the costumes and hairstyles. As he notes, "It takes a great amount of order to produce 'a sweet disorder,' a great deal of structuring to create a sacred play-space and time for antistructure."[71] Interestingly, Ryan Trecartin has made similar claims in regard to his work, saying, "What I have to deal with [. . .] is people assuming that the movies are improvised parties.

I spend a ton of time scripting the work on many levels, and the process is choreographed accordingly. Everyone involved works their asses off!"[72] Indeed, although shots move at frantic speeds, making the final product feel like a berserk mad-ride run awry, each camera angle is in fact meticulously orchestrated in postproduction.

While Bakhtin applies his theory of the grotesque and carnivalesque to literary works, Robert Stam continues the discussion in *Subversive Pleasures: Bakhtin, Cultural Criticism, and Film*, by adapting Bakhtin's theory to film. In his book, Stam reinforces some of Bakhtin's claims about carnival by reiterating that "carnival represents an alternative cosmovision characterized by the ludic undermining of all norms. The carnivalesque principle abolishes hierarchies, levels social classes, and creates another life free from conventional rules and restrictions."[73] Claiming that Bakhtinian notions of the carnivalesque and grotesque have "broad relevance for cinematic expression,"[74] Stam identifies a wide gamut of films that can be described as being carnivalesque, including films or film-related experiences that "strive to erase barriers between spectator and spectacle," such as *The Rocky Horror Picture Show* phenomenon, and those that "aggressively overturn a classical aesthetic based on formal harmony and good taste," such as John Waters's *Pink Flamingos* (1972).[75] Trecartin's movies also possess these characteristics. For example, *Any Ever*'s (2009–10) carnivalesque narrative is presented as an expanded cinematic experience that disrupts the limitations of the world of the film by placing interactive seating in the exhibition space, thus producing a work whose very essence is grotesque and transgresses the limits of "good taste." Stam argues that many films have been "misunderstood or misappreciated" because they have "been judged by the canons of 'good taste' or 'political correctness' rather than as prolongations of a perennial carnivalesque tradition."[76] The author's last argument broaches a critical concept in art: Is there such a thing as good art or bad art?

Destabilization of Taste

Francesco Bonami, curator of the 50th Venice Biennale, raises questions concerning the value of contemporary art in his article "The Good, the Bad and the Ugly." Bonami points out that before 1989, there was a general consensus, or "unwritten by-laws" among art critics who judged the merit of artworks. However, in 1989, he states, with the arrival of Jeff Koons's series, *Made in Heaven*, art criteria dramatically changed, as the spectacle marked "the beginning of critical chaos." First shown in 1990 at the 44th Venice Biennale, the work consists of paintings, photographs, and sculptures portraying Jeff Koons and ex-wife/pornstar, Ilona Staller, in explicit sexual positions. The piece created considerable controversy as it presented kitschy pornographic imagery as art, which some horrified viewers felt crossed the boundaries of good taste. However, others thought the show was of major art-historical importance. Certainly, due to the heated debate it provoked, the art world cognoscenti had to reconsider and adjust established critical standards and possibly even do away with them completely.

Bonami's article is particularly direct in calling attention to the fact that in today's art world, there is no such thing as bad or good taste—the good, the bad, and the ugly "have joined together to create a chaos from which it is hard to forecast a clear outcome."[77] Whether we are uneasy about the mayhem or thrilled by its undetermined outcome, we are in the midst of a time in art history that allows us to appreciate, without shame or fear of social repercussions, what was once considered tacky or vulgar. Embracing this situation, Ryan Trecartin writes,

> I also think that a lot of the time, with disturbing things, actually deep down underneath them something positive is shifting. [. . .] But then I kind of think that what's happening underneath is that we are all being a lot more comfortable with full-frontal ugliness, like showing everything that's running through our heads, and sharing everything, and not being afraid to be embarrassed and in a way that's kind of a positive shift.[78]

Trecartin employs the aesthetic tools of the grotesque, abject, and camp, because to him the "ugliness" is in fact symptomatic of change, which he sees as a positive process. He is deeply aware that the acceleration of interactive technologies is generating a new cultural momentum that is forcing this change. However disturbing that shift may appear at face value, he reminds us that change is necessary and natural. We will see throughout the manuscript that this philosophical undercurrent runs through much of his work.

Digital Camp

Much like Jeff Koons's seminal series, Trecartin's work is replete with camp imagery, which, like the grotesque, destabilizes aesthetic conventions. Caryl Flinn comments in "The Deaths of Camp," "Like the disunified grotesque, camp also works to violate the standards of 'good taste' [. . .]."[79] Camp aligns itself with the carnivalesque in its relation to playfulness. Susan Sontag writes in "Notes on 'Camp,'" "Camp is a solvent of morality. It neutralizes moral indignation, sponsors playfulness. [. . .] Camp taste is above all, a mode of enjoyment, of appreciation—not judgment."[80] While Sontag frames camp as a general phenomenon of mass culture, Jack Babuscio explains that camp is really "a creative expression of the gay sensibility."[81] Babuscio defines gay sensibility as "a creative energy reflecting a consciousness that is different from the mainstream; a heightened awareness of certain human complications of feeling that spring from the fact of social oppressions; in short, a perception of the world which is colored, shaped, directed, and defined by the fact of one's gayness."[82]

In recent years, there has been a shift from an oppositional binary definition of camp as an exclusively "gay camp" to a more inclusive notion of "queer camp." Aymar Jean Christian asserts that in the new era of camp, which he calls "camp 2.0," "the notion of 'queering' something is now fundamental to camp and suggests anything from blurring dichotomies—androgyny, confounding male and female—to challenging societal assumptions [. . .]."[83] According to Christian, online platforms such as YouTube have in fact humanized expressions of camp, as camp is no longer used to claim one's difference but one's individuality.[84]

Trecartin's playful sense of camp is more in keeping with this notion of camp 2.0 as his queer camp sensibility also challenges social norms. Thus, he departs from Sontag's interpretation, which, while playful, is devoid of criticality. The ever-shifting identities in *I-BE Area*, global corporate culture in *P.opular S.ky*, and the extension of consciousness via the internet are all examples of how the artist implicitly raises ethical concerns in his work—albeit while keeping a humorous distance. Jonathan T. D. Neil effectively sums up Trecartin's campiness as, "an air kiss and a bitch-slap at once."[85]

Trecartin's low-tech camp aesthetic also resonates with the masses' engagement with consumer-friendly technology. In a 2011 online interview, he disclosed that he used a small Canon camera, the kind "that fits in your hand," to shoot his series *Any Ever*, and edited the footage with iMovie. The audio was recorded directly from the in-camera microphones.[86] Trecartin is aware that artists are no longer the sole image-makers. He understands that in the age of digital reproduction, anyone can become a photographer, filmmaker, or graphic designer. Douglas Davis writes, "Only the unwary mind would deny the further inevitability that a 'neurasthenic' computer, programmed by humanoid codes [. . .] will shortly create paintings from first stroke to last."[87] Davis takes his cue from Walter Benjamin, who a century before made similar arguments to substantiate the claims for the populist appeal of photographic image-making.

As I discuss further in chapter 3, with the emergence of Web 2.0, online users are able to engage with works of art in unprecedented ways. YouTube viewers, for instance, not only interpret Trecartin's videos but are actively involved in shaping its cultural significance. Through the website's interface, they can share the work with other members, create discussion boards about specific videos, and even download, edit, cut, remix, and re-upload them for others to watch. What distinguishes interacting with Trecartin's early videos from viewing millions of others posted on video sharing sites is that the internet as a platform is an integrated component in the overall design of the work itself—not simply a venue for his videos to be exhibited. His aim is not for his movies to be separate objects contained within the interface of the websites, but rather to become extensions of the interface. In other words, there is no division between the content of the video and the participatory functionalities such as tags, comments, and feedbacks of the platform in which the movies are webcast. In fact, the artist encourages participation, contribution, and revision. As he comments in an interview for *Fillip* magazine, "I like people reading what they read: It's their edit."[88] The artist indeed responds to the content posted online by viewers and even develops collaborative relationships with some by enlisting them in his projects. When experiencing his work, one does not only watch the movie, but also follows audience participation and interaction with it. This mode of involvement with art has tremendous ramifications for discerning reception, as most of the comments posted are often raw and unprocessed. As such, they often dynamically reflect viewers' immediate reactions. Given the participatory nature, made possible through this online mediation, the inclusion of viewer feedback throughout this book is employed to address and illustrate important claims about his work.

Relational Aesthetics and Collaboration

In his book *Relational Aesthetics*, Nicolas Bourriaud claims that in relational art, the audience is conceived as a "micro-community." The artwork is more than just an object on display for the audience to passively look at; instead, this artistic practice produces intersubjective encounters. Through these encounters, meaning is created collectively.[89] The public is the source of "the aura." Bourriaud writes, "The aura of art no longer lies in the hinter-world represented by the work, nor in form itself, but in front of it, within the contemporary collective form that it produces by being put on a show."[90] Thus, he questions the notion of authorship. If, as he maintains, the viewer is the conveyor of meaning, then, can we still say that Ryan Trecartin is the work's author?

Trecartin is the first to state that his videos are the result of a collaborative process. As a director, he insinuates a word or line and then affords actors the freedom to improvise and create their own version of a character or a scene—thus everyone in his movies has "the authority in their relationship to being directed."[91] He credits his closest collaborators, especially artist Lizzie Fitch, who has performed in all his videos since they first met at art school. Fitch has contributed significantly as well to the design of the sets, props, and video installations.[92] In addition, Rhett LaRue has undertaken the application of special effects to his videos. Yet, Trecartin clearly affirms his vision through the editing and sound of his software-processed movies. As he states, "I write the script, although everyone influences it, and I direct, and then I edit, and they're all comfortable with that."[93] He is, in John Roberts's terms, a "bio-computational" author. Roberts writes,

> Artists no longer compose their works but rather "program" them. In this, previous artworks are no longer things to be cited or surpassed, but congeries of signs to be inhabited and manipulated, and, once these signs enter the realm of electronic space, a continuous means of generating other works and activities. The

> artwork, then, functions as a temporal nodal point in a larger flow or network of art's productive relations.[94]

As I argue in the final chapter, Ryan Trecartin gradually begins to conceive of his work much as a video game programmer does, as an experience intended for active participants who are engaged and able to navigate scenes. Trecartin explains, "I'm trying now to explore applications, hardware, and software ideas that would give more navigational agency to the viewer [. . .]"[95] In doing so, he attempts to transcend the barrier of the screen. In addition, the artist's view of the web moves beyond referring to the vernacular of the internet literally, as a subject, to acknowledging its networked platform as part of a collective social experience. As we will see in later chapters, the artist demonstrates how he conflates his philosophical perspective with formal art-making concerns in order to continue his quest to embrace change and fluidity.

Ryan Trecartin's work has been subjected to heated debates. On the one hand, it has been praised as groundbreaking, while on the other, it has been classified "as a cynical exploitation of the celebrity art market."[96] I believe that it is more fruitful to consider whether his work is contributing significantly to the broader ongoing discourse surrounding contemporary art. It is my hope that the following chapters will lay bare the complexity of Trecartin's art. I argue that Trecartin's movies are important because of what they reflect, what they say about a particular era and a generation in constant flux, while they simultaneously initiate and sustain an interactive dialogue with a global audience. That is not to say that he only produces art for his generation, as many reviewers have declared. Rather, Trecartin creates movies that demonstrate a way of thinking, a philosophical outlook that is open to all.

// 1 //

Early Baggage

Filmic Experimentation and Televisuality Retrieved as "Carry-On" Language

RYAN TRECARTIN CREATED *Early Baggage* (2001–03) during his tenure as an art student at Rhode Island School of Design.[1] The series consists of four individual short videos: *Valentine's Day Girl* (2001), *Yo! A Romantic Comedy* (2002), *What's the Love Making Babies For* (2003), and *Wayne's World* (2003), which are thematically and stylistically fully characteristic of his cinematic language. Viewers can already identify many of the defining formal elements that would firmly establish the artist's style—fast-paced editing, superimposition, oblique camera angles, repetition, fragmented shots, and discontinuity. *Early Baggage* also introduces us to Trecartin's recurring preoccupation with queerness, camp, the carnivalesque, and the grotesque and abject body. These early, pre-YouTube era videos clearly show that rather than gradually developing a visual vocabulary over time, he had already established a unique style at the outset of his career.

This is not to say that *Early Baggage* reveals all we mean when we speak of Trecartin's work. While it encompasses some of his formal approach, it does not contain many of the motifs the artist has explored and developed in the course of his career to date. He initially established his language by merging, inverting, blending shots, and utilizing postproduction tools, while breaking basic rules of filmmaking: 180-degree rule, rule of thirds, and leading-line composition. He borrows a myriad of stylistic references and techniques from experimental filmmaking and television for his arsenal of unlimited effects. He draws influence from a trajectory of avant-garde films, which concerned themselves with the formal manipulation of the moving image, often utilizing manual alternative processes. Through his use of Apple iMovie postproduction software with its multitude of special effects such as *overlay* to achieve a superimposition effect, *reverse* function that inverts images, and *instant replay* to repeat shots, he pays homage to a long-standing tradition of experimental filmmaking.

While Trecartin's digitally manipulated work may appear at first as a conglomeration of random software commands, these carefully selected effects play essential roles in inciting emotional responses from viewers. As I will be demonstrating throughout the body of this book, his aim is for his movies not to be simply watched but to be experienced. Trecartin's work enacts the manic and overwhelming experiential stimulus of virtual technology through fast-paced editing and an overload of images, computer-generated special effects, and iconography directly inspired by contemporary modes of communication.

In addition to new technology and experimental filmmaking, television plays a major part in shaping Trecartin's early work. The influence of TV and its effect on viewers is notable in *Early Baggage*, which is rich in pop culture references taken directly from television tropes such as the music video, commercial, soap opera, reality TV, and talk show, which he typically displays in rapidly expelled imagery and media sound bites.

Trecartin's first series of videos demonstrates an acute awareness of the ways mass media impacts youth culture by examining how young people readily identify with consumer culture and create and perform their identity(ies) around it. The four-part series begins with *Valentine's Day Girl*, a fantasy narrative about a teen girl, played by his friend and collaborator Lizzie Fitch, who has fallen victim to a holiday shopping obsession. *Yo! A Romantic Comedy* follows, featuring white suburban teenagers appropriating the vocabulary, body language, and street fashions characteristic of hip-hop culture. The low-tech creatures in *What's the Love Making Babies For* then communicate through a dynamic instant text messaging dialect about gender and reproduction. Finally, in *Wayne's World*, Trecartin ponders the significance of the content generated by mainstream forms of youth entertainment, by referencing MTV's music videos, reality programs such as *The Real World*, and homespun community cable programming. *Valentine's Day Girl* and *Wayne's World* make for particularly interesting close readings, as both not only comment on the effects of media on youth culture but also demonstrate the direct correlation that exists early on in Trecartin's art with avant-garde cinema and television.

Valentine's Day Girl opens with a black screen. No image appears within the first thirty seconds, yet the manic soundtrack playing in the background foreshadows the frantic action that is about to unfold. Although Trecartin's work is primarily visual in nature, he "intends his viewers to be listeners as well."[2] Linda Norden comments, "The best way to gain conversance in Trecartin's work is to watch it—and listen to it—repeatedly."[3] Indeed, the tumultuous opening soundtrack meshes well with its fast-paced in-your-face visuals. The brief silence at the commencement of the opening scene is shattered by a digital cacophony that takes the viewer by surprise as a loud discordant mixture of electronic sounds, including video game buzz and computer system crash warning signals, sound off at full blast. Although the relentless noise is at first unpleasant, if one listens to it repeatedly, a certain rhythm is identifiable, in which sounds are repeated in a sequential order that progressively accelerate until each note and vibration converge to create a sort of techno-clash melody. This overwhelming symphonic expulsion actually prepares us for full immersion into Trecartin's saturated visual style.

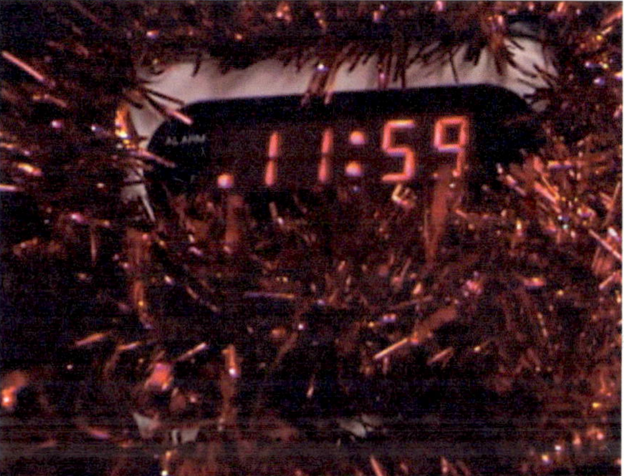

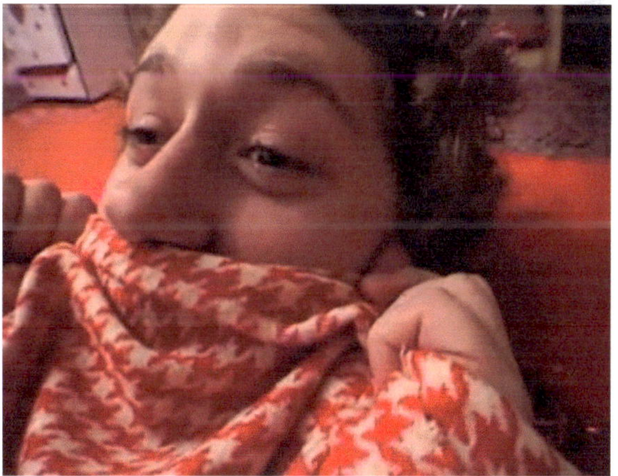

Figures 1.1 and 1.2 *Valentine's Day Girl* (2001)

An abrupt cut to a close-up of an LCD alarm clock swathed in a sparkly red garland is our entry point. The clock radio reads "11:59." Loud shrieks of excitement can be overheard in the background. Trecartin jump-cuts to a close-up of the protagonist's feet stomping on red linoleum flooring. The opening sequence is structured as a set of increasingly rapid crosscuts between close-ups of the alarm clock and an array of shots of Lizzie Fitch impatiently waiting for the clock to strike 12:00 midnight. Trecartin's stylistic decisions convey how the protagonist experiences the quickly shifting succession of moods. The artist translates a range of emotions that include anticipation, impatience, and finally euphoria. He accomplishes these fluctuations by employing rapid editing and artful cinematography that includes tilted camera angles, jump cuts, and claustrophobic close-ups. The video appears to be in a perpetual state of motion, as no shot lasts longer than three seconds. Flux is, in fact, a defining characteristic of all his work.

After jumping out of bed, *Valentine's Day Girl*'s heroine stretches her arms wide open as if waking up from an extended hibernation and exclaims, "I don't like Frederick. Boys are gross! Boys are gross!" Lizzie is then framed through an overhead shot as she casually explains, "I think I like girls this year." The high-angle prevents us from seeing her face. We do not know at this point if this sudden shift in her romantic preference is willed, or if it is a change that she has discovered after the fact, something that has happened to her spontaneously, without her consciously willing it. The unsettling background soundtrack comes to a sudden standstill and a close-up of the heroine fills the screen. The protagonist casts her eyes upward and for a moment of stasis appears to be wallowing in a state of ecstasy. She recovers and utters the name of her new love interest, "Ashley," in an exaggerated sensual voice. It is at this instance that we come to the conclusion that she is open to change; she accepts this shift and indeed embraces it. The lengthy five-second close-up reveals to us that the protagonist's switch is not involuntary. She then proceeds to erase Frederick's name from a long list of male and female contenders scribbled on a heart-shaped card she keeps tucked underneath her sweater, which further emphasizes Valentine's Day girl's fickleness. When asked to comment on the identity(ies) of the characters in his videos, Trecartin replied that he looks forward to the time when "we [can] reach a point where personality defines you more than your gender, sexuality, or career because nothing is fixed."[4]

Trecartin's understanding of "personality"[5] as nonfixed aligns itself with Doty's definition of queerness, as mentioned in the introduction. In the close-up described above, the protagonist not only expresses her choice but also affirms her queerness. Valentine's Day girl becomes a prototype for many of Trecartin's later subjects. It is important to understand that it is not because Ryan Trecartin and his characters do not set parameters for categorizing themselves that they are queer. It is because the artist and characters actively label themselves as individuals who cannot be labeled, that I understand them—and they understand themselves—to be queer. It is in this proactive labeling that they play a subversive role in the affirmation of their queer identity(ies). His characters are anything but passive; they seek "personal agency [. . .] in an age of infinite optionality."[6]

Trecartin frames his protagonists through partial views and tight close-ups that only reveal portions of their faces or bodies. In one close-up, for instance, the camera focuses on the protagonist's thighs as she sits on top of her kitchen table making her body appear truncated. She is overheard exclaiming, "I wish I had a penis!" The artist employs this fractional shot, as if it were a piece of a puzzle he is assembling. These in turn stand as symbols of the multidimensionality of his characters, made up of various options that he reconfigures, merges, or does away with. Valentine's Day girl may eventually decide that she will be a pansexual femme or a transsexual butch queen; either way, she, like all the other Trecartin protagonists who will come after her, occupies a queer space that is not contained within or described by a fixed gender/identity.

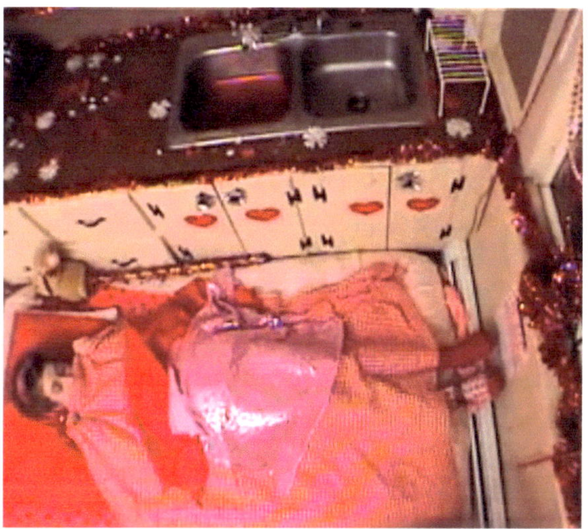

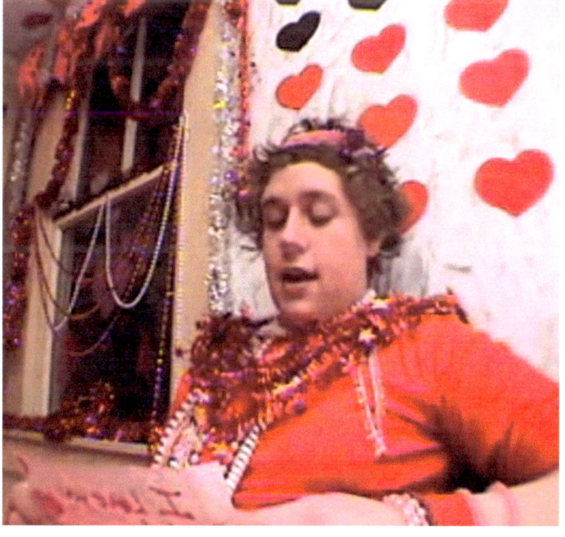

Figures 1.3 and 1.4 *Valentine's Day Girl* (2001)

As the scene unfolds, Trecartin provides wide-angle shots of the apartment's gaudy decor. Every nook and cranny in the low-budget set is replete with heart-shaped or cupid-inspired decorations and iconography. The over-the-top, campy mise-en-scène is strewn with carefully selected red, pink, and white party props, tinsel garland, and love-themed patterned fabrics. In her pivotal essay "Notes on Camp," Susan Sontag writes, "To emphasize style is to slight content, or to introduce an attitude which is neutral with respect to content. It goes without saying that the Camp sensibility is disengaged, depoliticized—or at least apolitical."[7] While Trecartin's campiness is playful, it is in no way disengaged. The oversaturation of sanguine colors and abundance of mass-manufactured plastic Valentine's Day tchotchkes point to the subversive nature of his commentary on the material culture of holiday commercialism. In addition, the protagonist's fanatical excitement is never justified, as she is never shown actually celebrating with anyone but herself. This facet of Fitch's character represents young consumers influenced by the media to anticipate and take part in capitalist seasonal festivities, even though they may not have any sort of real personal investment in them. The contrast between this alienation and obsession with Valentine's Day reinforces the irony.

Jack Babuscio notes, "Camp is often exaggerated. When the stress on style is 'outrageous' or 'too much,' it results in incongruities: the emphasis shifts from what a thing or a person is to what it *looks* like; from what is being done to *how* it is being done."[8] Interestingly, Trecartin has expressed that his characters do not represent people but social behavioral archetypes—they do not refer to themselves as human beings but as ideas.[9] He is more interested in what his protagonist represents than who/what she is. Extending Babuscio's analogy, Trecartin does not focus on *what* his protagonist does but on *how* she does it. For instance, when the character jumps out of bed to celebrate Valentine's Day, the mélange of crosscuts, jump cuts, and oblique camera angles aim to reinforce the protagonist's euphoria. Thus, the primary goal of Trecartin's montage editing is not to serve a narrative function but to convey emotion.

Soon after her initial burst of enthusiasm, Fitch receives an unexpected love letter from an unnamed character crouched inside her kitchen pantry. The note informs her that some treats are hidden under her oven. Through a series of quickly edited shots, reminiscent of a cartoon flip book, the heroine is seen running into her kitchenette retrieving and consuming the red sweets. Trecartin then captures the protagonist's dizzying slow-motion reaction to their consumption, while a mad soundtrack morphs into a deranged lullaby. We suddenly realize that the large bulbous treats she ingested seem to be laced with a hallucinogenic substance causing her whirling sensation. She finally regains consciousness only to realize that her private celebration has been invaded by a mob of Christmas-themed intruders. Rapid sequences of images catapult viewers inexplicably from shots of Valentine's decorations to nightmarish visions of Christmas ornaments. The heart-patterned fabrics hanging on the walls have been transformed into Christmas tree-patterned textiles, and the garland has been replaced with synthetic wreaths of green pine cones. This pseudosurrealist vision creates, as Amelia Jones puts it, an "alternative universe where seeing and knowing are split from each other such that vision promises nothing but uncoded, irrational images conveying [. . .] 'psychosomatic symptoms' of subconscious fantasy."[10] While these frightening images appear "irrational," they are not, according to Jones, "uncoded." Through them, Trecartin further develops his original commentary on the commercialization of holidays by disrupting his protagonist's Valentine's Day utopia, suddenly fast-forwarding her to Christmas, perhaps to comment on preemptive marketing strategies consumers are subjected to for holidays that take place months into the future. The director provides us with a point-of-view shot of the protagonist running across her living room as she tries to find a way to escape in vain from the Christmas coup d'état. The frenetic sequence suddenly ends where it all began—with a black screen.

The second act of *Valentine's Day Girl* opens with a point-of-view shot (from the protagonist's perspective) depicting a gang of creepy bedizened Christmas fairies directly facing the camera. They address the heroine in asynchronous and incomprehensible high-pitched voices that accentuate their fantastic nature, speaking what sounds like some sort of foreign dialect. The director then cuts to a succession of rapidly edited shots depicting the creatures partaking in a jubilant maelstrom while consecutively ravaging her apartment. Trecartin utilizes undercranking, dramatic high/low camera angles, and fast-paced editing to accentuate their high physicality: jumping, clapping, executing acrobatic moves, and dancing. Robert Stam describes

Figure 1.5 *Valentine's Day Girl* (2001)

such a spectacular and ostentatious form of play as carnivalesque: "an alternative cosmovision characterized by the ludic undermining of all norms."[11]

Trecartin chooses to forgo conventional rules of traditional storytelling by offering alternative temporalities that deviate from the fixity and linearity of continuity editing. The party scene in *Valentine's Day Girl*, in all its carnivalesque exhilaration, with its constant shift from high to low camera angles, long shots to extreme close-ups, fragmented shots, undercranking, and overall topsy-turvy editing, can be understood as a cinematic exemplification of Mikhail Bakhtin's logic of the inside/out. This entertaining and disorderly concept continuously shifts "from top to bottom, from front to rear, of numerous parodies and travesties, humiliations, profanations, comic crownings and uncrownings."[12] However, although the revelry appears at first as a randomly edited string of clips, each rapid shot in fact engenders the following one as a continuous extension. Individual cuts do not follow a cause-and-effect logic, but instead prolong or continue an action performed. Trecartin achieves this effect, for example, by cutting from a scene portraying a character in the middle of an action, to a shot of a different character continuing that same action. In one particular medium shot, we see a Christmas fairy clapping. The scene then cuts to another medium shot of a different pixie completing that clapping action. Subsequently, one creature jumps up in the air and the following shot shows a different character landing on the floor. This elliptical editing strategy unifies the individual characters into one unstable and unindividuated entity in a state of constant change.

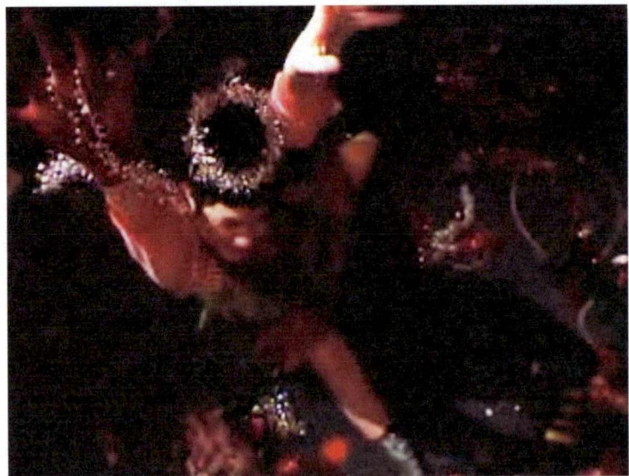

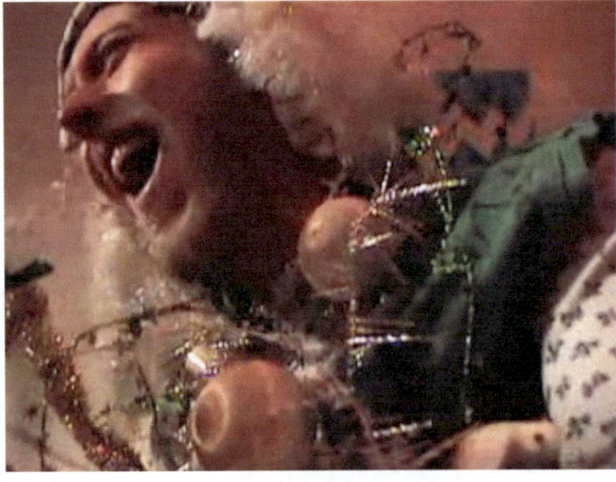

Figures 1.6 and 1.7 *Valentine's Day Girl* (2001)

The body of carnival, as represented by the Christmas characters' whimsical pandemonium, is indeed a body in flux and continuous creation, and thus grotesque. According to Bakhtin, the carnival, as the "feast of becoming, change," inscribes itself as the grotesque body par excellence, "a body in the act of becoming." It "outgrows its own self" as it is continually evolving.[13] This concept is visually translated through Trecartin's montage, which I coin the "grotesque montage," extended throughout much of his later work. Many of his subsequent videos climax in delirious party scenes in which characters come in and out of screens; shots are repeated and assembled in a nonlinear manner to fuse the performers into one body-in-motion, which gives the impression that these parties are ever-shifting entities or characters in their own right.

As the Valentine's Day festivities progress, we discover a shift in mood: the action accelerates, the characters' laughter turns menacing, and their smiles transform into grimaces. The creatures start puncturing balloons they had originally inflated and begin slapping each other. One evil garland draped performer slaps the camera lens, which causes the footage to shake. After this assault on the apparatus, a rapid succession of oblique angle shots creates a sense of nauseating delirium. The director turns the Christmas party into a perverse madhouse. He cuts to a close-up of a holiday reveler expelling a blob of viscid phlegm from his mouth. What originally seemed like playful shenanigans now turns into threatening degeneracy. The ecstatic Christmas creatures have shifted from grotesque to abject. While the abject disturbs notions of fixed identity by occupying a state of in-betweenness much like the grotesque in Bakhtin's account, "abjection, on the other hand, is immoral, sinister, scheming, and shady: a terror that dissembles, a hatred that smiles [. . .]."[14] The body of carnival in *Valentine's Day Girl* can thus be characterized as abject since it is both in a constant state of flux and traumatic. The dichotomy between abject and grotesque

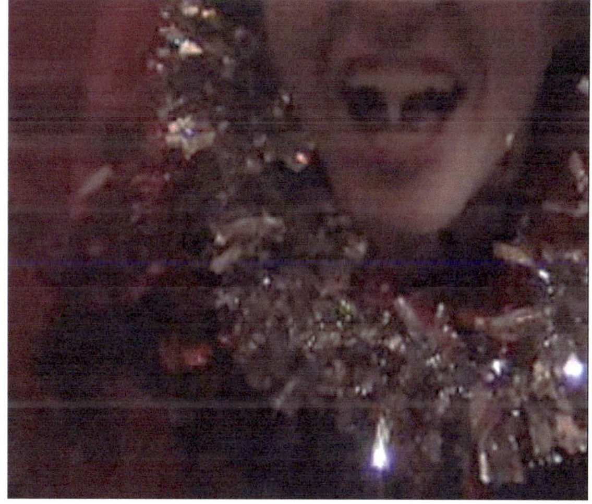

Figure 1.8
Valentine's Day Girl (2001)

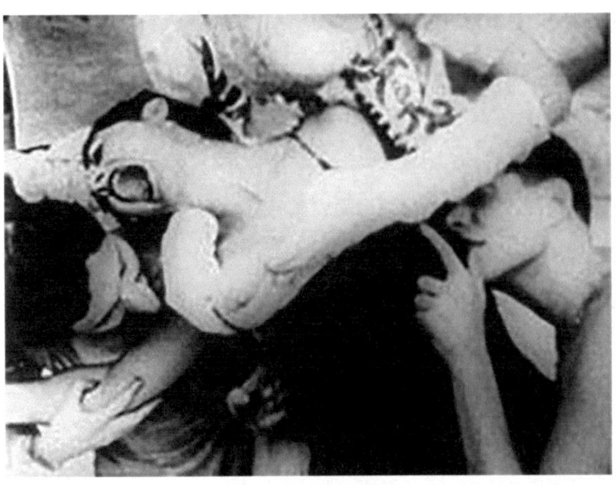

Figure 1.9 *Flaming Creatures* (1963)

and playful and menacing, are tensions inherent in the process of change and transformation.

Ajay RS Hothi and Christabel Stewart state, "Trecartin's films tread a fine line between comedy and horror."[15] However, by fully embracing both, his video actually obliterates the distinction. Much like Jack Smith's avant-garde classic *Flaming Creatures* (1963), Trecartin's polysexual and polymorphous fairies inspire both fear and laughter. In Smith's film, seemingly harmless androgynous characters, homeless junkies, and trannies all congregate to ravage a voluptuous young woman, Delicious Dolores (Sheila Bick). Similarly, in Trecartin's *Valentine's Day Girl* video, a wicked Christmas character is seen crawling toward the protagonist, who is gagged and strapped to a chair. As he slowly approaches, the villain flaunts his physique and begins to disrobe. Trecartin then cuts to a medium shot of the distressed heroine. Invoking the point-of-view of the villain, the camera surveys her legs and breasts in a slow, deliberate manner that suggests she is about to be victimized. Trecartin seems to be playing with the concept of the helplessness of consumers in the face of the commercialization of Christmas. While his deliberate camera angles are suggestive of an impending attack, *Flaming Creatures*' shots explicitly depict an orgiastic bacchanal. Jack Smith's overhead camera seems to take part in the all-consuming orgy as it surveys the mass of indiscernible entangled bodies.[16] It reveals Delicious Dolores being consumed by a horde of half-naked male and female creatures, close-ups of breasts, buttocks, vaginas, penises, and wagging tongues emerging intermittently from the helter-skelter. Much like *Valentine*'s *Day Girl*'s protagonist, Delicious Dolores is unable to escape and surrenders. Smith ends the scene with an unanticipated cut to complete silence. In a similar manner, *Valentine*'s *Day Girl*'s climax also comes to an abrupt ending, as Trecartin cuts without warning to a black screen. The demented soundtrack fades into a sweet lullaby, and we are confronted with an overwhelmingly disturbing close-up of the menacing Christmas character smiling directly into the camera.

Unlike *Flaming Creatures*, *Early Baggage* does not contain any shots of genitalia meant to challenge or shock spectators. Instead, Trecartin's videos are disturbing in what they leave unsaid, the questions they leave unanswered. As Wayne Koestenbaum writes, Trecartin's videos are like "slasher films without blood [or] porn [. . .]."[17] Trecartin understands that viewers have become desensitized to sex and violence, so both are presented with a tongue-in-cheek attitude. The whirlwind velocity of his editing, hybrid characters, and constantly shifting narratives destabilize viewers, who are reminded that what they are watching, in fact, represents a facet of the world they live in. However, the near seizure-inducing speed of his videos does not deny his genuine excitement in facing the unknown as Trecartin embraces change. In a revealing interview, titled "All-American Golden Boy," Trecartin commented:

> You know, a lot of the time terrifying aspects of our culture are really a symptom of something very positive that may be happening underneath. I think amazing things sometimes just seem superficial and negative at first because we have to change our moral codes before we can appreciate them properly.[18]

It is precisely his openness, his willingness to adapt to the unknown, that makes his work sublime and so true to life. His videos transport viewers on journeys of perpetual transformation that at first may appear disturbing and terrifying, but ultimately reveal themselves to be positive experiences.

Some of the feedback on YouTube regarding Trecartin's work is suggestive of the emotional impact his videos have on viewers. For example, after watching *Valentine's Day Girl*, member "crambearyyy" posted, "[. . .] I feel mostly engrossed, interested, happy, multidimensional but sometimes nauseous and self questioning. Nonetheless, I can't stop watching and I've seen all your stuff on youtube. You're one of my favorite artists of all time (&space) :]."[19] *Valentine's Day Girl* can even be described as destabilizing as it takes spectators on an emotional roller coaster, vacillating from humor to panic and finally leaves them pondering what happens to the protagonist at the end. Judging by the final haunting close-up of the villainous Christmas creature, our heroine appears to have been subdued by the onslaught of holiday merchandising. *Valentine's Day Girl* only

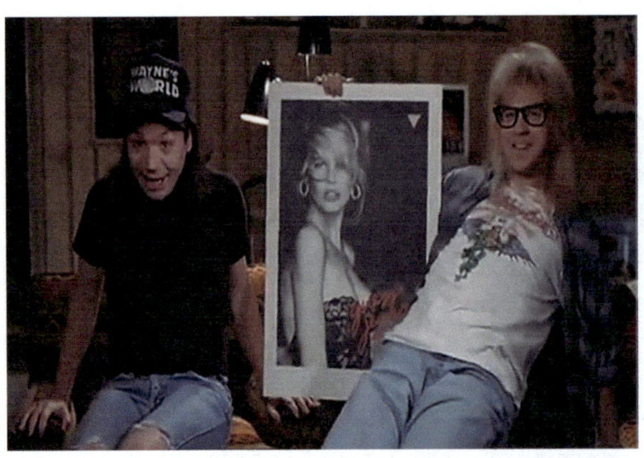

Figure 1.10 *Wayne's World* (1992)

constitutes the first episode of *Early Baggage*, however. It will not be until the last segment, *Wayne's World*, that the underlying positive message of the work is truly uncovered.

While *Valentine's Day Girl*'s heroine might be considered a victim of consumerism, the protagonists in *Wayne's World* are producers in control of their own representation. Much like the characters of the original *Wayne's World* film (1992), adapted from a sketch of the same name on NBC's *Saturday Night Live*, cohorts, Ryan and Lizzie, broadcast a low-budget cable access program from their basement.

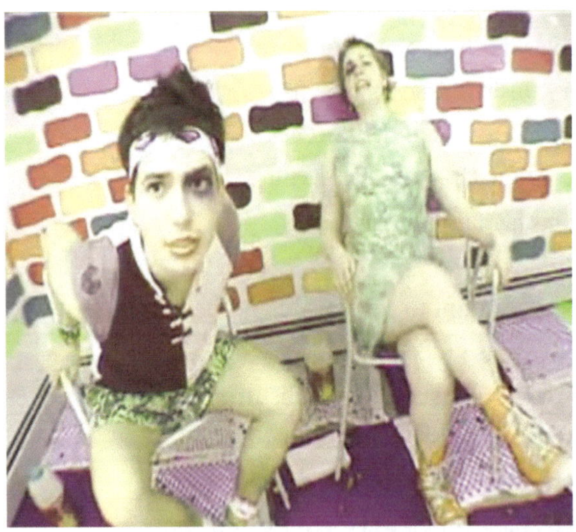

Figure 1.11 *Wayne's World* (2003)

Trecartin simulates the experience of watching television by incorporating many of the specific properties associated with it: immediacy, direct address, interruption, and segmentation. Trecartin's *Wayne's World* recalls an earlier video piece by Alex Bag who re-created the experience of channel-surfing in *Untitled* (*Project for the Andy Warhol Museum*) (1996) by jump-cutting back and forth between commercials, daytime and late-night talk shows, music videos, soap operas, and news programs, which all feature her as the protagonist.

Valentine's Day Girl's introduction confronts viewers with an opaque black screen, while *Wayne's World*'s opening shot directly references the music industry and privileges sound over image. The video opens with a series of hand-painted vintage-inspired graphics reminiscent of 1980s MTV promotional logos. The sequence crosscuts between jittering images of flashy geometric patterns and medium close-ups of Trecartin and Fitch's bright clunky sneakers moving in unison to music. In *Experiencing Music Video*, Carol Vernallis notes, "Music videos do not embody complete narratives [but instead] follow the song's form, which tends to be cyclical and episodic rather than sequentially directed."[20] While ballads might tell complete stories, Vernallis is referring specifically to the pop song format, which consists of a repetitive verse–chorus structure. Trecartin, however, manipulates the footage by fast-forwarding it, slowing it down, and repeating shots in order to create a visual rhythm in sync with the repetitive beats of his frenetic, discordant merry-go-round soundtrack. We are then provided with a full-frontal shot of Trecartin and Fitch's spastic choreographed dance. Although at first, it may appear as though one is looking in on and intruding on the characters' private universe, viewers quickly realize that the performers are actually inviting them to enter. This is made evident when the two protagonists look into the camera and address it, as if speaking directly to an audience.

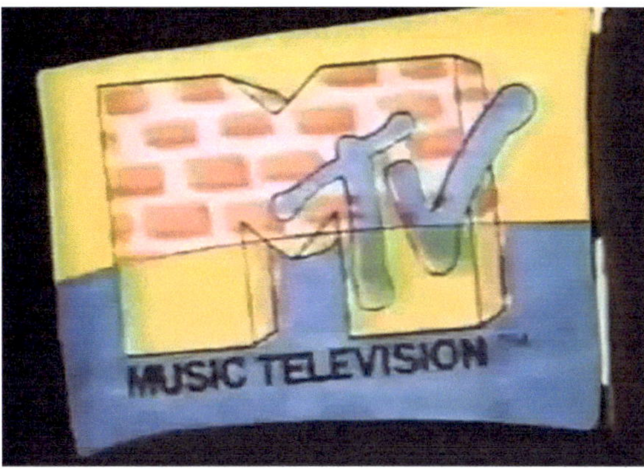

Figure 1.12
MTV Logo

The camera's presence is further emphasized when we observe the protagonists taking Polaroid snapshots of its lens. This self-reflexive nod to the camera informs us of their intent to acknowledge and call attention to the medium. We can trace this formal acknowledgment and recurring motif in the history of cinema from *The Great Train Robbery* (1903), *Sherlock Jr.* (1924), and *Man with a Movie Camera* (1929) to *Hold Me While I'm Naked* (1966) by George Kuchar. *Wayne's World* not only brings to our attention his awareness of metacinematic devices, but also the immediacy of the instant image produced by the Polaroid. In choosing to feature the device, Trecartin informs us that he and his audience belong to a generation used to performing in front of cameras, and

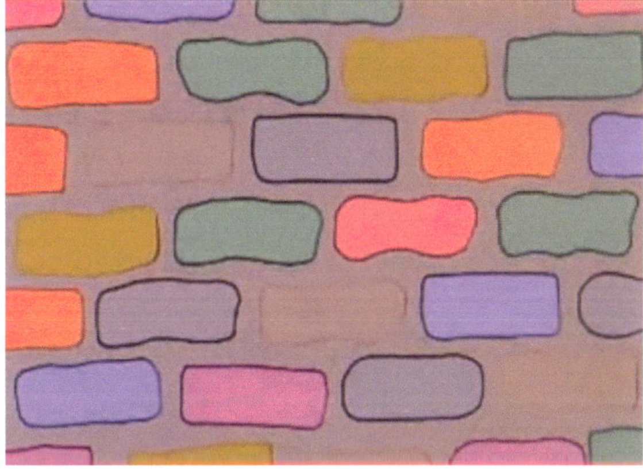

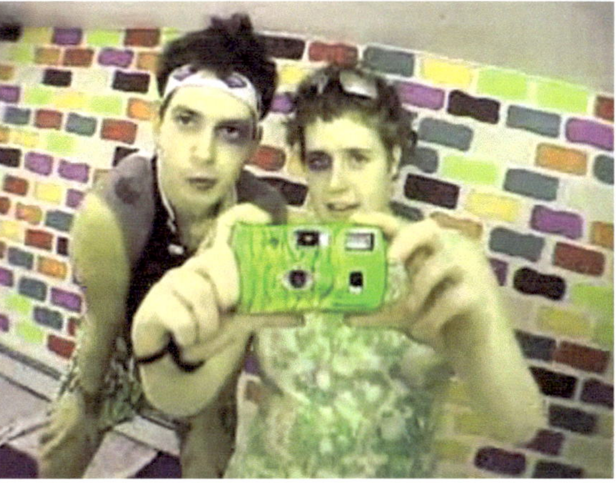

Figures 1.13 and 1.14
Wayne's World (2003)

attracted to the instant gratification that comes from the immediacy of the digital image.

Trecartin attributes the phenomenon of an entire generation of camera performers to the extensive influence of television. In an interview for *Another Man* magazine, the artist explained that early on in his career, he was mostly inspired by the way people responded to the medium.

> I feel I was really affected by my babysitters, watching them get excited by some TV show and how it affected their lives and how it changed the way they talked and how it added to their language and those other forms of intelligence that exist, like body language and accents. It's funny how everyone now is used to performing and translating ideas and using all forms of language.[21]

The artist's characters emit the same authenticity (or lack thereof) as reality TV stars, making it improbable we will embark on a journey of suspended disbelief. His decision to feature theatrical overacting ensures our understanding that they are putting on a show for us and it is scripted, fabricated, staged, and exaggerated. Even the close-ups do not allow the subjects to reveal themselves. Instead, Trecartin uses the close-up as a way to magnify affected facial gestures to inform us that they know they are being filmed.

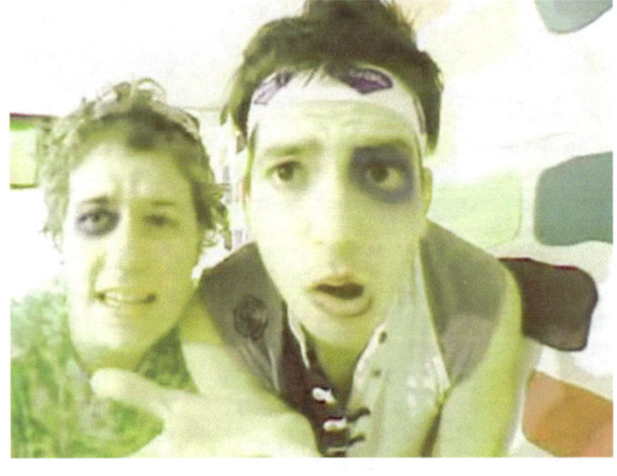

Figure 1.15 *Wayne's World* (2003)

Through a series of static camera angles, Trecartin is shown dancing and singing inside constructed environments fabricated to resemble sets straight out of the world of postpunk pop culture with the production value of a Jack Smith hand-painted set. Suddenly, the blaring soundtrack fades and the image slowly dissolves into an extreme close-up of a plastic bottle labeled "carrot juice 100% pure pressed"—an apparent nod to a commercial break. The image fades out once again, this time to present viewers with a tilted angle shot of Ryan and Lizzie preparing for a public access television talk show. However, before they engage in impromptu banter, the pair is interrupted by an overwhelming silence that appears to emanate from outside the frame. The background music comes to a halt. The characters prick up their ears in an attempt to ascertain this unfamiliar muteness, as if silence possessed a sound onto itself. Because they have been raised with the constant bombardment of media and data noise, this tidal wave of noiselessness overwhelms the scene with its foreign and unexpected stillness. Jessica Helfand notes in *Screen*,

> Silence, in contemporary life, is not only a commodity, it is an endangered species: hard to come by, harder still to sustain, and oddly associated with a kind of anachronistic world view: silence is the stuff of old media, a body of stillness, an inert mass.[22]

After recovering from the shock of the unexpected wave of silence, the camera offers us a back view of the protagonists opening the door to their basement in order to ascertain the disruptive yet inaudible source. As they attempt to uncover what lies outside their bunker-style underground shelter, they come face-to-face with a blinding tower of light. Pixelated two-dimensional bubble graphics explode from the glare and consume the entire shot. An effusion of translucent globes penetrates the protagonists' space, paralyzing them and leaving them confused. Both characters look at each other and simultaneously ask: "What what what what does it mean mean mean? What's the significance?" As if pondering the relevance of illogical sequences of images transmitted through TV and internet screens on a daily basis, the protagonists return to their seats and continue asking themselves "What does it mean?" Lizzie looks back at Ryan and simply responds, "Duh!" (as if the answer was obvious). Ryan looks at the camera and concurs "Duh!" Satisfied with Fitch's analysis, he moves on to the next topic. The artist does not attempt to provide answers, as he implies that there is really no complex meaning behind most of what is being shown on TV. Much like network-era television's discontinuous flow, *Wayne's World*'s plot is segmented into parcels, switching back and forth from talk show to daytime soap opera, to commercial, and to music video. This segmentation precludes a fluid viewing experience as TV constantly breaks its own flow. After all, as Jeremy Butler points out, "to the television industry, programs are just filler, a necessary inconvenience interrupting the true function of television: broadcasting commercials."[23] This instance of the video's self-reflexivity may raise the question of whether or not there is indeed any complex meaning behind Trecartin's video, since *Wayne's World* essentially tries to re-create a passive TV-watching experience with little to no intellectual content. However, it is through the very process of re-creating a televisual experience that Trecartin is able to take a distanced critical approach and dispel the myth of television, which makes his video so meaningful.

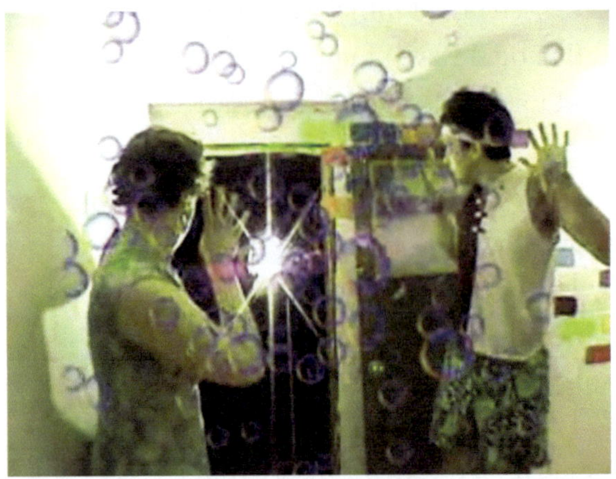

Figure 1.16
Wayne's World (2003)

Trecartin appropriates the televisual commercial format to comment on the consumption of youth culture. In her essay "Nothing Sells Like Teen Spirit: The Commodification of Youth Culture," Karen Brooks states that the media appropriate and objectify youth culture in order to sell products.

> In these television shows, youth is a performance, a "repeated ritualization" that can be imitated and consumed by audiences of all ages, perpetuating and commodifying what the dominant market forces imagine youth, in all its manifestations, to constitute. [. . .] Because of their apparent lack of political agency, young people are most often reduced to objects in this process: They are commodified and marketed back to themselves, stripped of any history, individual identity, or power. The commodification of youth and youth culture presents young people as important only when they are either products or consumers as opposed to critical, social subjects.[24]

The artist highlights this commodification in a scene in which protagonists parody a daytime soap opera. Employing direct address, performers playing fictional characters engage in clichéd breakup dialogue. The entire sequence is shot in medium close-ups—a tight framing tactic employed by TV directors to stress the "characters' heightened emotional state."[25] Ironically, *Wayne's World's* protagonists are completely detached from their emotions as they recite their lines in a mechanical manner, smiling and giggling at uncomfortable pauses. In presenting this contradiction, Trecartin emphasizes the apparent artificiality of the network drama.

In a scene where Lizzie pours her heart out in front of the camera, devastated from the demise of her "long-term" three-week relationship, Ryan (her boyfriend) responds by breaking out into song in order to express his emotions. He is only capable of processing and communicating his feelings through the structure of the verse and chorus of a pop ballad.

> Lizzie Fitch: "How could you break what you have been building, and the show was a thrill, and the cold has been frozen?"
>
> "I know that I am being very bad, I can't bring to say what I thought I could tell you."
>
> Ryan Trecartin: "Come on baby hold me, I love you. You'll always be my baby. Get a life."
>
> "Come on baby hold me, I told you, you'll always be my baby. Get a life."
>
> "When we talk for hours. It's dirty. I take a shower baby. don't send me flowers, oops, I told you."
>
> "Let me break it down. I told you, I told you it means nothing, it's nothing. Get over it."

The duet's antiromance/breakup ballad resembles songs by pop queens Britney Spears or Christina Aguilera. Trecartin is framed in medium shots swishing his hips in an exaggerated manner that recalls Spears's I'm a Slave 4 U's risqué choreography. He identifies and seeks to emulate his pop idols by reenacting a fictional storyline inspired by Spears's music video plot in Oops!... I Did It Again (2000), about a heartbreaker who toys with her lover's feelings. Trecartin's lyrics ("Come on baby hold me, I love you. You'll always be my baby. Get a life.) resemble Spears's "I made you believe we're more than just friends... Oh baby!" However, the primary difference between the two lies in Trecartin's use of irony. This distinction highlights the artist's criticality regarding the influence he reworks as an obviously exaggerated parody. We are meant to know that his take on Spears's song is in fact an imitation.

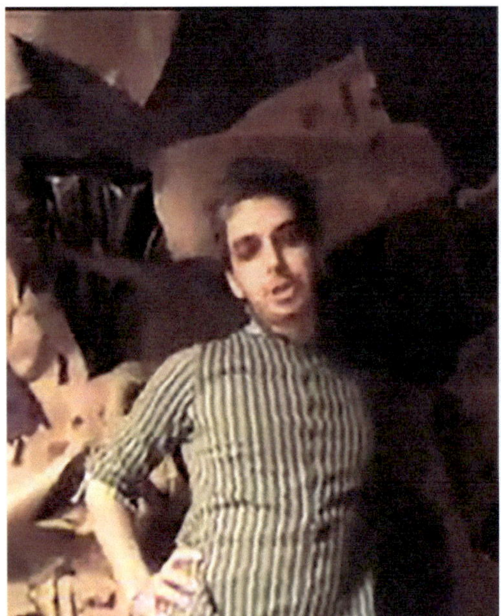

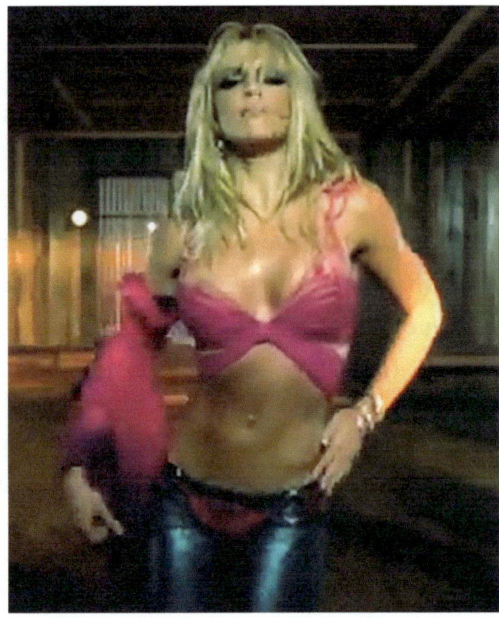

Figure 1.17
Wayne's World (2003)

Figure 1.18
Britney Spears, *I'm a Slave 4 U* (2001)

No matter how comical Trecartin's song may seem, it also conjures up a somber time for fans around the world who experienced the 2002 Britney Spears and Justin Timberlake breakup. Both pop stars publicly mourned the loss of their relationship. Justin wrote and performed "Cry Me a River" (2002), and Britney avoided dealing with her pain by going on her big-budget "Dream within a Dream" tour. Lizzie and Ryan attempt to find meaning in this sudden and unexplained pop fiasco by enacting what we imagine would have been the perfect way for Britney and Justin to have dissolved their made-in-pop-heaven union: an auto-tuned breakup duet.

Although the protagonists in *Wayne's World* may appear to be passive consumers of popular culture infatuated with celebrity relationships, they understand the codes and conventions of television and seek to challenge them. For instance, in one of their variety show segments, Lizzie reads a poem to Ryan.

Lizzie: I see Oprah on the TV screen. What does it mean? What does it mean? She sees herself on the TV screen. What does she see? What does she see? I see Oprah but she doesn't see me.

(Ryan interrupts his cohost and addresses the camera.)

Ryan: Bore Me to Death . . . Self-Reference! (laughter)

Trecartin understands that self-referentiality in TV lures viewers into thinking that they are empowered by making them privy to the ways media texts are constructed, however, this strategy may be employed "to further obscure the nature of media production."[26] Robert Stam writes, "Self-referentiality, far from demystifying the product or exposing hidden codes, conceals the deadly seriousness of the commercial—the fact that it is after the spectator's money."[27] As a savvy consumer, Ryan Trecartin is also well aware of advertisers' marketing tactics and appropriates and inverts them in order to take control of his own representation, thereby manufacturing his own version of himself.

Karen Brooks writes, "Youth are able to appropriate *themselves* as cultural products, place *themselves* within the circuits of consumption and so resist, challenge, and even, in a subversive gesture, celebrate the ideological imperialism that (re)creates young people as commodities instead of recognizing their potential as liminal subjects."[28] Brooks seems to imply that celebrating the commodification of youth and recognizing their liminality are mutually exclusive. However, Trecartin contradicts such implication by recognizing that each may be interconnected. He embraces consumer culture, as is demonstrated by his abundance of pop culture references. *Wayne's World*'s protagonists may appear to fetishize the objects they consume; yet, they readily dispose of them in order to move on to the next best thing. As the artist states, "We consume and consume and puke, more than fetishize the objects and information we use. [. . .] We don't act inside or outside of consumer culture, entertainment, or art culture, we consume and translate, we're a by-product of it."[29] By stating that he and his characters "don't act inside or outside," he emphasizes the concept of the "space in between," that is, their queerness. Furthermore, his reference above to puke and also to the term "by-product" evoking defecation, are part of what Bakhtin describes as "the main events in the life of the grotesque body, the acts of the bodily drama."[30] The concept of excrement as bodily discharge also aligns itself with Kristeva's notion of the abject. As Judith Butler writes,

> The "abject" designates that which has been expelled from the body, discharged as excrement, literally rendered "Other." [. . .] The boundary between the inner and outer is confounded by

> those excremental passages in which the inner effectively becomes outer, and this excreting function becomes, as it were, the model by which other forms of identity-differentiation are accomplished. In effect, this is the mode by which Others become shit.[31]

However, Trecartin does not see excrement as the "Other," rather, he embraces otherness in his affirmation, "We're a by-product." In fact, he "sees himself as a transitional figure."[32] He does not identify with the "inner" or "outer" but, rather, with "those excremental passages in which the inner effectively becomes outer." Therefore, the "by-product" that Trecartin refers to is not a fixed entity or "empty category" manufactured by "mainstream market forces,"[33] as implied by Brooks, but a complex and unstable being located within a liminal—an in-between and transitional—space.[34] The artist expresses this concept through his mise-en-scène: characters are never placed in the foreground or background; instead, they are shown in the middle plane of the shot. Furthermore, *Wayne's World*'s protagonists' flashy facial and body makeup colors match those of the various interiors that surround them. The characters can thus be seen as extensions, or "by-products" of the mise-en-scène—and vice versa. Therefore, there is no differentiation between bodies and other props in terms of their opportunities to be transformed. This is not to say that they are camouflaged within the set, since each truly demands viewers' attention as they double snap and prance during their respective performances.

With *Early Baggage*, Ryan Trecartin establishes a unique practice with an idiosyncratic style. Through his playful appropriation, extensive use of special effects, and delirious multilinear narratives, he generates content that feels like life run amok. However, while this loud and spontaneous approach might result in what appears to be an unscripted overload of stimulating imagery, I have demonstrated that it is much more complex. Every frame, cut, and shot is intentionally selected. Text, sound, and image operate synergistically to create an embodied and sensory viewing experience.

Kevin McGarry sums up the artist's video work as a "combination of assaultive, nearly impenetrable avant-garde logics and equally outlandish, virtuoso uses of color, form, drama and montage [which] produces a sublime, stream-of-consciousness effect that feels bewilderingly true to life."[35] What is terrifying in them is underwritten by something positive, their embrace of change. Through his art, the artist advocates for a flexible and adaptable world. But this revelation can only come to light by spending time with the work since, his narratives unfold at the speed of light. Unpacking them demands careful scrutiny as images advance faster than we can decode them on an initial viewing. Ryan Trecartin's impatience, apparent early in his career, clearly denotes an excitement toward the future and eagerness to grow as an artist.

// 2 //

A Family Finds Entertainment

The "Coming Out" Melodrama Remix

SHORTLY AFTER CREATING *A Family Finds Entertainment* for his BFA thesis exhibition in 2004, Trecartin rose to fame serendipitously, partly due to a series of extraordinary coincidences. As fate would have it, after uploading an excerpt of his video to the networking site Friendster.com in 2005, multimedia artist Sue de Beer was so impressed with the work that she decided to share it with former New Museum curator Rachel Greene.[1] A year later, *A Family Finds Entertainment* was exhibited at the 2006 Whitney Biennial of American Art and at QED in Los Angeles in a show called "I Smell Pregnant" curated by Elizabeth Dee.[2] The video has since become one of Trecartin's most popular works. This is due in large part to the queering and remixing of its narrative structure adopted from a beloved mode of storytelling: the Hollywood family melodrama.

In his book, *Hollywood Genres*, Thomas Schatz notes that most Hollywood movies may be described as melodramatic, since at its most basic level melodrama is defined as a narrative form that combines music or melos with drama to punctuate emotional effects.[3] However, he later explains that there is such a genre as the melodrama, which he refers to as the "family melodrama"—a term previously coined by Thomas Elsaesser.[4] According to Schatz, family melodrama's narrative formula is characterized by "its interrelated family of characters, its repressive small-town milieu, and its preoccupation with America's sociosexual mores."[5] Following Schatz, John Mercer and Martin Shingler proposed that the family melodrama "deals with highly-charged emotional issues, characterized by an extravagantly dramatic register [which] has the ability to provoke strong emotions in audiences, from tears of sorrow and identification, to derisive laughter."[6] Given its inherent intensity, it is not surprising that Trecartin would draw reference to the rhetoric of the melodrama, since one of his main concerns when writing scripts "is for viewers to leave his work with a deep emotional response to a reflection of their culture."[7] *A Family*

Finds Entertainment's dramatic logic, cinematography, mise-en-scène, performance style, and music accompaniment all borrow from the genre. Yet, Trecartin does not simply seek to produce a pastiche of melodrama's mode of address. The director revises it, transforms it, and ultimately, remixes it. Stefan Sonvilla-Weiss defines the cultural practice of remixing as one that may include "one or many materials, media either from other sources, art pieces (visual arts, film, music, video, literature, etc.) or one's own artworks through alteration, re-combination, manipulation, copying etc. to create a whole new piece."[8] While in a remix the end product in its entirety may not be a faithful copy of the original, the sources of the individual components that they comprise are identifiable. The individual influences that comprise Trecartin's remix of the family melodrama are clearly recognizable, as the artist does not attempt to conceal but pay homage to them.

Since the late 1970s, feminist film scholars have adopted the critical category of melodrama as a major area of debate, often investigating the extent to which patriarchal ideology is embedded within their narratives. Working within a revised feminist discourse in the 1990s, video performance artist, Pipilotti Rist, commented on the empowerment of the melodrama's female protagonist in her video installation *Ever Is Over All* (1997). Shot in slow motion to heighten its dramatic effect, a young woman dressed in a cocktail gown is shown walking down a city street smashing the windows of parked automobiles with a giant flower-shaped hammer. At the end of the piece, a female police officer passes by and smiles with approval. Introducing comic tension into this anarchistic final scene is Rist's way of challenging the formulaic predictable punishment of the liberated female protagonist in melodrama.

Similarly, Shana Moulton draws on melodrama's narrative strategies in her series, *Whispering Pines* (2002–present). The multimedia artist plays Cynthia, a hypochondriac housewife in search of her lost cat. Although Cynthia is placed within the context of heteronormative domesticity, the character deviates from this paradigm. Cynthia's sexuality is never directly addressed, but Moulton makes it clear that the character lives in a queer world where the time of reproduction is not ruled by her biological clock. She is unconcerned with child rearing, inheritance, or by strict bourgeois rules of comportment.[9]

In recent years, melodrama has become subject to critical analysis among queer studies scholars, building on earlier feminist work calling attention to the social constructedness of gender roles. As Jane Shattuc notes, "Gays [. . .] displaced their sexual identities onto the melodrama's heroine as a victim of patriarchal discourses on sexuality."[10] Openly gay film directors such as Todd Haynes have employed the language of melodrama to situate queer desire within mainstream culture. In *Far from Heaven* (2002), a pastiche of Douglas Sirk's *All That Heaven Allows* (1955), Haynes further queers the narrative by rewriting the original role of the protagonist's husband, Frank Whitaker (Dennis Quaid), from heterosexual to closeted homosexual. However, while Haynes's version weaves in this subplot, interestingly, Frank's storyline is secondary to Cathy's (Julianne Moore) interracial liaison with her gardener Raymond (Dennis Haysbert). Thus, *Far from Heaven* remains primarily preoccupied with heterosexual romance.

Ryan Trecartin goes a step further with *A Family Finds Entertainment* by placing queerness at the forefront of the family melodrama. In order to better comprehend how queerness operates in this movie, it is useful to consider some distinction between gayness and queerness. Elizabeth Grosz argues, "Simply being straight or being gay, in itself, provides no guarantee of an individual's stance as sexually radical: it depends on how one lives one's queerness or how one renders one's straightness as queer."[11] This differentiation between gayness and queerness provides a lens with which to examine the complex protagonists of *A Family Finds Entertainment*, as they are not only gay, but also aspire to live their queerness in a way that guarantees their radicality.

The narrative follows the (mis)adventures of three characters, each representing different stages of the coming out process. Lisa (Kelly Pittenger), a middle-class prepubescent girl, attempts to keep a secret from her mother while undergoing what Richard Troiden calls "sensitization," the first stage of the coming out process, which is characterized by feelings of marginality.[12] Skippy (Ryan Trecartin), an adolescent, struggles to come out of the closet in the next phase. Finally, Shin (also Ryan Trecartin), a third-sex character, fully comes out. The concept of "coming out" is illustrated metaphorically through the omnipresence of closets, windows, locks, and doorways. Characters are shown venturing to escape cramped spaces, which can be understood as attempts to openly declare to the world one's same-sex desire.

In an interview, Trecartin claimed that his movie is about coming of age rather than coming out.[13] However, it would seem rather unlikely that such recurring visual references are unrelated to the artist's own emergence during this period as a gay man. In 2011, Roberta Smith suggested that making *A Family Finds Entertainment* was his "way of coming out to his parents."[14] Although I argue that coming out is its overarching theme, the video itself was not primarily intended to help Trecartin divulge his sexual orientation to his parents, as Smith suggests. In fact, as he explained, he had come out to his parents a few years prior to the release of the video, during his freshman year at RISD.[15] Therefore, the artist's thesis project should not be solely understood as his way to reveal his sexual orientation but also as an affirmation of his queerness. In addition, the artist refers to "coming out" to express how he seeks to contribute to televisual and cinematic traditions. He situates himself "out there" in order to explore the vast, mostly uncharted, and limitless universe of the internet—a symbol for who he is, who we are, and who we are capable of becoming.

Figure 2.1
All That Heaven Allows (1955)

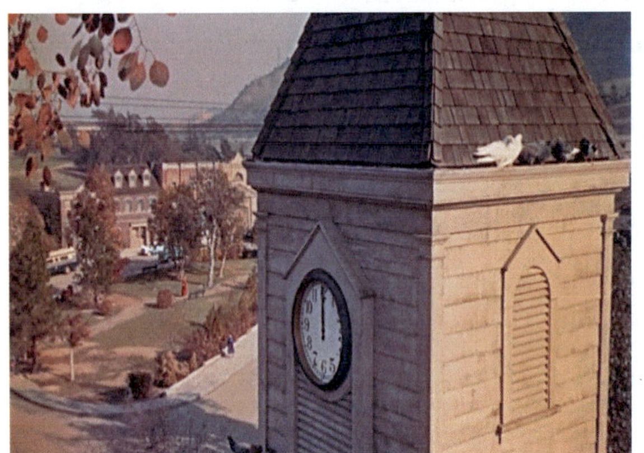

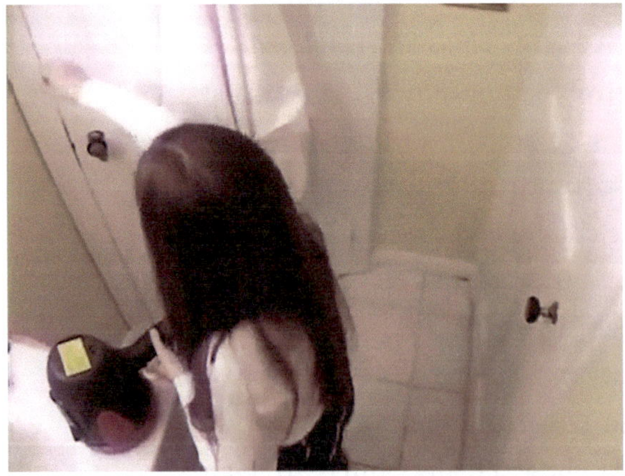

Figure 2.2
A Family Finds Entertainment (2004)

Unlike Douglas Sirk's melodramas, which often begin with sumptuous panoramic establishing shots, *A Family Finds Entertainment*'s opening directly transports viewers into a claustrophobic high-angle shot of Lisa locked inside a compact bathroom. The narrow interior setting, coupled with the close proximity of the camera, conveys a stifling sense of entrapment.

Lisa opens the washroom closet and a frightening derelict, Closet Monster (Ryan Trecartin), jumps out, taking her by surprise. Closet Monster, who appears to be held captive inside Lisa's bathroom linen cabinet, asks her, “Do I have to stay in here forever?” The scene then cuts to a point-of-view shot of her replying, “I don’t want to talk about it right now!,” as she forces the door closed to contain her prisoner. Lisa is seen in a low-angle shot, which reinforces her position of dominance while simultaneously rendering Trecartin’s character helpless. The image slowly fades to black while Closet Monster’s pleading is audible in the background muttering her name. Closet Monster sounds defeated, as if he already understands that coming out of the closet is not really an option.

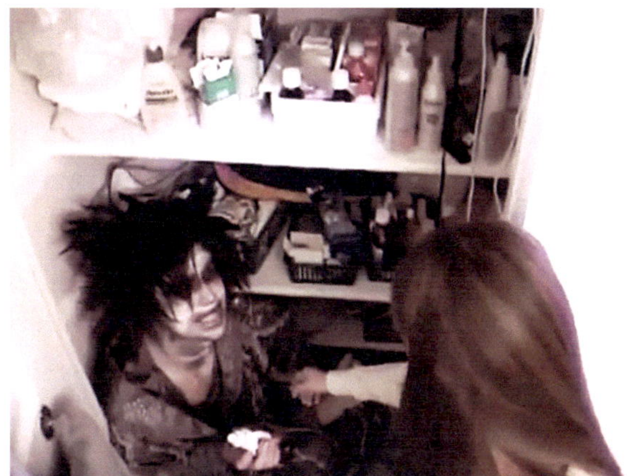

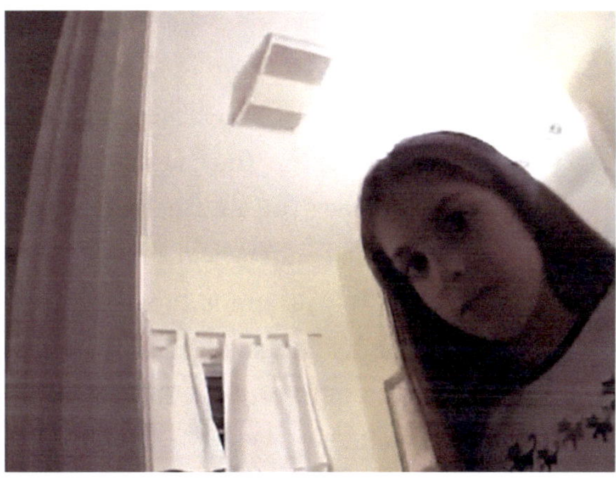

Figures 2.3 and 2.4 *A Family Finds Entertainment* (2004)

Within the first few minutes, viewers are introduced to the video’s primary theme. Family melodrama’s preoccupation with failure and hopelessness is invoked through the classic dramatic struggle to overcome an emotional crisis. As Barbara Klinger writes in *Melodrama and Meaning*, “melodramatic plots are particularly focused on the heights of dramatic conflict and the emotional affect such conflicts can arouse on the part of the spectator. Situations such as the moral plunge of a character [...] are manipulated to produce intense pathetic emotions in the viewer.”[16] Trecartin seeks to intensify the pathos of the entrapped character through stark high- and low-contrasted camera angles, as well as tight framing. Spectators are encouraged to feel a certain compassion for Closet Monster, despite his frightening appearance. While viewers may be emotionally invested in his plight, Trecartin does not make us privy to what happens next, as he is suddenly and completely dropped from the narrative. The artist cuts to a long shot of Lisa standing in the dark, adjusting her flashlight in front of the kitchen sink. The camera slowly advances toward her and a voice from behind the lens abruptly yells out “Lisa!” The young girl turns around and points her flashlight at the camera while giggling and singing, “I’m being as quiet as I possibly can, but you still notice me.”

Through this emblematic lullaby, I take Trecartin to be alluding to the ways queer individuals have learned to design their lives as a series of masterful compromises consisting of projections and exclusions. By shielding their nonconformity from public scrutiny, queers manage to construct an invisible identity within the epistemology of the closet.[17]

Lisa is seen running across the dining room as the camera follows and attempts to catch up with her. The character continues playing with the concept of invisibility as she is presented playing hide-and-seek with the camera. Her "performance of closeted-ness"[18] is made apparent by her avoidance of the camera's gaze, which conveys to us that there is something deeply personal she is concealing. Trecartin cuts to a medium-long shot of Lisa setting foot in the living room. A peroxide blonde, Booty Girl (Ryan Trecartin), enters wearing a midriff shirt and tight pants that accentuate her curves. The character is framed in the foreground of the living room posing in an alluring manner while seductively calling out "Lisa." This particular shot is held a few seconds longer than any other in the video, thus calling attention to itself, possibly to emphasize the dichotomy between Booty Girl's vulgar appearance and the mise-en-scène.

Trecartin contrasts what appears to be the epitome of the middle-class suburban American home with the nonconformity of his characterization. This juxtaposition results in an almost surreal effect, one which gives the impression that Booty Girl has been transported from the mise-en-scène of another video. She is clearly out of place in this suburban domestic setting. Together, both characters navigate through the dark mysterious interior of the house, flashlights in hand, traversing the unknown in search of safety. Trecartin invokes melodrama's theme of domesticity by making the home a site of social interaction and struggle. Thomas Elsaesser notes, "The setting of the family melodrama almost by definition is the middle-class home, filled with objects, [. . .] that becomes increasingly suffocating."[19] The home in *A Family Finds Entertainment* is not overcrowded with objects and furniture to create this effect. Instead, Trecartin opts to shoot the entire scene with the lights off in order to transmit a similar sense of oppression. He consequently turns the home into a somber labyrinth, lacking an established route, direction, or the familial support Lisa craves in order to come out.

Playing with similar conventional modes of representation, Matthias Müller challenges the ways classical Hollywood melodramas have traditionally placed female protagonists within the confines of the domestic sphere. Müller's *Home Stories* (1990), which consists of a montage of scenes taken from Hollywood melodramas of the 1950s and '60s, underscores the oppressive mise-en-scène in which these mainstream texts take place. In his short, Hollywood actresses such as Lara Turner, Grace Kelly, and Tippi Hedren are depicted as victims trapped in their own homes, attempting to escape, slamming doors, and running down hallways. Müller intensifies the overall sense of anxiety transmitted through the women's apparent despair by accompanying his edited collage with a foreboding soundtrack. Through its obvious nod to melodrama's stereotypical cinematic tropes, *Home Stories* exposes the restrictive and limited representation of female characters in these Hollywood motion pictures. While Müller fails to provide positive examples of self-reliant female protagonists, Trecartin creates character-centered narratives that feature actors who strive to find personal agency by confronting the forces that threaten their freedom. Lisa may find herself in a similar predicament as her Hollywood mainstream counterparts, however, it is Trecartin's intention to give her the opportunity to self-actualize.

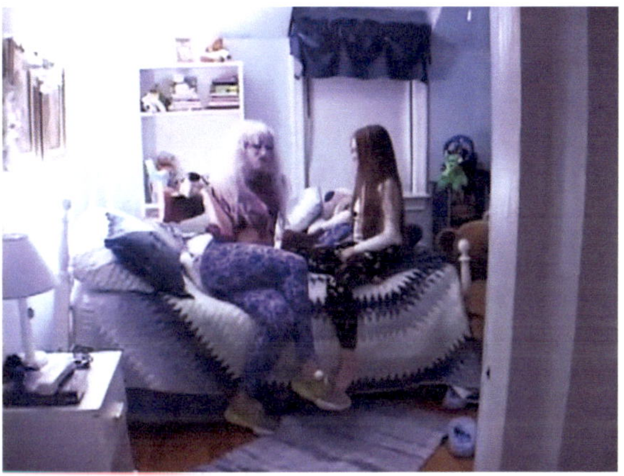

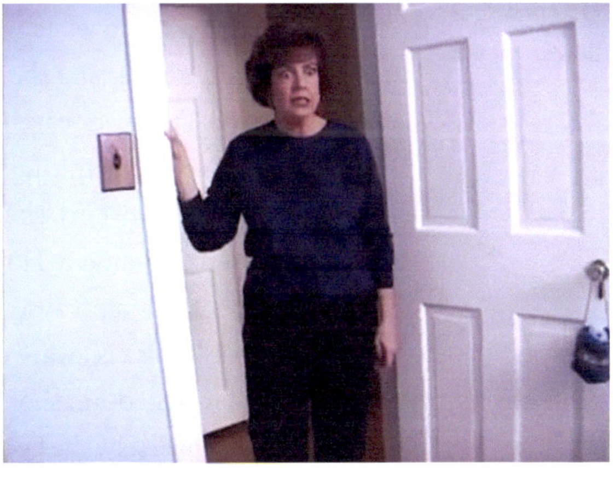

Figures 2.5 and 2.6 *A Family Finds Entertainment* (2004)

Booty Girl climbs up the stairs to join Lisa in her well-lit blue bedroom. A medium-long shot reveals them sitting on Lisa's bed. The shot is framed by the bedroom's doorway. The doorframe in the foreground symbolizes the border between Lisa's bedroom and the rest of the house. Her room represents a safe refuge. However, this private sanctuary is suddenly invaded by Lisa's mother (Shell Pittenger). A medium-tilted camera angle shows her standing in the doorway, upset that her daughter is still awake: "Lisa! What are you doing out of bed? It's midnight!" The scene cuts to a medium shot of Lisa standing on her bed as she nonchalantly mimics her mother's voice, "Lisa! What are you doing out of bed?" Booty Girl ends the repeated sentence with "It's midnight!" and breaks into laughter. For the first time since her first appearance, viewers are able to catch a glimpse of Booty Girl's face. We notice that she is the performer who played Closet Monster earlier (Ryan Trecartin). Booty Girl's mockery does not seem to faze Lisa's mother who responds, "I'm checking up on you." The mother's total obliviousness to Booty Girl's presence leads us to believe that she may not in fact physically exist. She may instead be a product of Lisa's imagination. Her mother smiles and affectionately says, as she exits the bedroom, "Lisa, it is you that I love." Lisa remains silent and closes the door behind her mother. As in maternal melodramas such as *Mildred Pierce* (1945), there is an emotional conflict and disconnect between mother and daughter, whereby the parent desperately attempts to step into the child's world, while the latter pushes her further away. Lisa's taciturn dismissal of her mom is partly motivated by her need to conceal a deep secret.

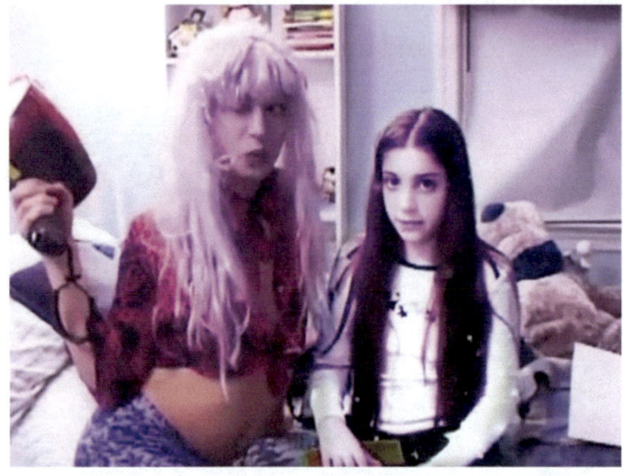

Figure 2.7 *A Family Finds Entertainment* (2004)

After shutting the door, Lisa turns toward Booty Girl and repeats, "Lisa, it is you that I love, as well." She retrieves a multicolored plastic pencil box while addressing the camera: "Look, I found something that is very dear to me. I've been searching for it. Inside is a story, something that I like. Be good and be thinking of for it. Like a bedtime story." Although Lisa is talking to Booty Girl, she does not look directly at her. Instead, she fixes her gaze on the camera. However, as the camera zooms in on her face, her eyes momentarily shift away from it as if trying to escape its scrutinizing stare. It is as if Lisa is aware of the camera's every move and intention. When framed in a medium shot, Lisa is more comfortable looking directly into the lens. Conversely, she becomes visibly ill-at-ease with the proximity of a close-up shot. She understands that the camera represents more than a recording machine. It is the point of convergence between the world of the film and the audience watching her. Looking into its lens would imply exposing her secret not only to the camera but to viewers as well. Lisa knows she is concealing something important from her mother and from us. She soon abandons her efforts to avoid facing the lens and decides to stare back at it. This intimate tight close-up declares that she can no longer hide her queerness from us. Her character can be interpreted as a surrogate for a young Trecartin struggling to understand and acknowledge his own queerness. This interpretation is reinforced by the fact that both Closet Monster and Booty Girl are played by Trecartin, as if to register that they do not represent individual characters but rather stand in for facets of compartmentalized identities. The camera then cuts to a close-up of the inside of the open pencil box, which suddenly transports spectators into a psychedelic third dimension, a parallel universe.

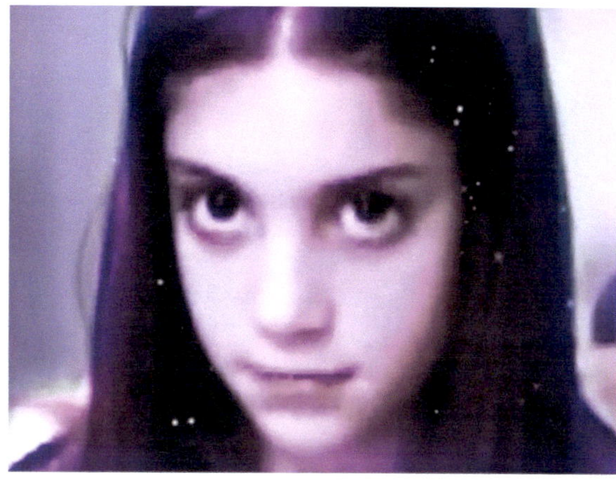

Figure 2.8 *A Family Finds Entertainment* (2004)

Through digital collages made possible by Photoshop, iMovie, and After Effects, Trecartin layers multiple two-dimensional animations on top of one another. The short animated sequence begins with a close-up of the moon. The camera slowly pans out until the scene suddenly cuts to a close-up of a goldfish swimming in a glass bowl. A lightning effect is superimposed on top of the shot. Trecartin then cuts to a two-dimensional bitmap of a beating heart. The animation continues with swirling spiral motifs resembling zoetrope patterns onto which he layers a projection of teenagers listening to a live garage band. The sequence culminates with a complex series of visuals in which a human anatomic model is layered on top of a tropical forest, and miniature animated beating hearts appear to fly in the air while moving across the screen.

The image fades, and we are transported to a bright-yellow living room in which teens are gathered playing guitar and singing. Veronica (Veronica Gelbaum) jumps from the couch and yells, "Skippy! Open that fucking fuckdoor of yours!" The scene cuts to a close-up of a half-open door. We are then introduced to the video's central protagonist, Skippy, a flamboyant teen with black teeth, whose skin color shifts back and forth between red and yellow. However, despite his disturbing appearance, he is privileged via close-ups that emphasize his emotional distress, thus evoking a high degree of spectator identification and empathy. Trecartin reclaims the use of the close-up, a cinematic mode of representation often used in Hollywood melodramas to facilitate viewers' cross-identification with the female protagonist, by inviting spectators to identify with a queer subject. In doing so, the artist subtly underpins the fact that gay and queer men, like women, have been portrayed as marginalized figures outside patriarchal power.

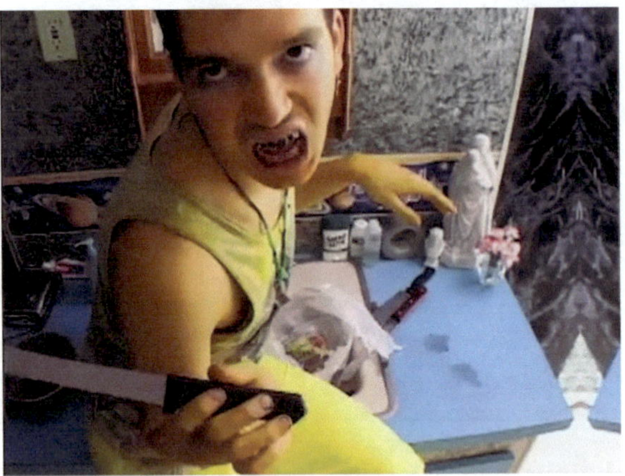

Figure 2.9
A Family Finds Entertainment (2004)

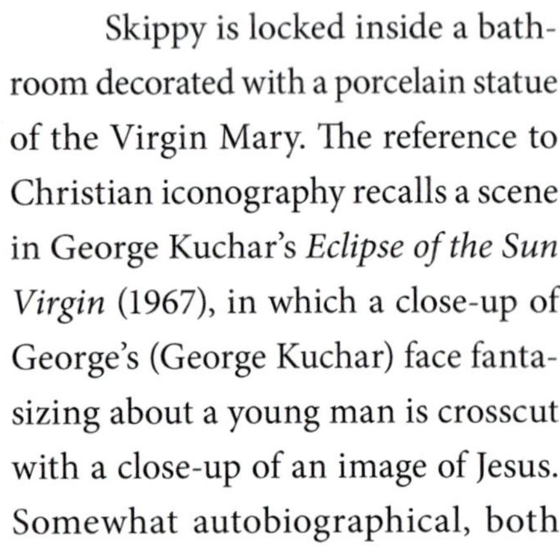

Skippy is locked inside a bathroom decorated with a porcelain statue of the Virgin Mary. The reference to Christian iconography recalls a scene in George Kuchar's *Eclipse of the Sun Virgin* (1967), in which a close-up of George's (George Kuchar) face fantasizing about a young man is crosscut with a close-up of an image of Jesus. Somewhat autobiographical, both videos can be read as therapeutic outlets that allowed the artists to reconcile religious dogma with their sexuality.

In an interview for Filmbrats.com, Trecartin was asked how much of *A Family Finds Entertainment* was drawn from his own experience. He replied by saying, "It's very personal. I get nervous."[20] While most of his work does not constitute a form of self-portraiture, *A Family Finds Entertainment* seems to be the exception to the rule. Skippy appears to serve as a stand-in (albeit an exaggerated one) for the artist. For example, both Skippy and the artist grew up in the Midwest, experienced their teens in the closet struggling with his sexual orientation, and each had to come to terms with family and religion.[21]

Veronica begs Skippy to come out as she stands in front of the slightly ajar bathroom door. The camera zooms in on the door to emphasize that it is unlocked. Veronica may be physically capable of opening it; however, only Skippy has the power to "come out." The recurring image of the half-open door signifies that Skippy is on the verge of taking the big step. Yet, despite pleas from his friend to come out, the protagonist remains ensconced in the bathroom. He is seen sticking a large kitchen knife to a mirror with tape, fumbling with bathroom accoutrements, taking Polaroid pictures of himself, and then cutting the images and flushing them down the toilet.

Sitting on the bathroom sink, Skippy looks at himself in the mirror and says, "I believe that somewhere there is something worth dying for, and

I think it's amazing… amazing!" The scene cuts to an extreme close-up of the character sticking his tongue out and smiling at his reflection. The recurring charged symbol of the mirror in the mise-en-scène is reminiscent of Douglas Sirk who "suggested that mirrors were of interest because they produce an image that seems to represent the person looking into the mirror when in fact what they see is their exact opposite. In Sirk's films, we see characters looking in mirrors when they are […] deluding themselves. Mirrors, then, represent both illusion and delusion in his films…"[22] Skippy deceives himself into thinking that death is the solution to his existential problem. As he stares back at his reflection, he appears to be expecting confirmation that there is indeed something amazing worth dying for.

The scene then cuts once again to a close-up of Veronica lying on the floor declaring, "Skippy, you can't keep things this way, you just can't…" The suspense mounts until the sequence reaches a traumatic climax in which Skippy is pointing a large kitchen knife close to his face. We are then assaulted with a disturbing shot of Skippy slitting his wrists. Fake blood gushes down from above the frame to his forearm, as if it were being poured from outside the frame. In true melodrama fashion, Trecartin intensifies the protagonist's inner turmoil by accompanying the scene with slow dramatic music. As John Mercer notes, in melodramas, "Music is used to mark the emotional events, constituting a system of punctuation, heightening the expressive and emotional contrasts of the storyline. In such moments, music makes these films much more dramatic […]"[23]

Figures 2.10, 2.11, and 2.12 *A Family Finds Entertainment* (2004)

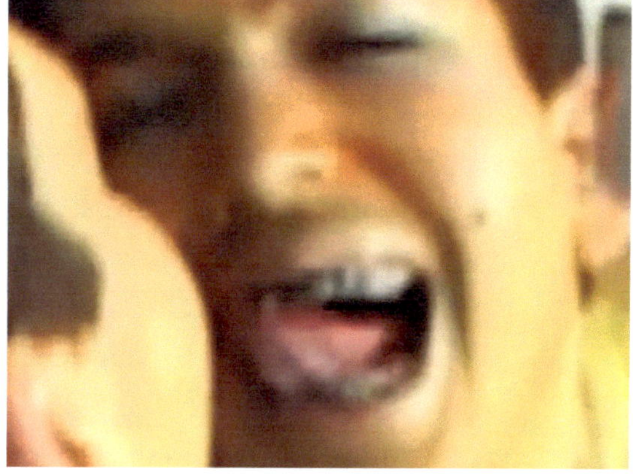

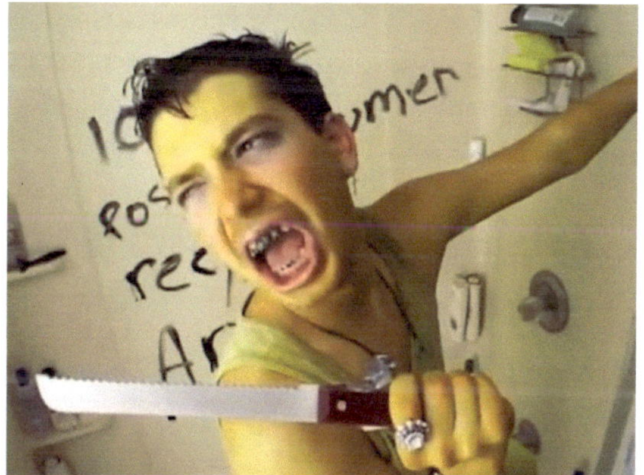

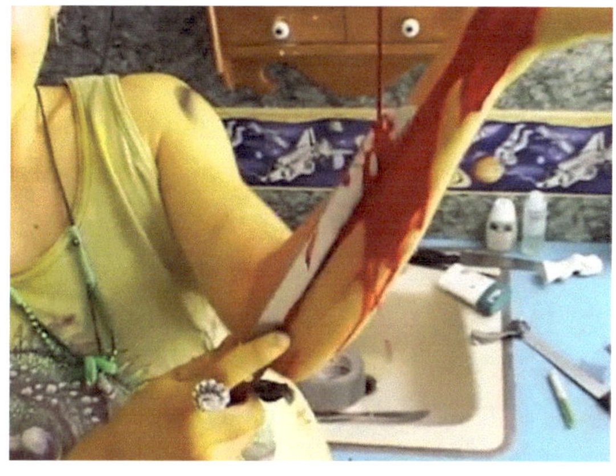

Melodramas privilege spectators by making them aware of the music accompaniment while the characters in the movie are oblivious to it. However, in Trecartin's video, the protagonist also possesses this knowledge, as he is seen singing along to the lyrics of the background music: "It's not that I want to keep things this way, it's just that I may be impersonating some people who are not me." The lyrics reflect queer individuals' struggle to construct and perform identities in order to function within heteronormative society. This survival mechanism leads many to structure life through binary oppositions: workplace/private life, sex/intimacy, and faith/sexuality. In doing so, the sense of self is lost beneath the fabricated facade. When Skippy looks at himself in the mirror, he desperately yearns to find his true self; however, he is left with the empty reflection of his projected image. Earlier in the scene, the protagonist looked at his reflection, searching for an answer to his question about whether there is something worth dying for. The fact that he later proceeds to slit his wrists may suggest that he found what he was looking for in the mirror. However, at this moment in the video, we are not made aware of such a revelation.

The scene ends as Skippy, drenched in blood, stares into the camera with a disturbing smile and proceeds to form a heart-shaped symbol with his fingers over his chest, while the soundtrack blares in the background. Despite Trecartin's apparent artificiality and campy aesthetic, he succeeds in producing a powerful emotionally charged scene. He accentuates the notion that verisimilitude is not a requisite for affective engagement. The emotional crescendo suddenly subsides, the music stops, and the image dissolves into a long shot of a house on a snow-covered block.

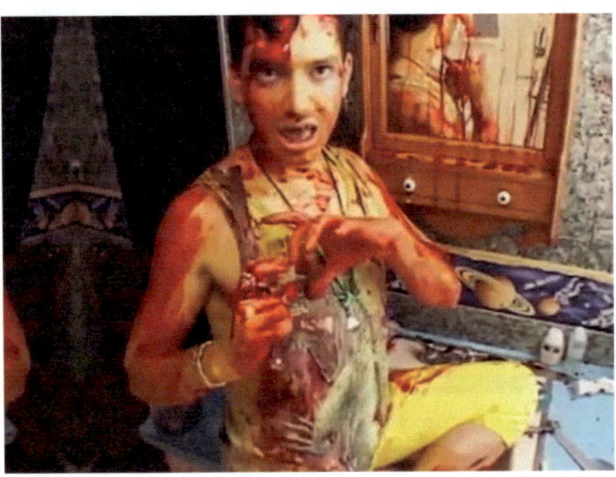

Figure 2.13 *A Family Finds Entertainment* (2004)

A character known as Snowy White Girl (Ryan Trecartin) ventures outside. Her arrival comes as a complete surprise; yet, I believe she does not represent an entirely new character. She is introduced immediately after Skippy's suicide attempt. Her blood-smeared face and clothes suggest that she in fact might represent a new incarnation of Skippy. The ensuing scene can be interpreted as a dream sequence that occurs while Skippy is lying unconscious in the bathtub. For the first time, a character is placed outside, engulfed in the gloomy exterior of the house. Here, as elsewhere, Trecartin employs color in a Sirkian manner, expressing emotion and inner conflict by contrasting the bright and colorful interior footage with the gray outdoor shots. Snowy White Girl is lost and in distress, running aimlessly across the frozen cityscape. She traverses a highway overpass, passing cars and pedestrians swaddled in layers of winter outerwear. Unlike the previous scene in Skippy's bathroom, shot almost exclusively via close-ups, this outdoor segment is composed primarily of extreme long shots. This stylistic decision creates a distance between spectators and the character that further reinforces our understanding that the protagonist is lost within the vast wintry landscape. The sound of wind, footsteps on the snow, and the character's gasps for air are echoed repeatedly. The outside world is depicted as threatening and potentially dangerous, away from the insulation of the home into a public arena, where one's queerness is at risk of being exposed. Judging by the bleak and ominous exterior scenery, Skippy is not yet ready to come out. The camera then zooms in on Snowy White Girl until her face is framed in an extreme close-up. Trecartin superimposes an image of a window over her face so she appears trapped inside the frame. The scene ends where it began: the character is placed back within the domestic setting—and inside the closet.

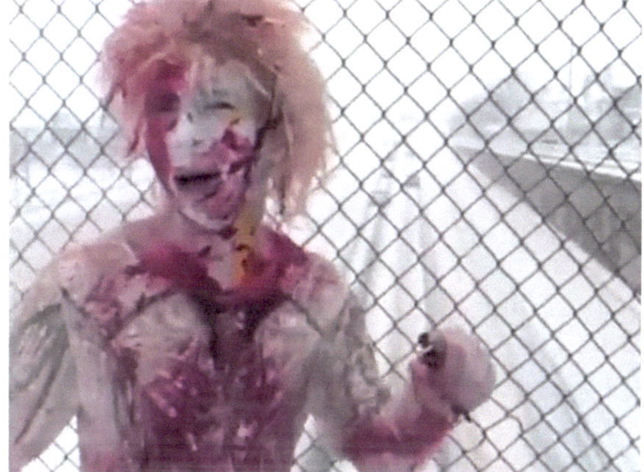

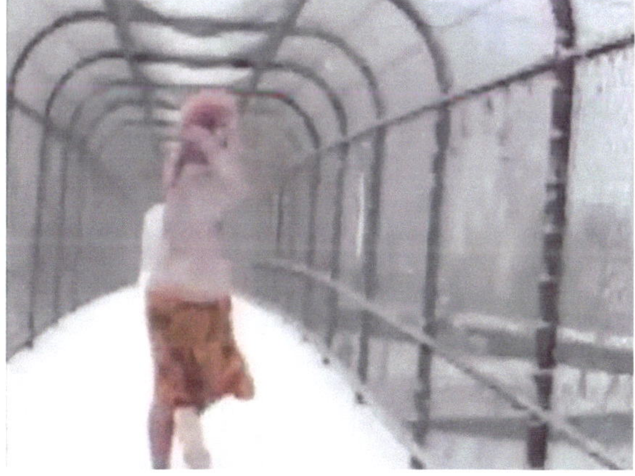

Figures 2.14 and 2.15 *A Family Finds Entertainment* (2004)

Snowy White Girl hosts a get-together in her living room with a group of friends (recalling Skippy's soirée earlier). The party quickly turns sordid as members of the motley crew begin verbally assaulting one another. Trecartin confronts us with an extreme close-up of Drag Queen (Taya Koschnick) with her eyes rolled back as if possessed by an evil force. As she regains composure she declares, “For an evening I'll hate you.” The camera then zooms in on Cosmos Bitch (Lizzie Fitch), who repeats, in a hostile tone, “For an evening I'll hate you,” while glaring at Snowy White Girl (Trecartin). The scene cuts to a close-up of a visibly perturbed Snowy White Girl who responds, “What?” The camera catches a glimpse of the other peripheral characters' astonished and anxious reactions. Cosmos Bitch follows with another menacing threat, “I'll give you a reason to die or kill!” Snowy White Girl laughs nervously, then abruptly adopts a serious expression. Cosmos Bitch's anger is palpable in an extreme close-up. Yet we are not sure what brought on this sudden burst of emotion.

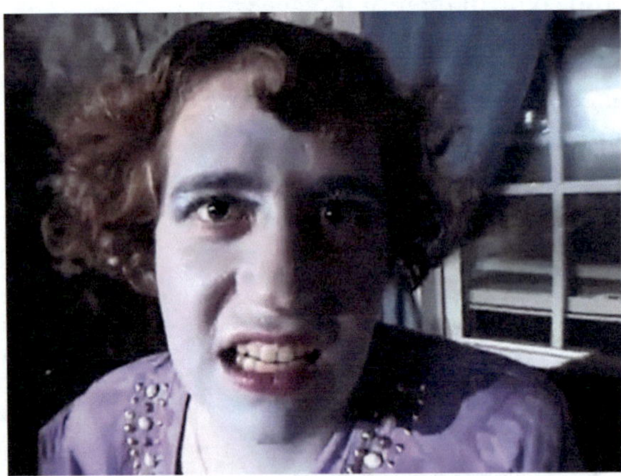

Figure 2.16 *A Family Finds Entertainment* (2004)

A series of extreme close-ups unravels succinctly. It is accompanied by an intrusive instrumental tune, a combination of electronic synthesizer sounds and xylophone pitches that break an agonizing silence. This sensational cinematographic interlude serves as a vehicle to transmit the heightened emotionality of the characters. The abundance of extreme close-ups, crosscuts, saturated colors, and digital manipulations, coupled with the abrupt soundtrack, provides a surreal audiovisual effect similar in impact to Trecartin's treatment of Skippy's suicide attempt. The tension between the characters builds up until the image dissolves into Snowy White Girl lying on the kitchen floor, soaked in blood, holding a knife. Her friends yell hysterically at her, “Why did you do that?” and she replies, “I did it for fun!” Death is presented as entertainment in the artist's videos because death does not really exist there. Trecartin's world is devoid of physical consequences—characters die and regenerate, much like pressing the replay button with video games and starting all over again. Death is only temporary, as spectators understand that the final outcome for characters is not final at all and thus, never tragic.

As we have seen, the artist views the body as a blank canvas onto which personalities are projected and articulated. He looks forward to a future in which humans no longer define each other, or themselves, by their bodies.

> I see people as being what their personality is at the moment of expression. I feel genitals hold us back a lot. They keep us connected to our older ideals of humanity [. . .] I think it's really interesting that there are a lot of trannies now who are in transition and want to be in transition—they don't want to be a man or a woman [. . .] The more nuanced we get, the more things people want to be.[24]

In *A Family Finds Entertainment*, queerness is not fixed to a singular body. This disembodiment, in turn, assures that viewers can identify with the characters because queerness is a personality trait that all Trecartin protagonists share, regardless of their body/gender. This disembodied queer subjectivity is reflected in the way he switches back and forth between individual characters' identities, as if each distinct personality were an expression of the artist's own queer subjectivity. For instance, directly after Snowy White Girl is presented covered in blood on the kitchen floor, the image fades to a shot of Skippy waking up in a bathtub full of blood. He notices the bandages wrapped around his arms and exclaims in disappointment, "What the fuck? Who fixed my bloody arms?!" The director then cuts to a low angle shot of Veronica lying on the floor complaining that the party is boring. Skippy righteously snaps his fingers and responds by directly addressing the camera, as if addressing us and Veronica, "Hey listen girl, I can for sure make choices, keep that in mind!" The protagonist's awakening can be interpreted as his rebirth. He decides to interpret his failed suicide attempt as an opportunity to come out of the closet and embark on the process of self-actualization.

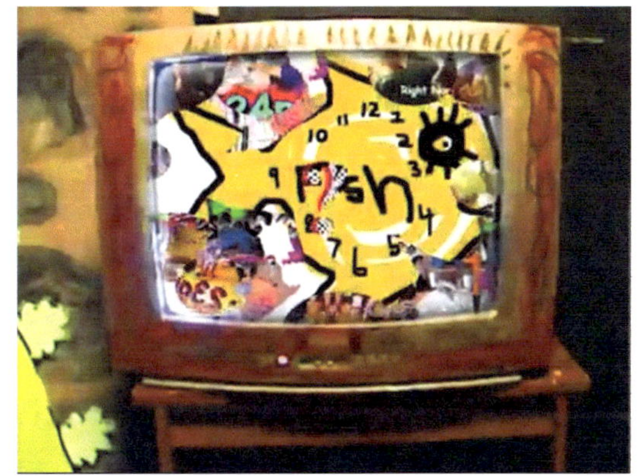

Figure 2.17 *A Family Finds Entertainment* (2004)

Shortly after Skippy recovers from his suicide attempt, Misunderstood Muddy Girl (Rachel Glazer) removes a tribal African mask from her face. She addresses the camera, "A digital relic from a future age of cyberchaos and analog holocaust." The camera zooms out until her image is framed within the rectangular screen of an obsolete CRT TV. The monitor is dingy, painted over with graffiti, and has the appearance of an excavated artifact of material culture.

The image of the TV monitor fades to white noise. Suddenly, the opening credits of a cable television game show, *Right Now*, dominate the screen. The program is interrupted by quick shots of the camera crew filming the participants while a monitor in the background plays back the video footage in real time. Through this metacinematic device, Trecartin highlights the mono-directional, insular, and closed circuit network of television. That is, the content being created by a select few, which is then directly fed to consumers. This does not mean that viewers are not active participants in creating meaning. While the television viewing experience has become more dynamic in recent years, due in part to added data services, video-on-demand, and real-time voting, in 2004, when *A Family Finds Entertainment* was released, TV did not entirely possess the same interactive capacity.

At the finale of the game show sequence, the word "INTERMISSION" flashes across the screen as someone flips a compact disc over to play the B-side, as if it were a vinyl record. This deliberately inaccurate anachronism draws attention to the layers of media archeology Trecartin excavates to mark technological shifts. From this significant point on, he transitions from addressing the aesthetic tools of the singular closed nexus of television to adopting the dynamic and open circuits of the web. The artist surpasses the limitations of television by embracing the inherent interactivity of the internet.

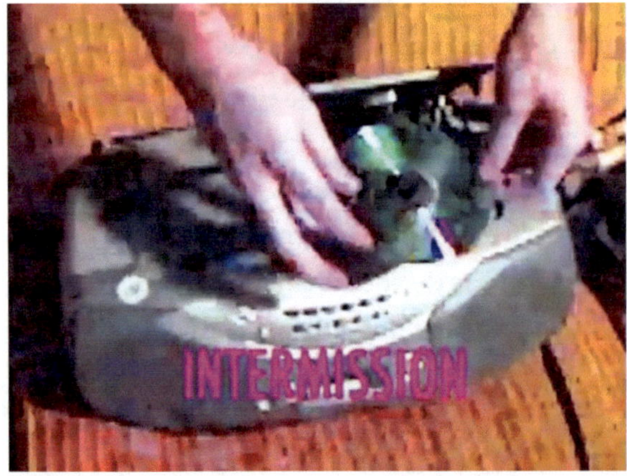

Figure 2.18 *A Family Finds Entertainment* (2004)

Trecartin correlates his embrace of the internet with the freedom associated with coming out. He projects these connections through his alter ego Skippy as he comes to terms with his sexual orientation on multiple screens that pop up as streaming footage of webcam shots. The artist provides these visual cues to signify his readiness to leave the refuge and shame of the closet for the public network of cyberspace with the help of his multiple personas and ensemble of friends.

Part of his hesitation to come out can be attributed to the fact that according to an interview, growing up during the onslaught of AIDS had a deep impact on him. Trecartin remembers being traumatized watching television news coverage of the AIDS crisis: "For me it was really frightening. [. . .] It turned me off from the whole idea of sex—'So sex means you die?'"[25] He also curiously mentions that during his closeted years in high school, he did not connect to the internet because he "was afraid of viruses."[26] It was at RISD that he finally managed to overcome his web-based "viral" phobia and accept his sexuality. Clearly, an ongoing connection exists between the artist's process of self-acceptance as a queer young individual and his relationship to the net.

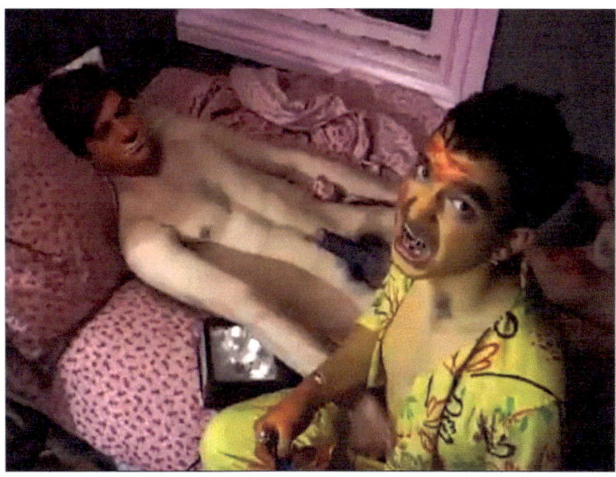

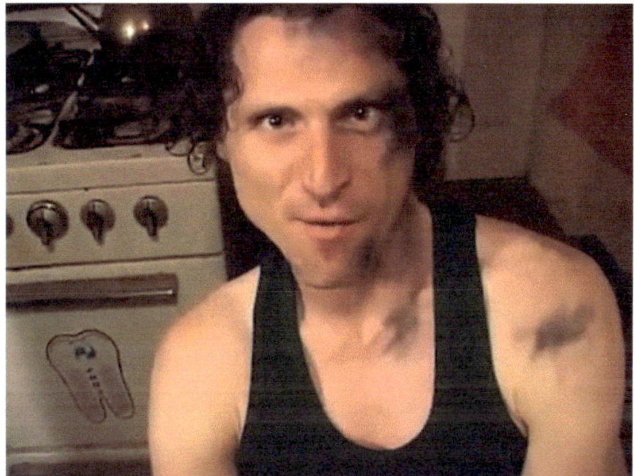

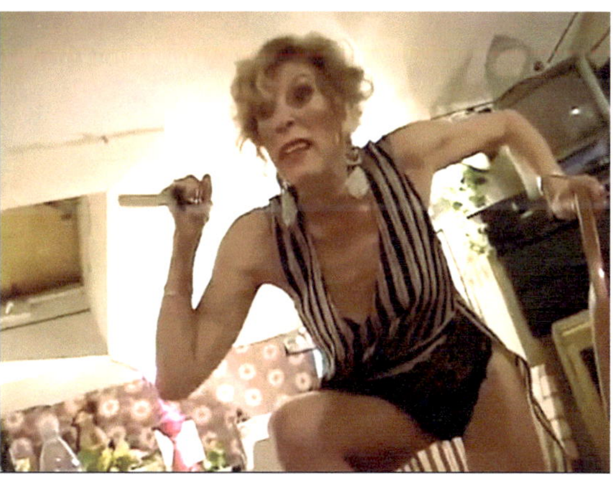

Figures 2.19, 2.20, and 2.21 *A Family Finds Entertainment* (2004)

In the following scene, Skippy is framed through a close-up addressing the camera, "Yeah, you know I have messy dreams, I need to be more *con-fi-dent*! You know, in my life, no more fake blood for me, I want the real thing . . ." The camera zooms in on Skippy's face as he is about to fit a condom over his boyfriend Billy's (Kenny Curran) erect penis. Skippy is no longer phobic about carnal contact and viruses (albeit while practicing safe sex). He has conquered the fear of the physical divide that prevented him from experiencing sex.

The protagonist's erotic escapade is suddenly interrupted by a jump cut to a close-up of his mother's (Annette K. Bonin) face. She engages in a conversation with someone off-screen, "Baby, I mean he is mad, he's like an alien, really." Skippy exits his bedroom only to be confronted by his mother, "Son you need to give it up! Yeah! This family is poisonous! Yeah! You need to find a new home!" Skippy's mother is primarily framed in low-angle shots that reinforce her dominance, while his father (Aaron Jungels) is mainly seen in high-angle shots sitting on a chair in the background. Skippy's Dad appears passive, emotionally detached, and ambiguous concerning his son's predicament. He makes homophobic comments that condemn his son's sexuality, only to later intimately kiss Skippy on the mouth. Dad provides us with a clue regarding his orientation when he comments on Skippy's naked boyfriend, "You look good guy." Perhaps, this is Trecartin's way of alluding to closeted homosexuals who feign heterosexuality in unhappy marriages. John Mercer and Martin Shingler point out that the father in melodramas is "the most unsympathetic figure, even more so when absent."[27]

However, while Skippy's Dad may be a conflicted father figure, he is certainly not the only unpleasant character. Skippy's mother is depicted as a shrew, or as Skippy calls her, "a snake." Not only is she callous, her presence is threatening. In one shot, she is seen holding a large kitchen knife exclaiming, "Shut your stupid hole or I'll knife it!" The tension escalates until she explodes: "I'll burn you like a witch, you butt plugger. I know your secret is kept very well. Go eat some estrogen you homo!" She opens Skippy's bedroom door only to find his naked boyfriend Billy sporting the iconic rainbow flag, graphic emblem of the LGBTQ community, like a cape. Skippy's mother provides her last bit of venomous analysis: "Son, family is poison. You need to go find your homeboys." She extracts a fifty dollar bill from her bra and hands it to him. "Be good and know that there is love." She kisses him on the cheek as a final farewell and tells him to "get the fuck out" of her house.

Although many of the elements in *A Family Finds Entertainment* are somewhat autobiographical, the dialogue between Skippy and his parents is clearly fictional. Trecartin's parents have admitted that at first they were surprised when Ryan came out due to his abundance of girlfriends. However, they soon embraced the fact and became very supportive.[28] While the artist did not experience the kind of dysfunctional family exchange portrayed in his movie, he nevertheless presents experiences of less fortunate queer teens, often homeless and rejected by their immediate families.

Skippy leaves his family in search of his "homeboys." This new family represents one he forms by choice, as opposed to relatives he inherits through procreation. A handheld camera trails behind him as he descends the staircase and exits the front door of his parents' home. Once outside on the porch, he draws the attention of a self-proclaimed documentary video artist, Zoey Spelling (Laura Callela). She informs him that she is producing a project about "medium-age kids all over the world." Zoey's point-of-view shot frames Skippy in infrared night vision. He proceeds to convince her that he is worthy of being in her documentary. The protagonist performs an exhibitionistic soliloquy in front of the camera. He exudes confidence and a diva-like attitude, snapping his fingers at the lens while emphasizing every uttered word. Skippy is no longer afraid to expose his queerness in front of the camera, especially because it affords him an opportunity to come out in a big way.

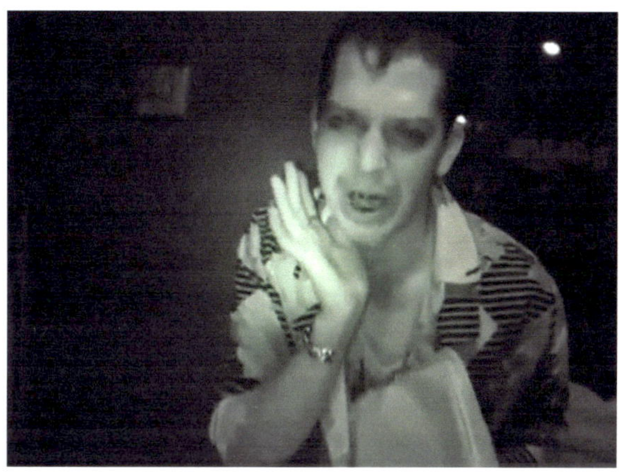

Figure 2.22 *A Family Finds Entertainment* (2004)

In her book *Melodrama and Meaning*, Barbara Klinger argues that melodrama "emphasizes the social mores of its time."[29] At the time *A Family Finds Entertainment* was made, coming out on TV had become a trend: Pedro Zamora was openly gay on the reality TV show *The Real World: San Francisco* (MTV, 1994),[30] Ellen DeGeneres publicly came out in 1997,[31] Rosie O'Donnell came out in 2002,[32] and *Queer Eye for the Straight Guy* first aired on the Bravo network in July 2003, featuring a group of openly gay men who provided aesthetic makeovers to heterosexual men.[33] Skippy's eventual decision to come out in front of the camera was therefore very much in tune with the general mainstreaming of queerness in American popular culture.

When Skippy finally commits to coming out, he embraces the decision as if he were making up for lost time. He marches into the street demanding, "Look at me, look at me," only to be fatally struck down by an SUV, an irrational twist of fate similar to those in Hollywood melodramas. Trecartin's movies feature contrived serendipity and reversals to advance the plot. As Steve Neale points out, "Melodramas are marked by chance happenings, coincidences, missed meetings, sudden conversions, last-minute rescues and revelations, *deus ex machina* endings."[34] Skippy's (temporary) death is a pretext to introduce us to a new character, Shin. While lying on the road next to Skippy's inert body, Zoey calls Shin (Trecartin) on her cell phone, asking what she should do. The scene cuts to a medium shot of Shin as s/he (or *ze*)[35] replies, "Zoey, just keep filming him." Skippy's storyline is temporarily placed on hold while Shin's is about to begin.

In the same vein as contemporary video artist Kalup Linzy, Trecartin's narrative follows a "to be continued..." format reminiscent of daytime soap opera. In his video piece, *All My Churen* (2003), a parody of the melodramatic soap opera, *All My Children*, Linzy introduces us to several family members (all played by the artist) talking to each other over the phone about an upcoming funeral. Far from the polished set designs and camerawork of the ABC sitcom, *All My Churen* is shot with a low-tech digital camera that frames the characters in static medium shots. Linzy follows some of the conventions of the daytime drama format. The narrative, however, is far from being related to the glamorous plots of its white upper-middle-class counterpart. Tyron, Mama, and Sister are arguing about who is going to finance JoJo's funeral. The characters address each other as "bitch," "child," or "girl," evocative of black drag-queen speak. Although Linzy and Trecartin both parody and refer to the rhetoric of the melodrama in their work, they do so very differently. Kalup Linzy seeks to transform dominant ideological practices by subverting established narratives, while Ryan Trecartin appropriates and remixes form and content without assigning either the original or the "revision" (Trecartin's term) a hierarchical value. Instead, he creates subversive work without directly attacking or counteridentifying with established conventions. Furthermore, both artists also have diverging views about the art of drag. Linzy in drag, portrays female characters adorned in European hair weaves or wigs and skintight dresses that accentuate his prosthetic curves. Trecartin, on the other hand, does not aim to create a campy female impersonation. Instead he claims, "I want a feminine moment, but it has nothing to do with performing a role that is the opposite of my being a man."[36] For Trecartin, gender is much more fluid and multidimensional.

Shin truly epitomizes Trecartin's concept of gender fluidity. Neither a drag queen nor a drag king, the "man-cunt" as ze is referred to by other characters, is a third-sex hybrid with an ambivalent sexuality. The ambiguous name Shin, a common Japanese male name, does not help us interpret his/her (or *zir*)[37] gender either. Depending on the kanji characters used, the name in Japanese, means "advance," "progress," "new," or "move forward."[38] Therefore, the name Shin represents this leap into the future, as it suggests the personification of the hyperactive internet new age. The character also possibly alludes to several gender ambiguous anime characters, such as Ed, the web hacker protagonist in *Cowboy Bebop*. Shin's constant verbal profusion, short attention span, and multicolored painted face are all characteristics that reflect the overabundant content generated online. Furthermore, the protagonist is almost always shown in relation to a portable electronic device, such as a cell phone or a handheld camera, to emphasize the character's connectivity and mobility.

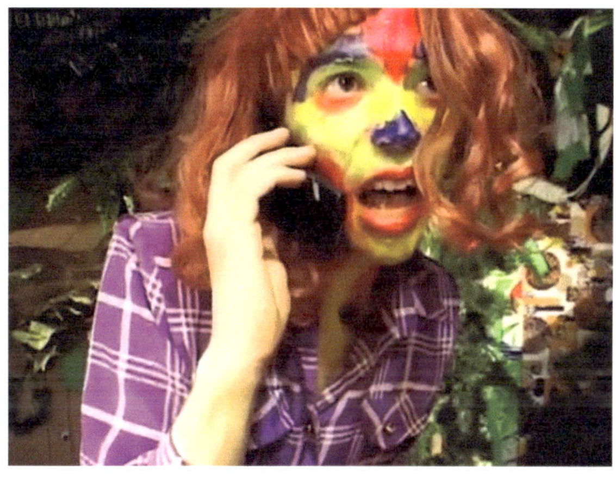

Figure 2.23 *A Family Finds Entertainment* (2004)

Shin's illogical verbal rants represent what Trecartin considers to be the bombardment of nonlinear streams of information on the net. In one instance, Shin directly addresses the camera while engaged in the following manic telephone conversation with a friend named Dameon (Will Gurley).

> Hey! Ha! Ha! Yeah! Dameon it's me Shin [. . .] anyway you should call me more often I'm throwing a party tonight I put a fish in my water I just went exercising it was really fun anyways I'm throwing a party tonight F-U-N it's called Experiments in Music bring everything that you own and well I just haven't been feeling like myself lately and I need to get back in the mood of things you know moods anyways so, hum, yeah, are you in the middle of a manly club meeting or something? What's going on?

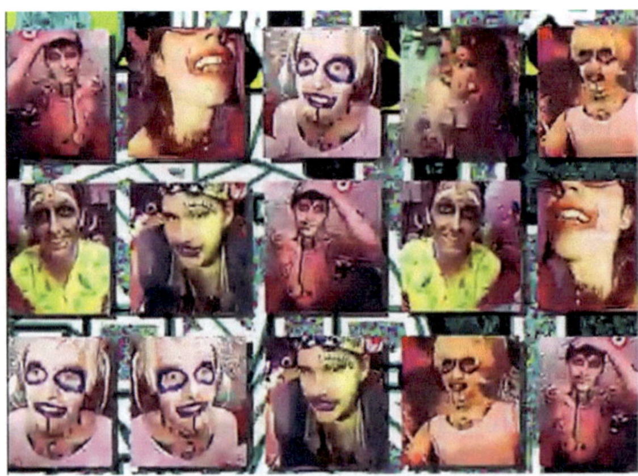

Figure 2.24
A Family Finds Entertainment (2004)

Fed up with the interaction, Dameon hangs up on Shin. Two separate layered partial shots of Shin are suddenly shattered into thousands of particles propelled toward the viewer, while the sound of a busy telephone signal pulsates in the background. Trecartin takes this opportunity to introduce us to an effect that will become one of his recurring visual motifs: multiple screens. He employs these much as Douglas Sirk used "frames within frames," as a visual device whereby characters appear contained within windows, doorways, and picture frames.[39] However, in Sirk's melodramas these devices symbolize isolation and confinement, while in Trecartin's videos they represent the multilinearity of cyberspace. Individual microframes each feature a character with a corresponding narrative, simultaneously streaming videos, akin to a computer screen displaying several browsers at once. The multiple screen motif is the quintessential symbol for the infinite freedom Trecartin insatiably craves. As Arthur Lubow puts it, "For Trecartin and many of his peers, 'all ways' is a much more appealing prospect than 'always.' "[40]

Shin steps outside the house and is welcomed by a group of colorful partiers dressed in vibrant colors, holding bright sparklers. This time, the outside is portrayed as festive, contrary to the earlier drab and disturbing outdoor experience that featured Snowy White Girl. No longer confined by interior spaces, the outside now appears welcoming. Doors open and doorways are crossed. Spaces are no longer divided by physical barriers and can be transitioned seamlessly. Shin holds a portable camera up in the air as a sign of victory and guides the group of friends toward the basement where jubilation is underway.

The helter-skelter party scene resembles the carnivalesque pandemonium of *Valentine's Day Girl*. Shin inquisitively meanders through the rooms of the house with a handheld camera in tow. Each room features distinct musical genres, including punk, classical, grunge, and electro-clash. Shin is mesmerized by what each space has to offer, yet only remains in each one for a few seconds. The sensory overload is so overwhelming that although not fully able to grasp all of it, Shin opts to continue on this exhilarating exploration, as if to make up for lost time. The protagonist enters and exits rooms much as web surfers navigate in and out of web pages, with hallways symbolically representing online search engines. Trecartin simulates the interactive nature of the internet, despite the limitations of single-channel video through the employment of these visual allegories.

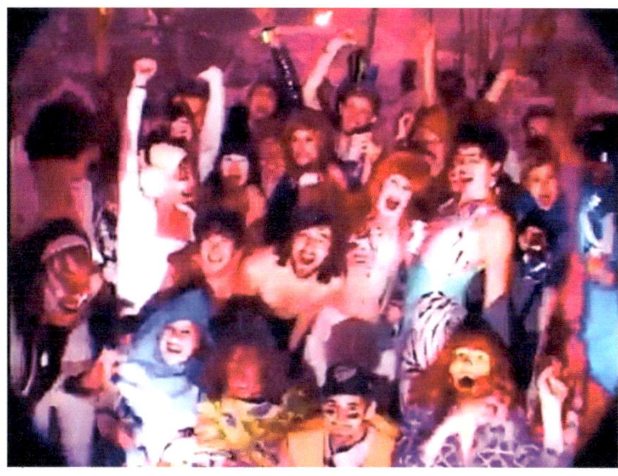

Figure 2.25 *A Family Finds Entertainment* (2004)

We are suddenly transported from the party to an overhead shot of Skippy's spirit ascending his body. Trecartin superimposes two digital layers depicting Skippy's body and reduces the opacity of the second layer to achieve this effect. Zoey Spelling's night vision camera captures his resurrection from death. "I hear music," Skippy says. Trecartin cuts to a close-up of the documentary filmmaker encouraging him to "follow it." Skippy snaps his fingers and with a fierce attitude exclaims, "*I will*!" The screen fades back to a close-up of Shin dancing, surrounded by partygoers congregated outside. The merriment culminates in a visual smorgasbord of special effects: overlay, fragmentation, and image reversal. The artist's editing abides no rules; images merge and collide in a mind-bending spectacle. The abstraction of shapes and colors meld and morph into each other to form a multilayered mass that conveys the characters' excitement and exhilaration.

The carousers gather around an inflatable pool filled with water, in which Shin's body is submerged as if for a baptismal ritual. We realize as Shin's wig falls off and makeup runs that it is no longer Shin we see but Ryan Trecartin. As he comes out of the pool, his gaze drifts upward toward the sky. The artist cuts to a point-of-view shot of the moon. The camera zooms in on the luminous lunar globe, a divine presence descending from the sky. The image fades to black, and the party comes to a close with a display of fireworks.

Consistent with melodramas' conventional storylines, *A Family Finds Entertainment* culminates in the expected happy ending. It has been acknowledged that a blissful closure in Hollywood melodramas was, in many instances, a requirement enforced by the studios and the production code.[41] For this reason, the endings of many of the 1950s and '60s melodramas seem forced and artificial. Working outside the mainstream Hollywood system, Trecartin, on the other hand, is not restricted by any constraints imposed on him. His use of clichéd symbols such as fireworks in the final scene, however, could equally appear as contrived as the motion picture subgenre he remixes. Yet, an eerie feeling still pervades throughout *A Family Finds Entertainment*'s final scene. As the block party comes to an end, the characters run in haste back to the house. Trecartin, standing outside by the front porch, glances at the camera one more time before joining his friends inside. It is as though the artist knows something we are not meant to know yet. The lack of resolution leaves viewers in a state of suspense, wondering what will happen next. *A Family Finds Entertainment* can thus be seen as a transitional stage for Trecartin, one in which he has successfully completed his rite of passage from the insular space of the closet to the queer world and the internet.

// 3 //

I-BE Area

Altermodern Time and Cyberqueer Place

A PIXELATED THREE-DIMENSIONAL WATERFALL EFFECT cascades down the screen. Through a slide-down transition filter, the image is then bisected to reveal a small frame in which I-BE 2 (Ryan Trecartin) addresses the camera. "I don't wanna see my original 'cause I already know what he wants to look like and I don't wanna look there." The protagonist is chatting online with his avatar (AV), Independent Avatar (Ryan Trecartin). A medium close-up shows him holding a computer keyboard in the foreground surrounded by his friends Cheeta (Rhett LaRue) and Jamy (Brian McKelligott). The digitization of the shot gives it the appearance of a video log filmed by a lo-tech webcam. A point-of-view shot of a Mac computer monitor displays I-BE 2's avatar framed within the computer screen. I-BE 2 is confronted by his overbearing online alter ego who appears to have hijacked his life: "I am assigning you a thirty-page historical paper with links to video and location. [. . .] And the only bibliography is your memory. And this event must take place outside of your lifetime."

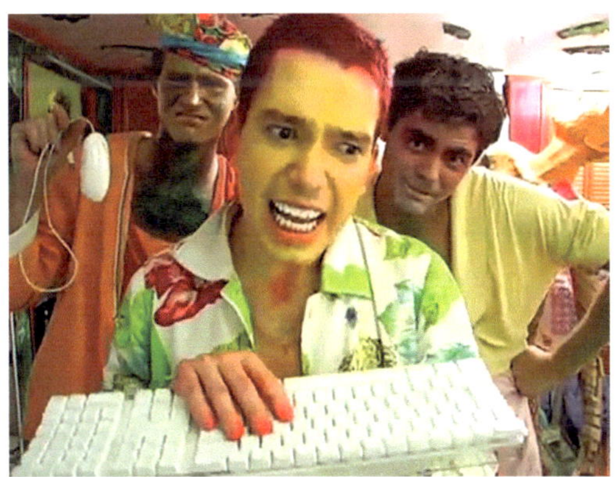

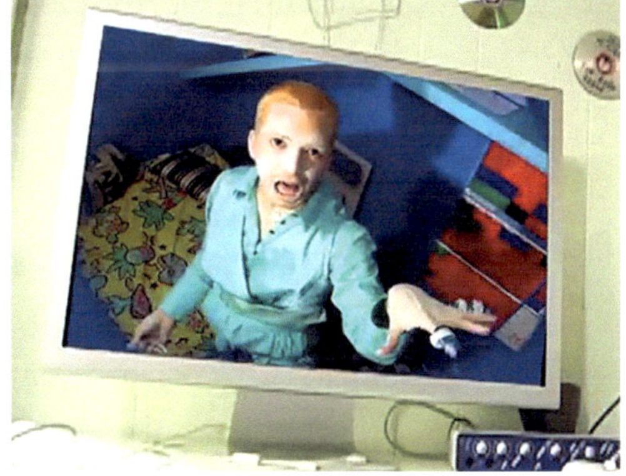

Figures 3.1 and 3.2 *I-BE Area* (2007)

Fed up with his virtual AV's litany, the protagonist proceeds to delete him. Trecartin cuts to an image of a desktop screen in which an arrow cursor clicks on a trashcan icon, followed by a black-and-white image of the avatar descending into a whirling vortex until it completely disappears, symbolizing its obliteration.

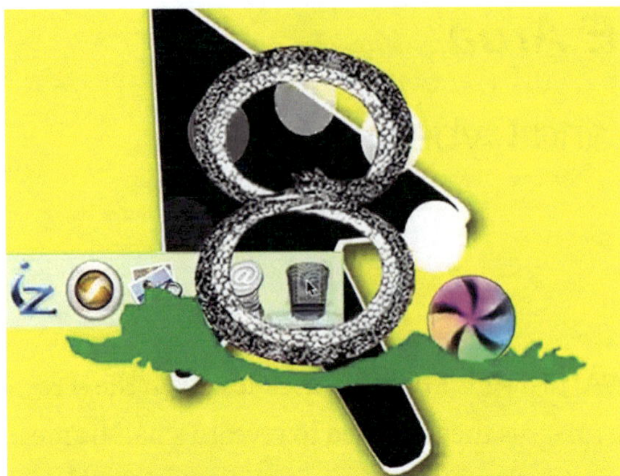

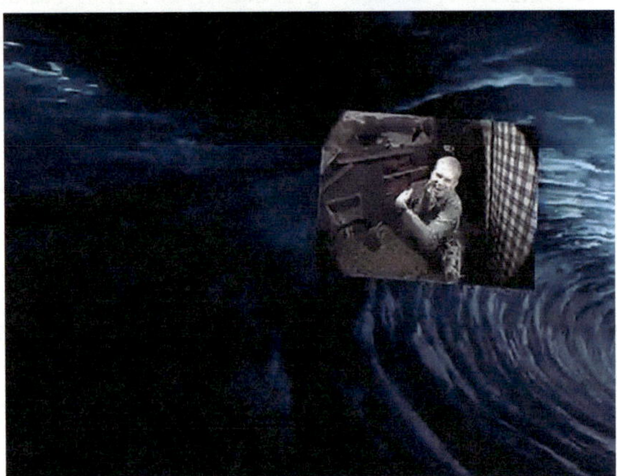

Figures 3.3 and 3.4 *I-BE Area* (2007)

This section of the feature-length video *I-BE Area* (2007) clearly reveals that within the virtual reality of the video, Trecartin and his protagonist are preoccupied with the plurality of representation afforded by the internet.[1] Understanding the relationship between that imaginary world and the existing one will reveal that for the artist, cyberspace does not exist outside real physical space, as he blurs the boundaries between virtual and corporeal realms.

I-BE Area follows the peripeteia of I-BE 2, a self-claimed "real-life mixed-media," clone of I-BE, the first "total original." The protagonist is in the midst of an existential crisis as he desperately seeks to abandon his original incarnation in pursuit of other identities. However, as a copy, he is unable to create entirely new identities, so instead he appropriates discarded ones from online users. As he navigates inworld across various virtual chat rooms, the protagonist drifts into new personae. I-BE 2 is the embodiment of the "cybersubject," "a fluid subject, [. . .] a 'feedback loop' constantly in formation through an interpenetration between self and not-self."[2] Matilda Tudor adds that the cybersubject is the "ultimate manifestation of queer theory as it [is] seen to transcend the physical world in a parallel space, where it freely and flexibly [can] pick [. . .] who to be,"[3] choosing from an infinite combination of mutable online identities. Nina Wakeford dubs some of these hybrid subjects, "cyberqueer." Wakeford suggests the term implies a "relationship between sexuality and space, where space is taken to be the arena accessible by computer-mediated interactions."[4] She identifies several types of cyberqueer spaces: chat rooms, websites, and newsgroups with a specific focus on the LGBTQ community, further elaborating as follows:

> Cyberqueer spaces are framed as new places within which lesbians, gay, transgender or queer experiences can take place, with a particular focus on the advantages compared to "real" physically-located space. Mainstream cyberspace has often been promoted as creating "virtual communities" and cyberqueer spaces may compensate for the social or geographical isolation of sexual minorities by operating as a medium through which contacts can be more easily facilitated...[5]

The emergence of cyberqueer spaces can thus be seen as an act of defiance. Following Wakeford's argument, Pramod K. Nayar proposes that

> These [cyberqueer] sites can serve as spaces of resistance to heterosexist cyberspace, where pockets of queer art can alter the nature of cyberspace representations. They are spaces of identity formation in a context where the "real" spaces of heterosexual, patriarchal technocapital have denied the queer his or her identity—the queer can begin the performance of identity (at least) in cyberspace.[6]

These cyberqueer spaces provide a mode of address for self-representation and transformation beyond transitional experiences in nonvirtual life. This is significant as they present opportunities to combat erasure and activate social visibility and inclusion within the canon for marginalized queer communities.

Interplay in cyberspace not only allows for extensive experimentation with identity, it also enables internet surfers to navigate across temporalities established within multiplatform computer interfaces. Trecartin takes advantage of unlimited opportunities to create virtual geographies and multilinear narratives. In doing so, the artist challenges previous notions of time and place by expanding their traditional roles through online mediation.

As such, *I-BE Area* can be seen as the cinematic exemplification of Nicolas Bourriaud's concept of altermodernism. In his "altermodern manifesto," he declares that

> We are entering the era of universal subtitling, of generalized dubbing. Today's art explores the bonds that text and image weave between themselves [...] This evolution can be seen in the way works are made: a new type of form is appearing, the journey-form, made of lines drawn both in space and time, materializing trajectories rather than destinations. The form of the work expresses a course, a wandering, rather than a fixed space-time.[7]

Trecartin navigates through a cultural landscape saturated with media imagery and forges new pathways between formats of expression (i.e., video, sound, computer graphics, internet). In Bourriaud's words he is a "'homo viator,' the prototype of contemporary traveler whose passage through signs and formats refers to an experience of mobility, travel, and transpassing."[8] This bohemian wanderer translates information from one format to another, from video to sculpture to multimedia installation, while appropriating and leaping through geographic location and history much like a "cultural nomad."[9] Many artists associated with this new generation are less interested in creating objects and more focused on presenting an artistic process or journey that may take the form of various formats (text, single video channels, performance, and/or sound). Indeed, Ryan Trecartin does not conceive of his videos as solely collectible products. His movies can be uploaded, downloaded, and even reedited if desired. In an interview with Cindy Sherman, the artist commented, "It would be amazing if we lived in a post-information world where we could truly transcend form and habit."[10] Trecartin shares with many contemporary artists a concern with democratizing new media's production and distribution. When asked why he chose to upload his videos on YouTube, he replied,

> I have very strong feelings about sharing. I make videos for people—the whole process is shared. [...] I think web 2.0 spaces relate tremendously to the logic and structures of physical space

> and plot sculpting in the movies. So I think it's an appropriate home that brings out a quality in the work that you may look over in the gallery. Plus videos are meant to be accessed and watched.[11]

I-BE Area emerged at a time of great technological innovation marked by the advent of YouTube and the explosion of the Web 2.0 infrastructure. Web 2.0, the second, faster generation of the World Wide Web, offers a more dynamic way of interacting with online multimedia platforms than what was then possible with Web 1.0. For instance, viewers can post comments on video channels in real time and later tweet them out to the rest of the world, thereby engendering a dialogue on a global scale. As Trecartin explains, "With the Internet, people are understanding that the camera is like a place of transaction, that both ends of it are subjective, a fluid tube."[12] Patricia Zimmermann notes,

> We are now in the midst of what feels like the amateurization of the entire media universe. It is a tsunami of user-generated, fan-produced, blogger-written, Twitter-feed practices. Developed on a wide scale over the last ten years, smartphone imaging, the user-friendly accessibilities of Web 2.0 for blogging, YouTube uploads, game-modding, the explosion of social networks like Facebook and Twitter, and the proliferation of fan culture engagements and modifications of commercial products from books, television shows, films, and games—all these present a monumental shift in media structures.[13]

This momentous change has caused, Massimiliano Gioni claims, "a profound metamorphosis [. . .] in the DNA of images."[14] Because new technology has become increasingly accessible, "art has lost any central role with respect to the image-making machine. Redefining the role of the artist in relation to this radical transformation of the image will not be a job only for this generation: It will be one of the most important challenges for the new century."[15] Lisa Phillips, director of the New Museum of Contemporary Art, comments in *Younger Than Jesus*: *The Generation Book*, that Millennials are "at ease with new technologies and new languages [and] has had a tremendous impact on the way we acquire, distribute, produce, and consume information, knowledge, and culture."[16]

Also known as "Generation Y," its members were born, according to Lauren Cornell, chief curator of the Hessel Museum of Art, on or after 1976.[17] In her essay, "Them," Laura Hoptman, curator at the Museum of Modern Art ("MoMA") in New York City, attempts to attribute a set of characteristics idiosyncratic to the Generation Y. She writes, "The Millennials (b. 1976–) are: very optimistic (!), totally wired, self-absorbed but socially conscious, presume wealth and are born consumers, and want what they consume immediately."[18]

Hoptman's statement may seem too broad, yet, one cannot deny that there might be a kernel of truth in her claim. In the technology-driven world we live in, iPhones, iPods, and iPads become bodily extensions. Millennials could be perceived as victims of their own time; anticipating the next best thing on their devices that will alleviate their FOMO (fear of missing out), however, some believe, the information revolution has actually empowered them. As Joel Stein notes, thanks to the internet, these young educated consumers are able to compete against big corporations: "bloggers vs. newspapers, [. . .] YouTube directors vs. studios, app-makers vs. entire industries."[19]

In an interview with LP Studio, Trecartin was quoted, "Technology and the infinite amount of data is not an overload for the new generation because they are in it, this is it for them, it's just a way of life."[20] This saturation of encrypted information has led to the creation of new forms of expression, of a new language—one that is concise and abbreviated enough to function within text messages and engage our fleeting attention span. Who still has time for "I love you," when I ♡ U is all we need? Massimiliano Gioni posits,

> One has to [imagine] the relationship between generations and individuals as something similar to the relationship of language as an abstract set of rules on one hand, and language as speech, as its actual use on the other [. . .] Quite significantly, a new obsession with language seems to emerge precisely from the works of many artists born in and around the 80s. There is a linguistic explosion on all sides, an unstoppable flow of words.[21]

Ryan Trecartin's technical vernacular inspired by software programming languages. For instance, in one scene in *I-BE Area*, the protagonist exclaims:

> I-BE 2: Look I think I just saw a highly advanced, 3-D text message of my future self giving me the middle-finger and I'm gonna fuck right back in his face. [. . .] Yeah Have yall been downstairs lately? It looked different. [. . .] I think they had a '70s filter on a very low percentage 'cause it reminded me of all the memories that I hate from that decade.
>
> Jamy: It's not a filter. It's called Linda, a hidden decade from the present.
>
> I-BE 2: Listen Quit explaining shit to me, Jamy. You think I don't know about all the decades that they be hiding? They must have slipped me some computer pills or some shit because I had no control.
>
> Cheeta: I-BE, I can't translate your rants. What the hell you mean?
>
> I-BE 2: Buy my Rosetta Stone.

While Trecartin's version of the popular instructional language course might facilitate deciphering his highly programmed lingo, many online followers already intrinsically understand it, as illustrated by a comment posted by "Scandibilly" on Trecartin's YouTube channel.

> No one has ever captured my mind. I didn't think it possible. I didn't know this film was possible. It was perfect. That one hour, 48 minutes was the closest I'd come to someone who could understand me. Thank you! Thank you! I understand![22]

The comment, representative of many other posts online, clearly evidences that the artist is able to tap into the consciousness of many members of his virtual community. It is through his twenty-first-century dialect that Trecartin is able to interact with a techno-centric fanbase. Terry Smith notes that the concept of interactivity is an essential component of contemporary art. He states that contemporary artists' works "involve methods of social exchanges, interactivity with the viewer within the aesthetic experience being offered to him/her, and the various communication processes, in their tangible dimension as tools serving to link individual groups together."[23]

The artist created the website riverthe.net, an auxiliary internet project launched in 2010 in collaboration with Tumbler founder David Karp. The site functions as an endless stream of unflagged, unrestricted short ten-second videos uploaded by anonymous participants. Each randomly streaming video is tagged with three key words. Videos with similar tags are linked together in order to create playlists. Viewers may click on the tags associated with a particular video as they watch it, which in turn directs them to a new related playlist. This innovative participatory viewing experience not only allows spectators to generate content but also directs what they watch by enabling them to pick and choose from endless streaming pathways. As Trecartin explained during Rhizome's Seven on Seven Technology and Art conference in 2010, the rationale behind the creation of the website was to build a platform in which the user interface is integrated within the video. He expressed a desire to enhance the interface of video sharing sites such as YouTube, pointing out that all of the participatory elements such as tags, comments, and feedbacks, are broadcast *outside* of the video. Trecartin's goal for the project was to contain the interface *inside* the content, rather than surrounding it.[24]

Although *I-BE Area* was released three years before the launch of riverthe.net, the feature can be understood as the artist's first attempt at simulating the dynamic interface of online platforms within his movies. Its visual language incorporates earlier stylistic devices such as fast-paced editing, repetition, and fragmented shots, but its repertoire is expanded with the integration of pop-up windows, shattered screen effects, computer desktop wallpapers, three-dimensional effects, digital pictograms, and graphical user interface-inspired designs. Viewers are transported into a "sensory enactment of technological immersion"[25] akin to surfing not *on* but *within* the internet.

Unlike *A Family Finds Entertainment*, in which the multiple screens were simply used as a visual device, in *I-BE Area*, they also serve a narrative function. That is, the action taking place inside the screens-within-the-screen has a direct consequence on the action surrounding it. Consequently, this effect creates heterogeneous temporalities in which narratives merge and unravel simultaneously.

This concept is best exemplified in a scene where I-BE 2 is rejected by his "clone-intolerant family group."[26] The protagonist grabs a clear plastic suitcase from a family member—signaling his departure. He then retreats upstairs to his bedroom in an attempt to avoid a possible confrontation. I-BE 2 is filmed through a long shot opening a door leading to a staircase. As he exits the living room, the director cuts to an over-the-shoulder shot of Cheeta sitting in front of a computer watching I-BE 2 ascend the stairs on the monitor. The scene unfolds as if it were live footage recorded by a security camera. Trecartin then zooms in on the computer screen, which displays the protagonist entering his bedroom. Cheeta is then seen through a back shot as he watches himself onscreen talking to I-BE 2, "I-BE, I just watched the living room channel. I thought you were gonna fuck some shit up." The director zooms in on Cheeta's face until the edges of the monitor disappear completely from the frame. The characters continue their rapport, however, we are not sure if what we are viewing is now taking place in the protagonists' physical world or within the computer-mediated sphere of Cheeta's desktop. Trecartin purposefully maintains this ambiguity as he aims to erase the distinction between both. As James Bridle notes,

> While the idea of cyberspace has proved useful for some time, it posits the digital realm as an elsewhere, a separate domain of experience, interaction and memory, with a clear frontier—which is contrary to our own experience. A planet-wide digital infrastructure; mobile devices; pervasive connectivity; social and private networks and other forms of communication; all point to a world in which the virtual intersects with the physical at every moment.[27]

In Trecartin's virtual utopia, cyberspace and the physical environment coexist concurrently. Indeed, the artist "looks forward to a time when people no longer distinguish between their technology and their humanity [. . .] I think technology is us, not something we invented. [. . .] I think we are more psychic now because we have cell phones and you can look and see who's calling you. When people start seeing technology as us, as humanity, our whole idea of what existence is, is going to shift."[28] The artist perceives new media not as a form of representation but as a means to augment reality and become more human. However, the goal is not to reach a fixed destination or identity but to be in a constant process of becoming. As one character states in *I-BE Area*, "I need to feel endless in both directions."

I-BE 2 never remains a fixed identity as he constantly searches for a new one to adopt. The protagonist is thus always in a transitional state. In one of his incarnations, he takes on the identity of Oliver (Jessica Williams), a teenage girl from Ohio who sells her identity so she can buy a plane ticket to Brazil and start a new life. Oliver is introduced through a digital media player screen similar to a thumbnail pop-up window. She is presented from a static frontal view reminiscent of a YouTube clip via direct address.

> Hi, my name is Oliver. I'm five feet eleven inches and I look like this. I'm just sick of this though. [. . .] I'm talking about my lifestyle vibe. My horoscope, my attitude, my e-mail address, my fucking mother everyone. [. . .] Rewind. I could leave any day and just go. [. . .] My one-way plane ticket to Brazil costs 995 international dollars. My address should appear now, send me a one-way money order and you get this box.

Oliver, like millions of internauts worldwide, divulges an abundance of personal information on her online digital diary. Indeed, there are thousands of videos on YouTube titled *The Real Me*, which function as webcam-recorded confessionals. These days, almost anyone can be a director, producer, or a self-made online celebrity generating thousands of views and endorsements. Amateur videographers post advertisements online via Google AdSense in order to generate more and more revenue from sponsors as their videos gain popularity. This is a phenomenon that has taken over social media sharing platforms. However, becoming popular on the web is an arduous endeavor since, according to YouTube's statistics, "100 hours of video are uploaded to YouTube every minute."[29] Thus, bloggers must constantly compete against one another in order to stand out and be noticed.

Trecartin alludes to the competitiveness of the web in the introduction of *I-BE Area*. Soon after the opening credits, a faded freeze frame of a smiling young girl (Jade James) appears onscreen. The word "AVAILABLE" in block letters flashes over the image. The director cuts to a close-up of the character addressing the camera while holding a cell phone, "Hi Charity, it's Nicole. Guess What?" Nicole suddenly begins her self-promoting sales pitch, "Hi, my name's Nicole. Adopt me now. Get into it! I'm worth it! Five, six, seven, eight. Watch me now." The young girl executes an overly cheerful choreographed dance in front of an assumed audience. The scene abruptly ends with the opening freeze frame of Nicole repeated, this time with the word "SOLD" in bold red letters superimposed over the original shot. The director then jump-cuts to another amateurish video featuring Steven (Jack Ironstone), a nine-year-old boy also hoping to be adopted.

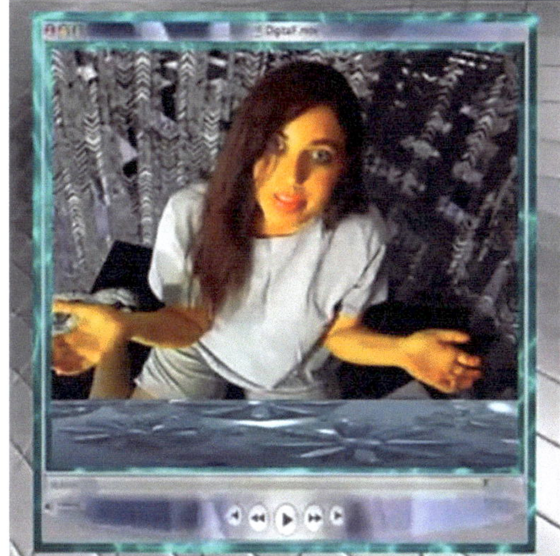

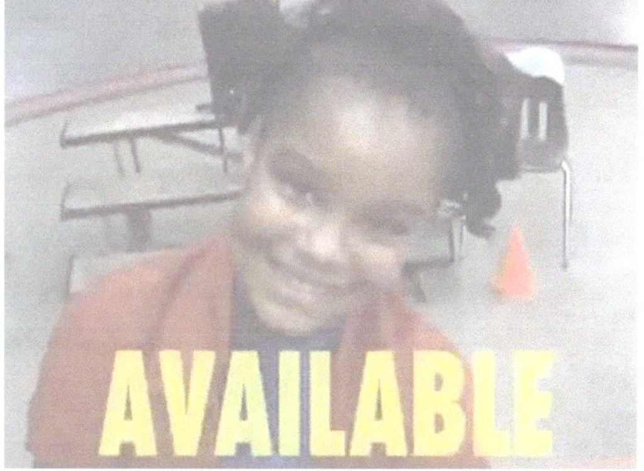

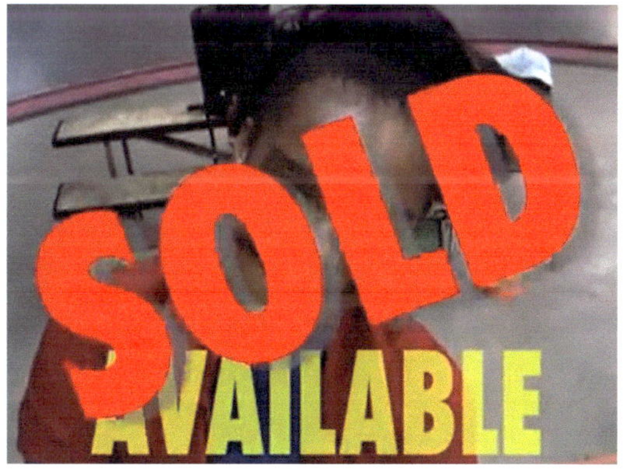

Figures 3.5, 3.6, and 3.7 *I-BE Area* (2007)

> Hi. My name's Steven. I'm nine years old, seventy pounds and four foot five. Hi. My multi-professional parents don't raise me. They act like I'm see-though. [. . .] I am something inside of me to give, something that everybody needs. I know the world would pick me out of a crowd. [. . .] Someone please adopt me before the talent show. [. . .] If you're surfing the Adoption Network, stop.

Much like Nicole, Steven attempts to showcase his talent by performing a tap dance routine in front of the camera. Both characters are aware of the camera's presence and thus perform understanding the powerful impact of posting their stories online.

By juxtaposing these two scenes side by side, Trecartin emphasizes the duality between both characters. Each is competing for attention, which is clearly illustrated by their impulse to display their physical prowess as if trying to impress the judges of a talent contest. In doing so, both attempt to stand out by claiming their individuality. However, Hal Niedzviecki notes that this kind of exposure is not meant to show how special or exceptional we may be, it is about showing how "deserving of everyday human interaction we are."[30]

The concept of adoption, a recurring theme in *I-BE Area*, is expressed throughout the narrative in various forms: as the legal guardianship of children, the longing to connect and belong to a community, or the co-opting of someone's online profile. This last example is manifested in I-BE 2, who takes on an alternate identity, or as Trecartin prefers to call it a personality, of an avatar. Lisa Nakamura describes this concept as "identity tourism."

> Users of the Internet represent themselves within it solely through the medium of keystrokes and mouse-clicks, and through this medium they can describe themselves and their physical bodies any way they like; they perform their bodies as text. On the Internet, [. . .] it is possible to "computer crossdress" and represent yourself as a different gender, age, race, etc.[31]

Massively multiplayer online role-playing games (MMORPGs) allow users to create and customize virtual characters by selecting from a wide variety of features such as gender, hairstyle, body type, skills, and age, among other options. In recent years, the practice of selling customized advanced characters online has gained much popularity. Websites entirely dedicated to the buying, selling, and trading of avatars have emerged, such as epicnpc.com, playerauctions.com, and marketplace.secondlife.com. Ranging from one to thousands of dollars, buyers can choose from an impressively wide variety of characters, including animals, fantasy creatures, and male, female, or in-between humans, as is illustrated with the avatar named Jeffree, a transgender AO (Animation Override) on sale for one thousand Linden dollars (Second Life's currency), which equates to approximately four U.S. dollars.[32] As explained by the seller, Jeffree comes with a modifiable shape, skin with hair base, sexy latex suit, eyebrows, and forty-six animations.[33]

Jeffree's list of customizable features can be compared to the panoply of choices included with the purchase of Oliver's personality. Pointing to her clear plastic suitcase, she states,

> Inside is my cell phone, outfit, all my passwords slash keys, plus a live subscription, hard copy PDF file of all the people I know in my life, how we relate and why I do the things I do. [. . .] Please. It's easy. I'm knowable, memorize this shit and save me.

As her prolix monologue comes to an end, the media-player screen suddenly swirls uncontrollably and is subsequently minimized until it disappears. I-BE 2 simultaneously enters the frame sporting clothes and a wig, which are identical to Oliver's. With his new feminized voice, I-BE 2 (now Oliver), shouts with excitement, "Hey, guys. Cheeta, Jamy, I'm gonna do it. I'm gonna be her." The protagonist snatches a pink cell phone (which belonged to the original Oliver) and proceeds to call her new mother, "Hello, Mother Mercedes?" Trecartin cuts to a close-up of Mother Mercedes (Susan Birmingham), an angry middle-aged butch lesbian on the hunt for a new rock band to adopt. Surprised by her daughter's unexpected call, she replies, "What the hell are you doing? I don't get it. [. . .] Oliver, Mayfly said you ran away." The scene cuts back to I-BE 2 posing as Oliver exclaiming, "Cheeta, I like this, I already like being her." Cheeta replies, "Yeah, but Oliver's a dumb name."

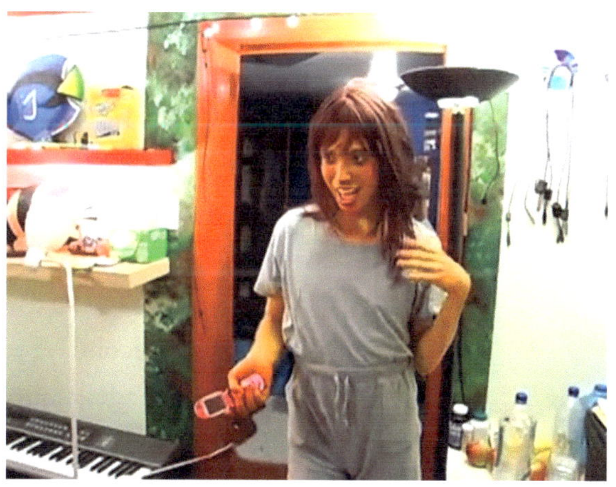

Figure 3.8
I-BE Area
(2007)

Unhappy with his adopted name, I-BE 2-Oliver-poser opts to change it to Amerisha. Similar to the way internet users customize and personalize their avatars, I-BE 2 refreshes Oliver's history in order to establish his own. However, although he has appropriated Oliver/Amerisha's persona, I-BE 2 still comes through. We notice this when the protagonist alternates between his initial masculine vocalization and the latter feminized one. I-BE 2 consciously modulates the pitch of his voice to make it sound more feminine. Therefore, we understand that I-BE 2 does not become Amerisha but performs Amerisha. Although his appearance closely resembles Oliver's, I-BE 2's impersonation is indubitably exaggerated. His flamboyant hair flips and affected mannerisms resemble internet sensation Chris Crocker's YouTube drag performance, *The Hairflip*!, which at one time had 6,448,010 views, where he expounds on the therapeutic effect of the hair flip.

Although Amerisha is intended to represent a female character, her flat chest and slight pelvic bulge make this quite questionable. Therefore, the wig and attire merely serve as props that enable viewers to recognize I-BE 2's impersonation of the original Oliver, while simultaneously allowing Trecartin to emanate from the performance. For Ryan Trecartin, blending gendered characteristics is not solely an attempt to destabilize gender categories but also his way to pluralize being-in-the-world. His campy portrayal of characters such as Amerisha symbolizes what he understands himself and all selves to be: a multiplicity of selves in constant flux. We understand this because Amerisha, I-BE 2, and I-BE the original all coexist and are channeled simultaneously through Trecartin.

The last shot in the scene exemplifies the protagonist's polymorphous existence. After saying her final goodbyes to Cheeta and Jamy, Amerisha is seen through a medium-long shot exiting I-BE 2's bedroom for her "amazing next life." Her image is projected onto a mirror hanging on an adjacent wall. However, Amerisha's reflection is not in sync with her gestures. Trecartin visually expresses this disconnect by presenting Amerisha's mirror projection in slow motion while maintaining Amerisha at thirty frames per second, producing an effect that transmits to viewers that the mirror image has a life of its own. This intentional directorial decision produces a dichotomy that further reinforces the character's inherent plurality.

As is customary in Trecartin movies, the next scene transports viewers into a completely different locale and introduces us to a brand new cast of characters. The sequence opens with an establishing shot depicting a young woman, Care-Inn (Tammy Zapotechne-Kelley) and a child, Jango (Solomon Kelley) standing in front of the entrance to a thrift shop. As they are about to enter the store, the camera slowly zooms in on the child, but we are unable to see the child's face as their backs are turned to the camera. A hypnotic flickering light bathes the shot, as an eerie accompanying musical score coupled with slow-motion cinematography reinforces the overall sense of mystery surrounding these two new characters.

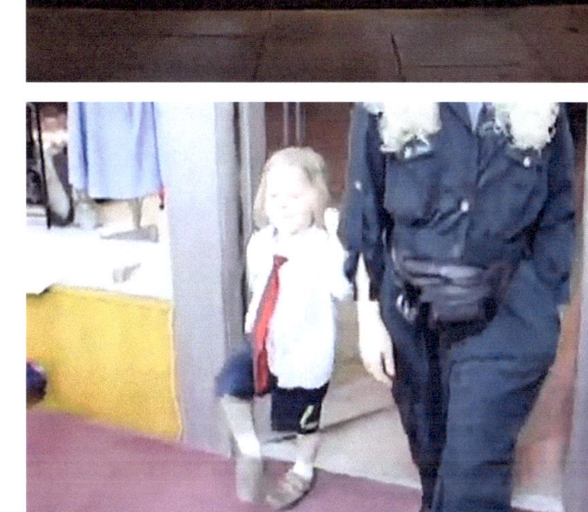

Figures 3.9 and 3.10 *I-BE Area* (2007)

The director cuts to an inside shot of the storefront. The camera, while extracting the young woman's head from the interior of the frame, zooms in on what we discover to be a boy's face. Although Trecartin directs viewers' attention to the child, little is known about him at this point. His relationship to the woman accompanying him is also obscure. She is seen walking into the store, her back turned to him, oblivious to his presence. A store employee named Daisy (Lizzie Fitch) yells out with excitement, "Care-Inn!" BeadStoreGirl (Ryan Trecartin) greets Care-Inn, then immediately addresses her mini-sidekick, "Fresh off the freakin' boat. Hey, buddy, can you say buddy?" Care-Inn interjects with disdain, "He can't talk yet." The camera then cuts to the boy, whose name is Jango. Smiling at the camera, he says, "When do I get to kill you?" The clarity of the child's speech contradicts Care-Inn's claim that he cannot yet speak, leading one to infer that she has little knowledge of the child and may not be directly related to him. She suddenly drags him forcefully by both hands across the floor and shoves him into a dressing room. Unaffected by Care-Inn's brusque behavior, BeadStoreGirl enlists her coworkers, "Let's steal these beads, girls. We got a career to start!"

The director suddenly jump-cuts to a frame within a frame in which the entire staff of the shop is seen facing the camera, reciting in unison, "The bead store, where culture is a way of life! The bead store, where culture is a way of life!" All the employees mechanically deliver their lines into the camera, as if they were addressing customers in a no-frills infomercial, "I need everything in this friggin' store! [. . .] Seriously, the whole world is right here in little beads. This is amazing!" Jango interrupts the production and asks Care-Inn, "When can I be adopted?" She quickly replies, "Jango, be quiet. [. . .] If you want me to adopt you, you're going to have to be a better person." Much like Nicole and Steven, the two young characters featured at the beginning of the movie, Jango seeks to be adopted. However, it is not clear what motivates such a desire since Care-Inn is portrayed as a less than caring prospective parent. The camera cuts back to Jango sitting in the dressing room talking to himself. "Care-Inn's amazing. She's gonna give me a house and everything . . ." His delusion comes to an end as he realizes that his mother-to-be is keeping him locked inside the fitting room.

Soon after Care-Inn withdraws to the basement of the store in order to "figure some things out," the bead store girls gather to discuss the child's future.

> BeadStoreGirl: Okay. I think we should show him the color yellow for a year, and then the next year only the color green.[34]
>
> Faye: I feel like he's gonna be a thornless rose.
>
> BeadStoreGirl: And modest. And modest.
>
> Meddy: He's gonna be amazing.

Jango's role within the narrative is still unclear. We are left to wonder what function the character really serves, as he appears to occupy such a prominent role throughout the scene despite his minimal onscreen presence. Trecartin does not provide us with an immediate answer, and instead introduces us to yet another character (or so it seems).

Daisy receives an impromptu phone call from an unknown person. The director then cuts to an explosion of a three-dimensional orb into liquid particles while Daisy's voice is overheard calling out, "Pasta?" Shortly after, a shot of a red Dodge SUV parked on a quiet sunny suburban street follows. A new character with bright-yellow painted skin emerges from the car and scampers toward a toddler (Penelope Wright) shown playing alone on the sidewalk. Like I-BE 2, Pasta (Ryan Trecartin) is a "mixed-media humanoid."[35] With blond pageboy hairstyle, coordinating denim outfit, bright skin tones, and unisex name, Pasta is an uncategorizable gender-ambiguous character, much like Shin in *A Family Finds Entertainment.* Although Shin possessed what could be considered some gendered characteristics, such as a long wig and a purple dress, Pasta, by contrast, has no identifiably traditional gendered signifiers.

In addition, unlike I-BE 2, Pasta does not seek to appropriate the forsaken identities of others; rather, the character is obsessed with the idea of stealing children. Mesmerized by the infant, Pasta seizes the child and scurries across the sidewalk to an apartment. Squeals of excitement resonate and once inside, Pasta places the child on a wooden rocking horse. The camera offers us a wider view of Pasta's living room. The array of children's toys and miniature strollers scattered around the room signals to us that Pasta has had previous contact with other children.

Pasta momentarily exits the living room only to return shortly to show several photographs to the toddler. The child attentively inspects one of the images and exclaims, "Baby, baby!" The camera manages to catch a glimpse of the photo as it dangles from the toddler's hand. We suddenly realize that the child in the photo is none other than Jango. Spectators are led to believe that Jango may have encountered Pasta on a previous occasion. Again, Trecartin presents a view we cannot accurately interpret because he purposely withholds information to keep us in suspense. Although his videos unravel at supersonic speed, they do not readily provide us answers to many of our queries. Instead, they slowly reveal themselves and the artist's intentions.

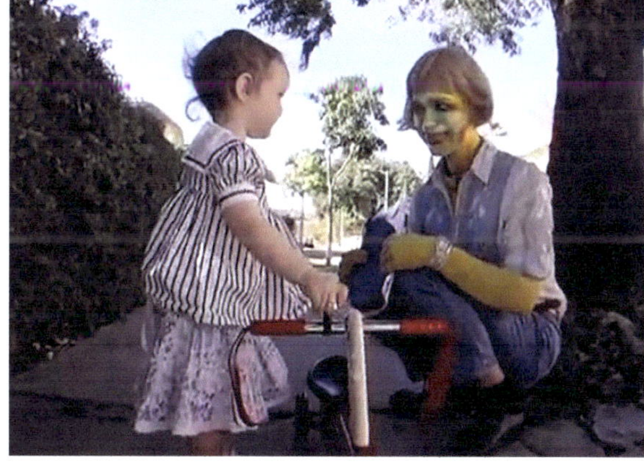

Figure 3.11 *I-BE Area* (2007)

Pasta grabs the child, carries her into a bedroom, retrieves a new set of photos, and shows them to the infant. A close-up of Jango's portrait fills the screen. In the background, Pasta can be heard saying, "Polly, when I was your age I looked like this and my name was Jango. I changed it. Best decision of my life." We now understand that Pasta was, and still is, Jango. The confusion of past, present, and future reflects the fact that Trecartin's abrupt transitions do not convey a sense of the passage of time. As we recall, the previous scene that takes place in the store ends when the shop girls receive a phone call from Pasta as they are contemplating Jango's future. Trecartin thus destabilizes temporal logic by giving the impression that these two scenes happen concurrently. As Kevin McGarry observes,

> [...] It is revealed that Pasta too was stolen as a child, before [s/he] had changed her name from Jango. Before is misleading, because her scenes and Jango's take place simultaneously. Pasta has developed [him-/herself], Jango, into another person in order to seize maximal control of her options. Jango the child continues to live in temporal coexistence with Pasta the adult, perhaps unaware of Pasta yet destined to one day invent [her/him].[36]

McGarry's observation points to the fact that Pasta coexists as both child and adult and thus can be seen as living in a perpetual state of adolescence. This nondistinction between childhood and adulthood is, according to Jack Halberstam, an attribute characteristic of queer subcultures: "For queers, the separation between youth and adulthood quite simply does not hold, and queer adolescence can extend far beyond one's twenties."[37] He further claims that while "heterosexual men and women are spending their weekends, their extra cash, and all their free time shuttling back and forth between the weddings of friends and family, urban queers tend to spend their leisure time and money on subcultural involvement: this may take the form of intense weekend clubbing, playing in small music bands [...]"[38] Pasta may share some of these traits, but fundamentally diverges from the author's queer paradigm as the character does not partake in "subcultural involvement." Instead, Pasta's main preoccupation revolves around the idea of parenting and fostering children, a seemingly normative endeavor.

Halberstam postulates that queer time and place exist outside the traditional reproductive or familial time. Although the author notes that, "Not all gay, lesbian, and transgender people live their lives in radically different ways from their heterosexual counterparts,"[39] he subsequently maintains that "part of what has made queerness compelling as a form of self-description in the past decade or so has to do with the way it has the potential to open up new life narratives and alternative relations to time and space."[40] The issue at play is that Halberstam's notion of queerness exists outside heteronormativity.

Trecartin does not oppose nor does he seek to comply with the conventions of hetero- or homonormative society for that matter. Having to choose to support or reject any of these models would create limiting boundaries that would deny him the unrestricted freedom he so desires. Pasta is both queer and concerned with child rearing. Yet, the character does not identify with mainstream gay culture. If contemporary gay-rights movements focus on marriage equality and adoption, Pasta is seeking an even more radical alternative life narrative. The character does not seek permission from an authority figure, since s/he operates outside the socio-judicial system as s/he steals children. Nor does s/he seek to build a family. Indeed, Pasta's insatiable baby cravings can only be temporarily satisfied by acquiring a new child while doing away with the old one. As Pasta tells Polly, "In twenty-five years we won't have Polly anymore... We just won't need her."

Pasta receives a phone call from a friend, Sen-teen (Alison Powell), requesting help babysitting two abandoned twins in Old New Jersey. After some consideration, Pasta decides to leave the toddler alone in the bedroom. Once outside his condo, Pasta revs the engine of her/his white MINI Cooper and drives off to Old New Jersey. A close-up of the character's face behind the wheel is crosscut with a panoramic view of a virtual landscape advancing forward. The polygonal environment in this scene consists of infinite rows of smooth surfaced mountains lining an endless highway. Far from the urban cityscape imagery often associated with new technology and the World Wide Web,[41] Trecartin's digital space-making is devoid of the kinds of futuristic infrastructures one would envision finding in a high-tech virtual world. Although this desolate site might surprise some viewers at first, Tom Boellstorff points out that virtual landscapes, such as those found in the MMORPG Second Life "often have a rural feel to them—newcomers to Second Life

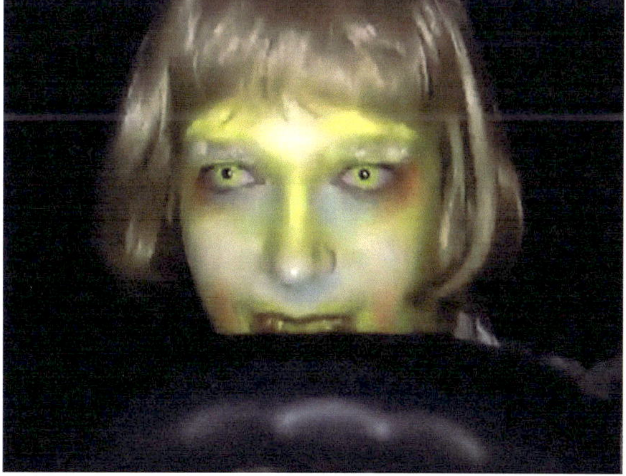

Figure 3.12 *I-BE Area* (2007)

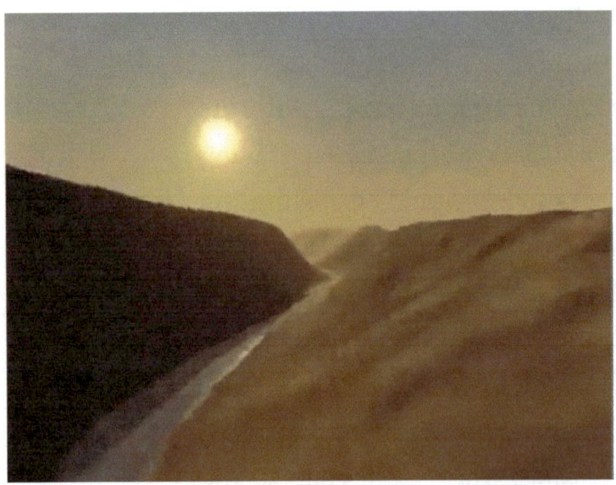

Figure 3.13
I-BE Area
(2007)

often say it seems empty or abandoned. One reason for this is that to distribute server load, only a certain number of objects can be created or 'rezzed' on a parcel of land."[42]

By situating Pasta within a digital rural environment, Trecartin challenges the theory of metronormativity in which queer subcultures thrive primarily in urban areas.[43] Halberstam argues that queer individuals feel more threatened in rural areas as they stand out more. Moving to the city becomes a survival strategy, or as the author states, a necessity. The queer place is thus a safe space in which various communities coexist and allow for diverse cultural expressions outside of the dominant culture. Although the claim is nuanced by noting that "many queers [later] yearn to leave the urban area and return to their small towns,"[44] the statement still suggests that queers have to move to the city before venturing back to rural life. In reality, queer individuals today no longer have to move to the city in order to find and/or build support systems thanks to community building and outreach made possible through social networking sites and other online platforms. Steve Silberman further remarks that, "In the past, teens had to wait until they were old enough to get into a bar to meet other gays and lesbians. Now, online interaction lets teens find other gay youngsters—as well as mentors."[45]

Furthermore, the erasure of established geographic demarcations through globalization and constant satellite surveillance makes categorizing specific locales as queer or heteronormative politically obsolete.[46] In *I-BE Area*, Trecartin seeks to eliminate such divisions by placing much emphasis on his characters' mobility. The protagonists are able to move seamlessly from one place to another almost telepathically: pop-up windows simultaneously display the same character in different environments, jump cuts and crosscuts also transport them to disparate situations, and fade-ins and -outs give the impression of spatial unity despite the fact that the scenes are shot in completely unrelated locations. Unlike

Kuleshov's concept of creative geography, Trecartin here does not seek to combine various segments shot at distinct locations, so they all appear to occur at a fixed location during a continuous time. Instead, he purposefully eschews continuity editing and pieces scenes together explicitly unrelated to each other in order to emulate the internet's constant stream of imagery.

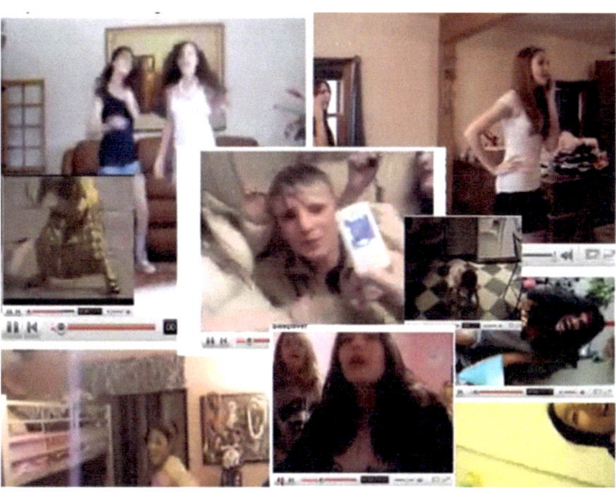

Figure 3.14 *I-BE Area* (2007)

The director also refers to the characters' portability through dialogue. For instance, Pasta requests that his confidant, Mayflyflowna (Katrina), a suburban housewife, cash a check, purchase a plane ticket, and provide an opportunity for limitless travel on an endless journey: "I wanna a one-way, no-way ticket to the end." Pasta begins to count down from five to zero as the acoustics of a space rocket blasting off slowly rises in volume. When s/he reaches zero, the image cuts to a three-dimensional rendering of the sky, which then dissolves into an aerial shot of actual sky footage in which a minuscule silhouette of a plane can be detected on the horizon. This furtive shot quickly leads to a three-dimensional rendering of a desolate beach at night bathed in bright moonlight. This uncharacteristically romantic, almost idyllic vision is interrupted by the sudden (re)apparition of Amerisha. Then we are provided with a pitch-black long shot of a cornfield at night. An indistinguishable figure observed from a distance runs frantically across the field, struggling to find a way out of it. As the character advances toward the camera, we recognize the outfit and wig previously worn by Amerisha. Yet, when we are presented with a close-up of this mysterious intruder, we realize that the performer playing Amerisha is no longer Trecartin but Kenny Curran, a recurring cast member in Trecartin's projects.

This latest version of Amerisha should not, however, be interpreted as a new character, since it is later revealed in the credits that it is named "No name I-Be corn Glitch." As such, Kenny Curran, as Amerisha, appears to be nothing more than a temporary computer system malfunction. We are left pondering what is causing this character such distress and why she is so eager to escape the cornfield. Interestingly, cornfields represent a region in *Second Life* that consists of a "mythological status where once naughty avatars were sent to think about what they had done."[47]

Although we are not told what has led to Amerisha's demise, we understand from her alias and location in a cornfield that she has become a naughty avatar—an avatar with design flaws, or, even worse, an avatar containing a virus. Working within a similar entropic logic, artist Cecile B. Evans and creative technologist Alice Bartlett recently developed a computer app that creates a "bad copy" of your online identity on the social media site Twitter.[48] The app, available at http://sevenonseven.herokuapp.com, hacks into Twitter profiles and changes behavior patterns randomly: adding strangers to the list of followers, and un-following others.[49]

In this particular scene, the glitch of the character is highlighted by its nonsensical rant: "Stupid retro reality vote people fucking off TV can suck my... building." Something off-screen momentarily catches the avatar/glitch's attention. Like an insect drawn to light, Amerisha rushes madly in its direction. After crossing busy roads and a forest, the character arrives at her destination. She momentarily pauses and points to a modern glass edifice nestled under a full moon and hypnotically declares, "Building, I'm gonna buy that building."

Unable to resist the bewitching magnetism radiating from the superstructure, Amerisha races toward the perplexing corporate erection. The next shot shows the character entering the building. However, she has regressed back to her original version impersonated by I-BE 2 (played by Trecartin). Once inside, Amerisha wanders through dark gloomy halls, in search of "another soul." The scene cuts to a point of view shot of the character seen through glass windows hurtling across a corridor. An unidentified figure in the foreground of the screen, her back turned to the camera, is observing Amerisha, as we are. The protagonist seems to be trapped inside this oppressive industrial structure that appeared so alluring earlier. The camera zooms in on an image of a spinning vortex overlaid atop the indistinguishable character. The visual recalls a previous spiral effect that appeared in the scene where I-BE 2 dumped his Independent Avatar into the computer trashcan icon. This parallel may be foreshadowing the fact that Amerisha is about to experience the same fate as I-BE 2's previous avatar. The image fades and we are now transported inside a bright-green classroom.

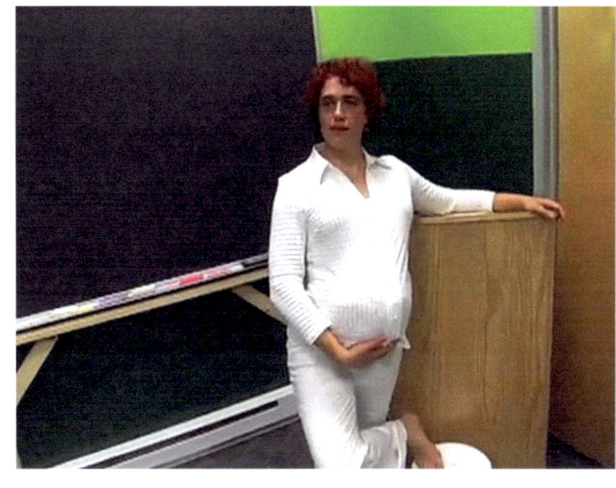

Figure 3.15
I-BE Area (2007)

We have entered Jaime's (Lizzie Fitch) area, a workshop in which trashed avatars are reformatted. Jaime is an inimical pregnant drama teacher in charge of reprogramming these discarded avatars. With her protruding belly, she represents the motherboard-mother figure. Referred to as "the fate creator" by the other characters, Jaime possesses the power to control all of the avatars ensnared in her territory or disk drive. Although she calls herself a drama teacher, Jaime primarily educates discarded avatars about consumerism and corporate culture.

> You're in front of a store. It's overstylized and controlling. They have dumb designs that fall apart and a scary smell [...] Don't be about the employees. It's a guilty prop [...] It's cool. You can deal. Ask to see the manager and then his girlfriend, the CEO [...] They're like a young hip company. Kind of cool, kinda fair, kinda researched, all around wish-wash.

Jaime pauses from delivering her corporate jargon-infused rhetoric to enlist her students in a game of truth or consequence. Based on their response, she chooses a door to open that will determine their doomed fate. Her lecture is momentarily disrupted by the entrance of a new character, Jeff (Kevin McGarry), an obstreperous computer bug, who disruptively storms out of a school locker. The character is framed through several oblique camera angles, vacillating between

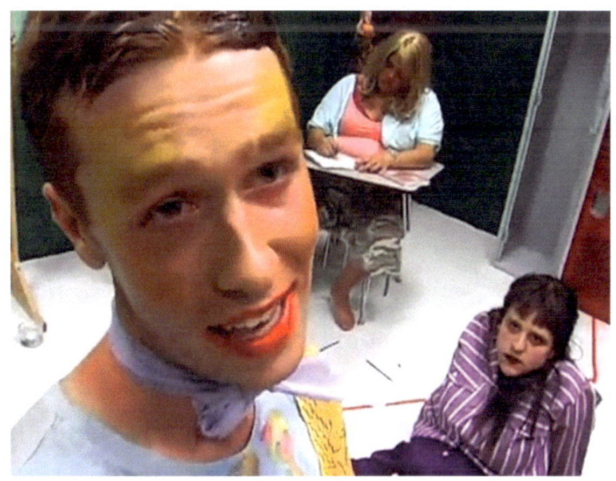

Figure 3.16
I-BE Area (2007)

close-ups and medium shots, to reinforce the sense of confusion he generates. Although Jeff's role within the narrative is minimal, his brief onscreen presence is important insofar as his sudden teleportation into the scene is paradigmatic of the recurring concept of mobile fluidity.

I-BE Area's mise-en-scène can be perceived as an online chat room within which members may decide to join and participate or to leave. Jeff's entry into Jaime's area through the locker portal can thus be read as barging in, uninvited, into the chat venue, further accentuated by flooding the room with repetitive senseless messages.

> I'd like Orbit my Orbit silly Boo [. . .] Outer space like seeing yourself out there, fluffy poo-poo cakes. Like I care. My outer goo-boo so fresh in poo-poo [. . .] I have five boyfriends to go sketch so open says me Out like a prefab in a tornado. I have five boyfriends to go sketch. Open says me out like a prefab in a fornado. First, I'm gonna call my best friend to beat the fuck up out of Jeff, hello.

Jaime's area is intercut with another chat room conversation. In it, three teen girls preparing to go clubbing discuss their lifestyle blogs and followers. Brief shots of Amerisha navigating aimlessly through the channels of the various chat rooms punctuate the scene. As a newcomer, Amerisha has been reformatted by Jaime and is now renamed "No Name I-BE." Like the rest of the forsaken avatars, No Name I-BE has been stripped of his identity and is now at Jaime's mercy. Lost in Jaime's area, No Name I-BE comes across a mirror painted with the phrase, "Sally was here." No Name I-BE looks at his reflection in the mirror, intrigued by the writing, as he desperately seeks to adopt a new identity—most probably Sally's discarded one. Before he is able to do so, Jaime's dictatorial voice surges from afar as she orders the protagonist to "become an official Sally man now." No Name I-BE acquiesces to Jaime's command and proceeds to remove his wig, but unable to commit to a new look, he asks Jaime which outfit he should wear to fulfill his newly appointed role as SallyManNow. However, Jaime remains silent. As a result, he is left on his own to select his new wardrobe. This significant point in the narrative marks the first instance in which the character takes control over his representation.

No Name I-BE proceeds to grab a towel from a locker, wipe his face, and remove sections of the yellow makeup he wore when he was assuming Amerisha's identity. The central protagonist creates his own version of Sally without relying on other online users' hand-me-down identities. No Name I-BE, thus, becomes SallyManNow, or as Kevin McGarry describes it, a "self-authored identity."[50] We understand that I-BE 2 has come a step closer to becoming the agent of his own destiny. He represents Trecartin's prototypical protagonist: a character seeking "personal agency [. . .] in an age of infinite optionality."[51] This is central to Trecartin's philosophy, since for the artist the internet is not only a tool external to us, but it is us—it helps us become more human, and thus helps us to exist. By authoring his own identity, I-BE 2, or SallyManNow, creates a unique online profile that helps him affirm his place within cyberspace.

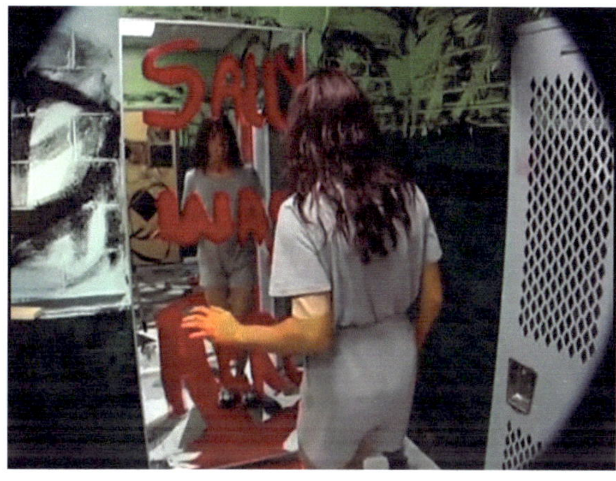

Figure 3.17 *I-BE Area* (2007)

Following his transformation, SallyManNow confronts the tyrannical Jaime. We realize through her exasperation that she is unable to control the fate of this self-authored avatar. The intensity of their conflict progressively escalates until Jaime and SallyManNow enter into what they call "a civil war." Much like Trecartin's earlier videos, *I-BE Area* ends in pandemonium: characters ravage their environment, destroying furniture, and throwing buckets of paint all over the walls. As Jaime's area turns into a battlefield, her crew begins to shout, "I pick Sally." SallyManNow checks out his reflection in a mirror as he shouts, "That is me. Mirror, Sally, that is me. I look like how I feel now [. . .] This is who I am. This is how I feel now."

Initially, we may not realize that the mirror motif is utilized by Trecartin to highlight the character's ongoing process of self-realization. This is due in part to SallyManNow's temporary state of existence—emphasized by the character's reiteration of the word *now*, signifying the temporary present. Although Trecartin's protagonists constantly shift between temporary identities, this does not discount their ability to evolve and therefore the significance of the process of ongoing personal growth.

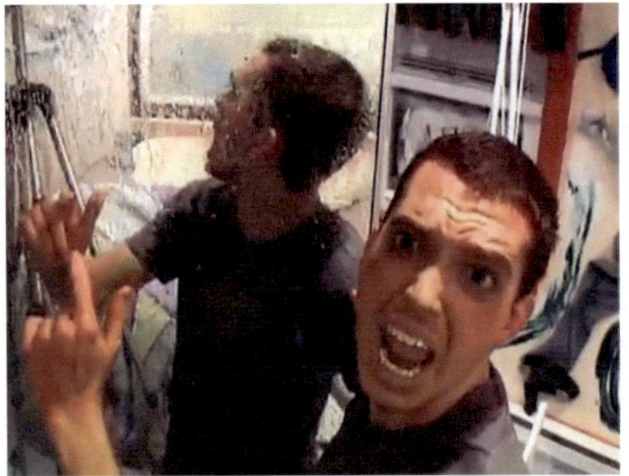

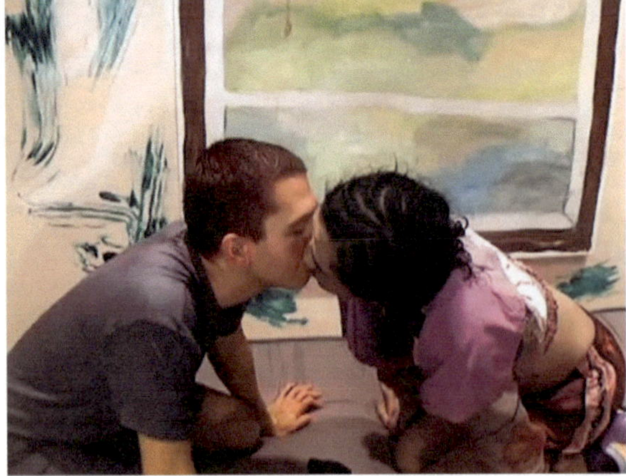

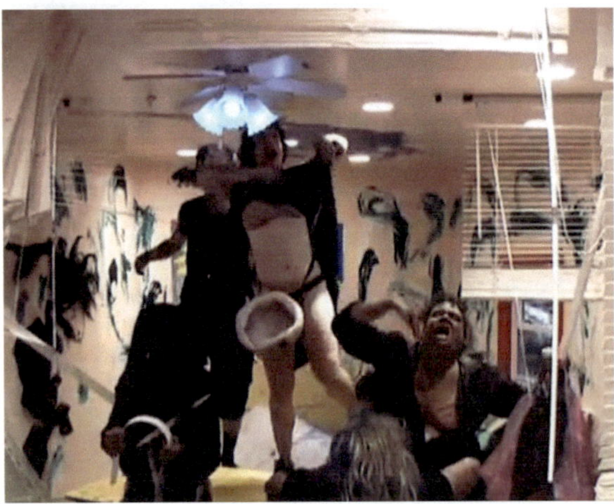

Figures 3.18, 3.19, and 3.20 *I-BE Area* (2007)

This process does not occur in one continuous trajectory, but instead happens in sections, scenes, or multiple screens.

In a final attempt to annihilate the protagonist, Jaime instructs her minion, Ramada Omar (Raul de Nieves), an avatar she has completely programmed, to kiss SallyManNow. By orchestrating the peck, Jaime attempts to transfer some of Ramada's genetic coding into SallyManNow. In turn, this will facilitate the takeover of the protagonist. As the two kiss, Jaime pauses them indefinitely, illustrated via freeze frame. McGarry points out that, "In doing so, Jaime portrays I-BE 2's entire personal narrative as a snapshot: finite, objectively knowable, and stripped of any potential futures. This is death in Trecartin's world."[52] However, I believe that the pause serves instead as a regenerative transition that allows characters to reboot and start afresh, since death is a foreign concept in Trecartin's video universe.

"Sometimes it's really cool when things don't move," declares Jaime in front of the camera. Behind her, we see a Polaroid depicting I-BE 2 and Ramada Omar smiling, pinned to the wall along with their clothes. The director cuts to Jaime surrounded by the demolished set—symbol of the eradication of her chat site. Stripped from the area that defines her, she gives up her role as motherboard and transmutes into a generic avatar by detaching her prosthetic belly. "This was nothing but a power prop! I did it for power! I did it for power!," she repeatedly shouts while undressing. By removing her clothes, Jaime liberates herself from her role as the central control agent of her area.

The madness suddenly comes to a halt with a cut to a rotating 360-degree panoramic view of Jaime's ravaged bedroom. The camera's lens surveys the wrecked room as if documenting the aftermath of war. The great emphasis placed on the mise-en-scène shows a clear connection between Jaime's relinquishing of power and the destruction of the space she inhabits. Trecartin explained in an interview that one of the messages he wished to convey was "that what identifies people is not necessarily their bodies anymore; it's all the relationship they maintain with others. You are your area, rather than you are yourself."[53] Much as web users update their Facebook pages, Twitter, Instagram, and Vine accounts, broadcasting their branded image to online social sites, the characters in *I-BE Area* also inhabit a virtual space within which they create and promote their self-generated fictitious profiles. Space(s) and personality(ies) appear to be interrelated. However, it would be reductive to read Trecartin's work as mere commentary on technology and social networks. The artist also embraces and explores—and invites us to embrace and explore—the multidimensional modalities of existence the World Wide Web makes possible. In doing so, he frees us from the constraint to define ourselves in fixed linearity. Trecartin's utopian cyberqueer world heralds a future in which technology helps us move beyond limitations and "unlock new realities that are already inside us."[54]

// 4 //

Any Ever

Stardom, Fashion, and Consumption

RYAN TRECARTIN WAS INVITED TO MIAMI during the Great Recession in 2008 by Silvia Karman Cubiña, director and curator of the Moore Space, for a funded artist residency to work on a short-term project.[1] Soon after his arrival, however, the artist and his troupe of performers were forced to relocate after the nonprofit exhibition space founded by eminent contemporary art collectors Rosa de la Cruz and Craig Robins closed unexpectedly in October 2008.[2] With the help of Elizabeth Dee Gallery (his art dealer at the time), private collectors, and maxed-out credit cards, Trecartin moved to a rented house in the Miami Design District and began to expand the piece originally commissioned by the Moore Space into what would become an ambitious epic series totaling close to four hours of footage titled *Any Ever* (2009–10).[3] Conceived as a diptych, *Any Ever* is comprised of seven videos divided into two sections: *Trill-ogy Comp*, which contains three videos—*K-CoreaINC.K (section a)*, *Sibling Topics (section a)*, and *P.opular Sky (section ish)*; and *Re'Search Wait'S*, which consists of four videos—*Ready*, *The Re'Search*, *Roamie View: History Enhancement*, and *Temp Stop*. However, *Any Ever* may be understood as a single movie, as individual sections are interconnected through recurring characters, narratives that begin in the middle of one and end in another, and actions abruptly interrupted only to be resumed minutes later in a different video. Therefore, I will read the work as one continuous piece while distinguishing between its various parts, in order to extract its complex, sometimes disjointed structure and meaning.

Any Ever takes viewers on an overwhelmingly stimulating ride, bombarding them with mass-media imagery and symbols. While contemporary media and advertising seek to produce passive consumers by overstimulating their senses in order to dull them, Trecartin's maximalist style conversely invites viewers to become active editors involved in curating the content, thus allowing them to extract their own meaning out of a clash of adjacent shots. Trecartin explains,

> Well, I think meaning is a responsibility, and the blah, blah, blahs might be an exercise or a foreshadow to a very important shift in reality that seems to be in the air. I think we are becoming really good editors. It's now a personal responsibility to curate your own understanding of the larger cultural mud we are all contributing to and navigating. The easier it becomes to participate in making culture, the more meaning is in the eye of the reader. And reading involves an act of writing. It's no longer a handout that is consumed. It's possibly a different kind of intelligence that is currently underappreciated, but nevertheless we are being forced to flex this muscle a lot in current, contemporary culture. I don't see any of this as a negative.[4]

The idea that "meaning is a responsibility" is central to *Any Ever*, as the artist assigns significance to objects beyond their function, turning "a careerist goal into living room furniture, an accent into a hairdo, or an ideology into a body language, or designer skin tone."[5] Trecartin and his friends parade the streets amid foreclosure signs in eccentric accoutrements and asymmetrical multicolor makeup. Indoors, the action carries on as characters continue to act out in constructed sets overloaded with objects and furniture sold at retailers such as Target and Ikea, specifically selected for "their ubiquity and faux-designery corporate blandness."[6] Although at first glance the work may seem like a glorification of a consumerist society and its values, on closer inspection a more nuanced commentary on the economic crisis at the time, global corporate culture, and personality branding becomes apparent. *Any Ever* (2009–10) deals with a complex and intricate system in which individuality and subjectivity are homogenized.

The protagonists in the series reflect the visual accumulation of the signs and symbols they so readily assimilate, which are transformed into an idiosyncratic perspective on the grotesque in fashion and style. While his work always appears to be imbued with a fashion-forward stylization, in *Any Ever*, it is taken yet a step further. Fashion constitutes a language of its own, offering deeper insights into the narrative. Therefore, sartorial analysis serves an important role in unpacking his work. In the interrogation of the relationship between his art and its connection to fashion, it is useful to analyze the editorial spreads Trecartin art directed for *W* magazine in 2010 and 2016. Diana Crane notes that the fashion industry often partners with art as a way to confer meaning on fashion products and acquire "cultural capital for the occupation."[7] Reciprocally, artists may benefit from this association as it provides them with an entry point into the mainstream that subsequently has the potential of turning them into public figures, thus potentially increasing the value of their work. Contemporary artists thereby have agency in creating their own brand. This chapter closely examines Ryan Trecartin in various contexts: artist, brand, and pop figure.

Employing the visual language of advertising, Trecartin creates a world where high art and mass culture products, luxury brands, and industrial design, coexist seamlessly. For the artist, there is no "distinction between what's 'high' or 'low,' anymore, what's professional or amateur, all those dichotomies [. . .] inhabit the same media space now."[8] Trecartin's perspective vis-à-vis advertising and conspicuous consumption is more complex than meets the eye. As Lauren Cornell puts it, "Trecartin's work is not—to use a word that gets bandied about in the films—'anti.' Rather, it's radically 'pro' or constructive, absorptive and forgiving."[9] While there is much truth in this statement, I propose that his work is neither "anti" nor "pro." Unlike other contemporary artists whose work is often interpreted as direct critiques of consumer culture, particularly as it pertains to the fashion industry, such as Tom Sachs, who creates sculptures from luxury brand packaging, or Sylvie Fleury, who glamorizes the fetishistic trappings of consumerism, Trecartin does not adjudicate on our social practices. The artist elaborates as follows:

> I enjoy exploring ideas more than judging them, and often when I see something in the world that feels destructive, disturbing, or ugly, I don't necessarily see it as a bad thing [. . .] Sometimes when people watch my movies, I feel like they will say something like, "Oh my god, you're showing how ugly our culture is, just an inch underneath," and I'm like, no, I think that I'm showing, in a different way, why these things are potentially creative and positive.[10]

However, this does not mean that *Any Ever* is devoid of any social commentary. The series clearly functions as an exaggerated magnification of our consumerist social practices. Yet, although his critique of our economic and sociopolitical systems may sometimes appear negative, the artist always finds a way to punctuate it with humor, perhaps as a mode by which to instill positivity in the collapsing system depicted in his work. When asked to comment on the idea of entropic decay in his videos, the artist simply replied, "I think it's more about celebrating transition as a generative process."[11]

I consider *K-CoreaINC.K* (*section a*) to be the introductory section in the series (although Trecartin does not designate an order). The video opens with a rotating three-dimensional model of the earth surrounded by four satellites. The monochromatic color scheme consisting of gray font superimposed over a gray globe transmits a sense of blandness, which is further emphasized by the allegorical message,

> Dear HeyK, Please Don't Accept your Progressaphobias in work flow by Brand Washing My Global Blanky with SAME Page. I really need a case of atmosphere. Are you finding Position? It's such a Hunt.

Within the first few seconds, Trecartin introduces us to the central theme expressed throughout the seven videos: the commodification and standardization of contemporary culture. This concept, however, is not a new one. Theodor Adorno and Max Horkheimer had taken notice of this phenomenon by the middle of the twentieth century, when they wrote that "Culture today is infecting everything with sameness. Film, radio, and magazines form a system. Each branch of culture is unanimous within itself and all are unanimous together."[12] Trecartin reexamines this concept of post-twenty-first-century globalization, where singularity has become a myth. However, for Trecartin sameness does not necessarily represent a loss of individuality, but an opportunity to connect with others.

K-CoreaINC.K's opening scene quickly transitions to a medium shot of an office worker (Xavier Cha) standing in front of her desk, sporting a platinum-blond wig, white powdered face, and a pristine white shirt. "GSAK" appears in the foreground as an acronym for the character's name, General South AmeriK. GSAK faces the camera while addressing another member of her team off-screen, as if communicating through video conferencing technology. Unlike previous videos, *K-CoreaINC.K (section a)* takes viewers outside the domestic context and transports us into a corporate environment.

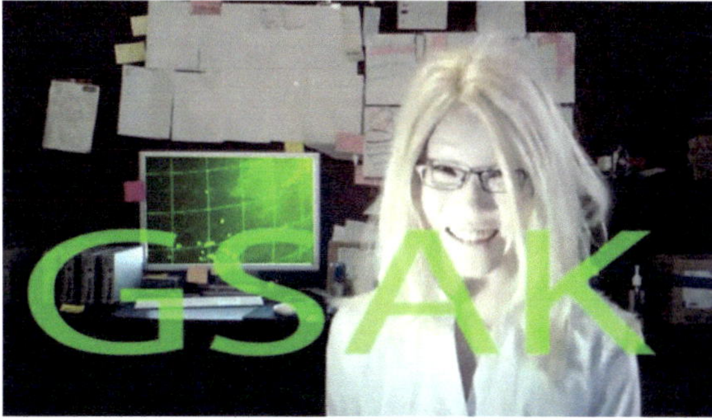

Figure 4.1 *K-CoreaINC.K (section a)* (2009)

Trecartin then cuts to a fast-paced montage sequence, employing his signature multiple screens motif to quickly introduce the video's protagonists: a homogeneous team of clone-like office workers of a global corporation named Korea Inc. Individual staff members are presented onscreen alongside their acronyms such as NAK (North America Korea) or MK (Mexico Korea). Their names, devoid of any human signifiers, are instead based on the company's international trade exchanges with other nations. Global identity is visually expressed through monotonous uniformity. Workers are assimilated into the white cubicle aesthetic of corporate interior design and have become as sterile as the decor itself. They have lost all sense of individuality, which is repeatedly emphasized through their repetitive utterances: "Oh my god! You look so beautiful, you look like me! We are you!" Korea's employees have merged into a standardized corporate collective programmed to factory presets.

The last shot of *Temp Stop (Re'Search Wait'S)* also calls attention to this global trend toward homogenization. A static headless plastic mannequin modeling a generic denim skirt suit is on display in the foreground of the screen. In the background, countless replicas of the same ensemble line the aisles of a department store. A monotone voice in the background debates: "Should we get it? I like it. Let's get it."

The characters' readiness to be subsumed into the masses threatens their individuality. However, the artist understands their willingness to adopt a uniform appearance as a way to adapt to the situation at hand and connect with one another. The protagonists purposely evade uniqueness and embrace homogeneity in order to belong to a community. The trend forecasting group, K-Hole, calls this phenomenon "Normcore." Although Normcore refers primarily to an attitude, the term has been conflated by mainstream media with another K-Hole concept called "Acting Basic," a fashion trend consisting of dressing neutrally with casual wear such as T-shirts and hoodies to avoid standing out. In their issue, "Youth Mode: A Report on Freedom," K-Hole observed that

> Normcore doesn't want the freedom to become someone. Normcore wants the freedom to be with anyone. [. . .] In Normcore, one does not pretend to be above the indignity of belonging. Normcore moves away from a coolness that relies on difference to a post-authenticity coolness that opts in to sameness. [. . .] Normcore seeks the freedom that comes with non-exclusivity. It finds liberation in being nothing special, and realizes that adaptability leads to belonging. Normcore is a path to a more peaceful life.[13]

Of course, the concept of Normcore cannot be endorsed verbatim. Particularly problematic is the statement's last and most radical claim, which states that "Normcore is a path to a more peaceful life." While the power of this theory lies in its potential to unite individuals, it can also lead to their alienation. The need to belong to a community might impel some to significantly compromise in order to be accepted.

This is the case with characters such as USAK and JJ Check (both played by Trecartin), who have forgone their personality and fashioned drab corporate facades in order to fit in at Korea Inc. The employees' erratic verbal exchange comprised of sentence fragments and incomprehensible business-like jargon refers to the technicalization of language: "I copy-pasted the e-mail I just cc'ed you." The characters deliver their lines mechanically, detached from any recognizable emotion. They appear to have lost touch with their humanity. Both protagonists struggle to reconcile their own individual aspirations with their duty to conform and serve the organization. JJ Check and USAK's micro-vignettes illustrate the ramifications of the accelerated corporatization of culture. The two protagonists attempt to escape the control exercised by the omnipotent Korea Inc. in order to reclaim ownership of their own destiny. Yet, although a gleam of hope remains by the end of their respective adventures, we are still uncertain of their fate as Trecartin leaves us hanging. The director deliberately denies viewers closure in *Any Ever* so that its open-endedness might encourage them to navigate content in the order that they wish. This provides an opportunity to extract one's own meaning from the experience. However, what is left clear at the end of *K-CoreaINC.K* (*section a*) and *Roamie View: History Enhancement*, in which both protagonists resign from their positions, is that Korea Inc.'s cutthroat system allows no room for nonconformist or inefficient workers.

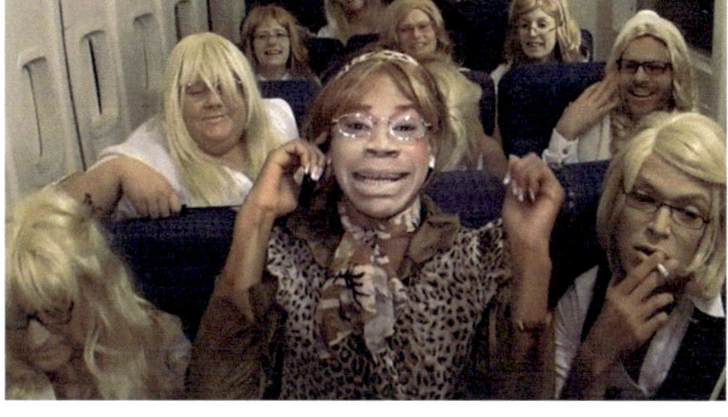

Figure 4.2 *K-CoreaINC.K (section a)* (2009)

While a certain corporate discipline exercised through a dress code is mandatory for most Korea, Inc. employees, Global Korea (Telfar Clemens), a devilishly manipulative, yet thoroughly entertaining character is exempt from the requirement. In her essay, "Fashion and the Fleshy Body: Dress as Embodied Practice," Joanne Entwistle applies Michel Foucault's theory on the relationship between bodies and power in *Discipline and Punish*, when she explains that "particular strategies of dress such as the imposition of uniforms and dress codes at work, are utilized by corporations to exercise control over the bodies of the workers within."[14] Global Korea manages to exert great control over how she attires her body. Unlike the rest of the employees whose office drag consists of dull white business shirts and khakis, GK infuses pizzazz into her look. Global Korea is seen sporting a leopard-print top with a brown satin knee-length skirt. She differentiates herself from her coworkers by employing her wardrobe as a tool to establish her superior rank and spirit of nonconformity. GK appears to be working within the corporate system but subverts it via sartorial choices. However, she does not merely set herself apart by establishing visual differentiation. She also neglects to attire herself with undergarments, often flashing her penis at the other employees—as a form of *power dressing*—to reinforce her dominance.

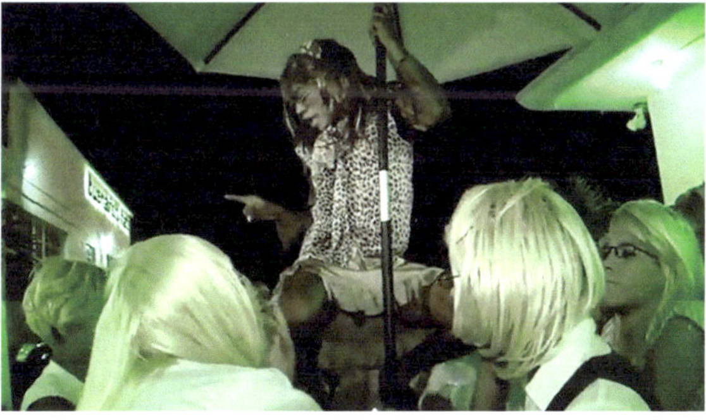

Figure 4.3 *K-CoreaINC.K (section a)* (2009)

In *The Language of Fashion*, Roland Barthes writes, "Dress is, in the fullest sense, a 'social model,' a more or less standardized picture of expected collective behavior."[15] Therefore, not adhering to institutional dress protocol can be regarded as an act of defiance against the unity of the incorporated body and may subject one to disciplinary action from management.[16] In the ensuing scene, a recalcitrant stewardess (Ryan Trecartin), dressed in a head-to-toe latex suit, rebels against the company by smashing a porcelain plate on the floor in front of Global Korea. The camera momentarily focuses on the debris splattered across the room to emphasize the gravity of this act of rebellion. In true diva form, GK raises her finger in the air and exclaims, "Oh no she didn't!," while the employee sitting next to her replies, "Oh yes she did!" Trecartin cuts to a medium close-up of the stewardess as bold yellow letters flash "FIRE HER" across the screen. Ironically, Global Korea takes the order much too literally and proceeds to set the disobedient employee on fire.

Standing outside the building, GK drenches the rebel with gasoline while the rest of the crew witnesses the incendiary through the window. The contrasting festive ambience surrounding the scene is unsettling. The employees laugh and clap, as GK smokes a cigarette and commences to giggle while pouring fuel over the stewardess who sensually gyrates her body as the flammable liquid saturates her torso. The camera then zooms in on Global Korea as she says, "I told you." She proceeds to throw a lit cigarette at the stewardess and Trecartin adds an After Effect flame filter that consumes the screen.

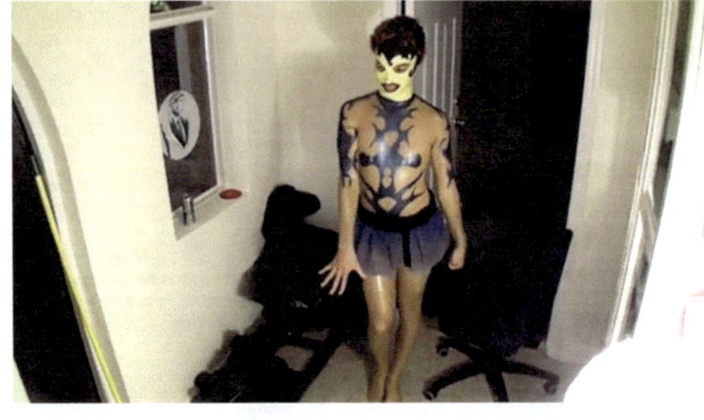

Figure 4.4 *K-CoreaINC.K (section a)* (2009)

Although the stewardess's on-screen appearance is brief, her limited presence nevertheless suffices to disturb the rest of the employees who immediately join in her annihilation. The character is a threat to the conglomerate, not solely because of her rebellious attitude, but also because of her destabilizing image. Unlike Korea's workers' uniform look, the stewardess's latex body suit, typically considered fetish gear, exudes individuality and embodies a kinky sexuality. It is worth noting that her face is completely covered, thus, her characterization is primarily constructed through costume. In doing so, Trecartin presents a hybrid, almost cartoonish figure that is difficult to read: is it human, cyborg, or should it be interpreted as a sculptural form? The stewardess is thus not simply a performer, but a designed character.

Character design, including those incorporating animals with anthropomorphic features and two- or three-dimensional human-like characters have inundated our cultural landscape, existing in various forms and contexts, from video games, to cartoons, animation, art, and fashion. Fashion designers and performance artists have explored and transcended the limits of the body through dress that features the expression of un-human-like characterizations.[17] Deviating from standardized ideals of beauty, these visionaries have created amorphous designs of exaggerated proportions. They play with fabrics, shapes, and colors to transform the body into an abstract grotesque figure. Often featuring humorous, fetishistic, or even frightening silhouettes, Japanese designer Rei Kawakubo, for instance, has introduced feather down padding in her collections to create a distorted female form featuring protruding bodily appendages. In doing so, Kawakubo challenged Western fashion's contemporary silhouettes, which often sexualize the female form with body-hugging garments that accentuate the body's natural curves. German designer Bernhard Willhelm, U.S. designer Jeremy Scott, and Belgian designer Walter Van Beirendonck take on a more festive approach to their confections. The garish patterns and playful geometric shapes of their garments transmit a cartoonish quality. In 2008, Scott began a collaboration with sportswear brand Adidas to work on a collection of footwear and apparel. In line with his bold aesthetic, the collection featured winged high-tops and wildly patterned tracksuits. British designer Gareth Pugh's futuristic cybergothic pop fashion eschews vibrant colors for a monochromatic color scheme derived primarily from dark-gray hues. Nick Cave creates fantastical soundsuit sculptures for performance pieces from a combination of manufactured and handmade fabrics constructed with unexpected materials such as toys, dyed human hair, and bottle caps.

On the edge between sculpture, art, and fashion, these garments extend beyond the bodily borders of the model. When examining the grotesque in punk fashion, Patrizia Calefato applies a Bakhtinian perspective: "the body has no impenetrable surface, no insuperable limit: every inch of skin can be pierced by a safety pin, slashed by a blade or used for the exhibition of an unusual object, like a toilet chain or a sanitary towel."[18] Expanding on the intersection between Bakhtin and fashion, Francesca

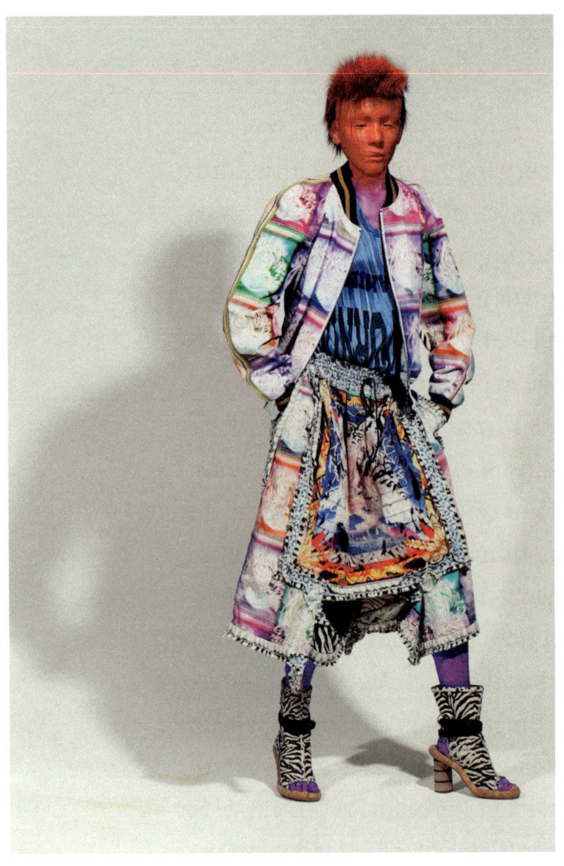

Figure 4.6
Photo by Dan and Corina Lecca,
fall/winter 2011,
Walter Van Beirendonck Collection

Figure 4.5
Photo by Petrovsky and Ramone,
spring/summer 2013,
Bernhard Willhelm Collection

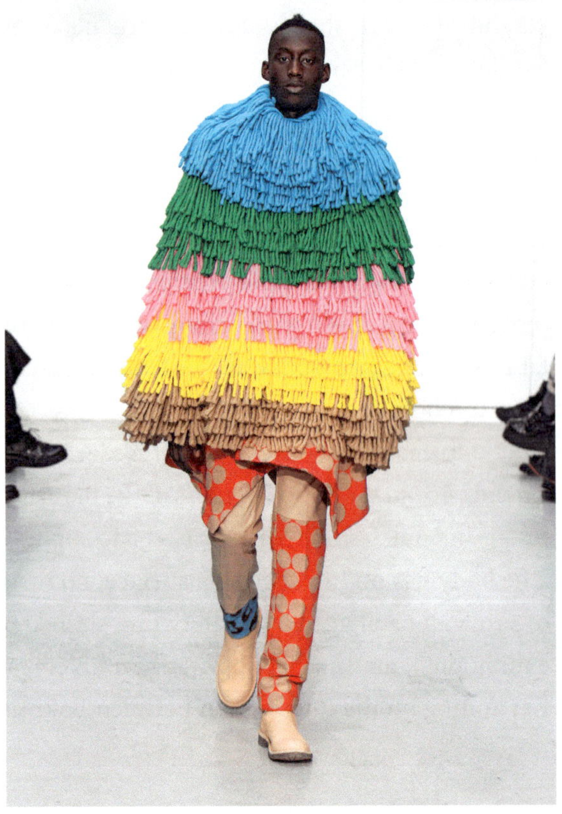

Granata posits that contemporary experimental designers create sartorial manifestations of the grotesque body, "an open, unfinished body, which is never sealed or fully contained, but it is always in the process of becoming and engendering another body."[19] Trecartin's designed characterizations are grotesque in their discharge of surplus information. Unable to be contained, they confound the boundary between the inner and outer body. These highly stylized protagonists symbolize the accumulation of the mass-media expulsion they have internalized. Each look is a collection of diverse signs and symbols from contemporary visual culture collectively assembled and layered on top of each other. At the end of *I-Be Area*, for instance, Lizzie Fitch, along with her horde of minions, disrobes in front of the camera, detaching her prosthetic pregnancy belly in the process. Fitch's naked body contorts hysterically as she delivers an aggressive manifesto, while surrounded by scantily dressed goth friends sporting wigs and fishnet stockings over their faces. The faux belly strapped onto her body represents a mutable grotesque body par excellence as it possesses the possibility of outgrowing itself. Bakhtin writes that, "The [grotesque] body discloses its essence as a principle of growth which exceeds its own limits only in copulation, pregnancy, childbirth, the throes of death, eating, drinking, or defecation."[20]

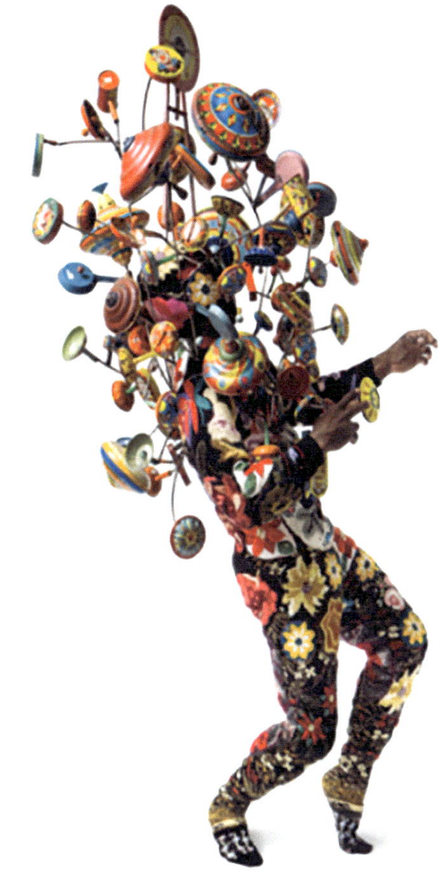

Figure 4.7 Nick Cave, Soundsuit

In addition to placing emphasis on alternative hybrid body shapes, conceptual designers have also aimed to detract attention from or conceal the human face. They achieve this depersonalization through stylistic devices, including intricate masks or makeup, in order to direct focus onto the clothes and away from individual facial signifiers. Known for creating one character look per year and wearing it twenty-four hours a day during

365 days, performance artist, fashion designer, and club personality Leigh Bowery introduced the complete head-to-toe latex bodysuit which completely wrapped his face. Attired in conspicuous, outlandish, sometimes monstrous confections he concocted, Bowery manifested genderless fantastical queer creatures with concealed visages designed with a variety of cunning strategies. Trecartin's constructed personae, such as the disobedient stewardess outfitted in a latex full-body suit à la Leigh Bowery in *K-CoreaINC.K* or the BeadStoreGirl in *I-BE Area*, represent posthuman characters endowed with camouflaged features. Similar to fashion designers blurring facial signifiers, the artist applies digital special effects to his protagonists to further obscure their appearance, enhancing their open-endedness and the expression of their fluid queer "personalities." Granata understands the concealment of the face as a way for designers to comment on identity.

> In its playful and amorphous quality and in its insistence on shielding the locus of subjectivity represented by the face, their work corroborates an understanding of identity as constructed, in flux and inherently unstable. In doing so, it illustrates and partially explains the centrality of fashion, and particularly experimental fashion, to contemporary culture and to our ability to negotiate a complex and multisided existence as pluri-cultural subjects in a globalized society where identity is no longer fixed.[21]

In fall 2010, the year *Any Ever* made its national debut at the Museum of Contemporary Art in Los Angeles, Trecartin directed a fashion shoot for the annual artist issue of *W* magazine. Instead of engaging traditional models, the artist cast his friends and recurrent performers from his films: Lizzie Fitch, Veronica Gelbaum, Telfar Clemens, and Ashland Mines. The overall styling of the photographs is very similar to *Any Ever*'s aesthetic: the models pose in overly accessorized intricate garb, sporting designer goods mixed-matched with mass-manufactured items from department and novelty stores. Although the stillness of the images do not convey the frenetic pace of his video work, Trecartin manages to transmit his narratives' themes in the editorial spread, thus recording his models as freeze frames of the characters in his movies.

Lizzie Fitch's theme, "Negative Beach," portrays a Valley girl sporting tan lines in all the wrong places on the first page of the spread. Fitch holds a bottle of Penta purified water filled with guppies swimming around a buoyant red BlackBerry. On top of her head, a shiny camouflage-print eye mask serves as a headband. First-Class Forever stamps attached to mosquitoes embedded in chunks of amber dangle from her earlobes. A tooth is accessorized with a brass hoop piercing and in an effort to blur the character's gender, an Adam's apple was added in postproduction. The complete look is accomplished with the application of multiple customized spray-tan lines, which contour Fitch's face and body in distorted hypo- and hyperpigmented skin shades.

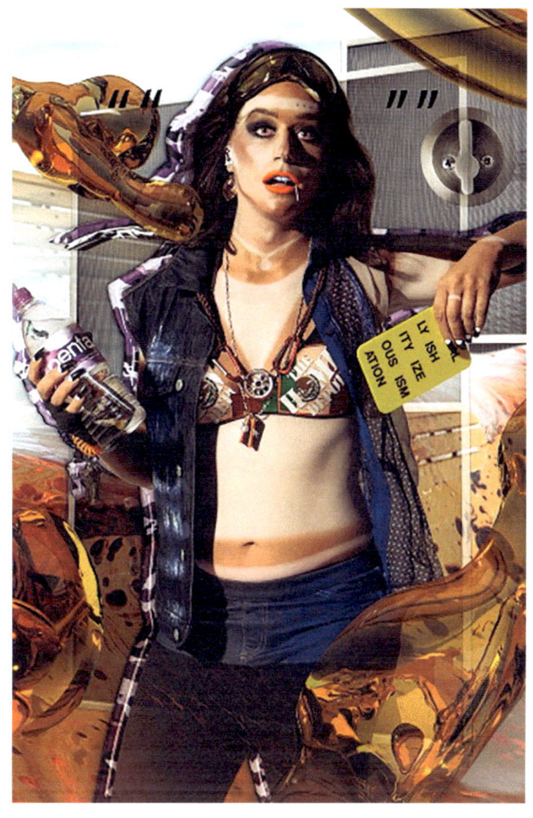

Figure 4.8 *Negative Beach* in *W* magazine, November 2010

Trecartin dissects a secondhand Ann-Sofie sleeveless black blouse and reassembles it with half of a gray-and-blue Dries Van Noten shirt, in order to create Fitch's top for the shoot.[22] Much like fashion deconstructionists, Martin Margiela and Ann Demeulemeester, or punk-style guru, Vivienne Westwood, who originated the incorporation of exposed seams, unfinished edges, and ripped fabrics into her creations, Trecartin takes apart garments and reassembles them in peculiar and unexpected combinations.

Fitch's Southern California teenage-girl persona in the *W* spread is quite distinct from her role as Able, a self-important careerist in charge of the Human Resources department in *Ready* (*Re'Search Wait'S*). Her character "Negative Beach" appears to be completely oblivious to the camera's presence, while Able is quite conscious of it. Able is always presented through frontal views addressing the camera while showing off her legs, either wide open

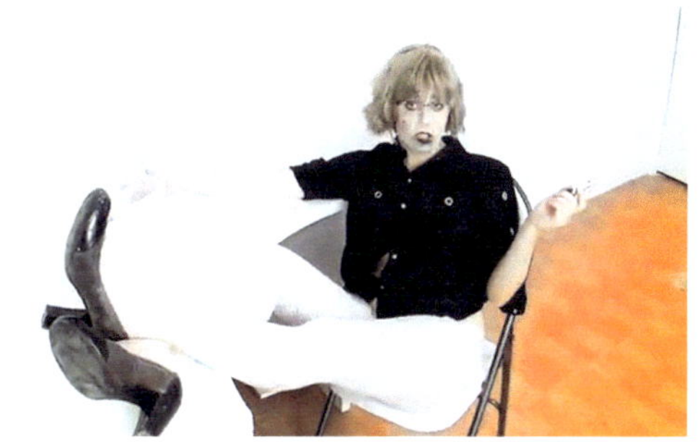

Figure 4.9 *Ready* (*Re'Search Wait'S*) (2010)

or up in the air. Yet, she does not face the camera to be seductive, instead, she confronts it in order to exert her authority. A power struggle appears to be at play between Able and the camera, visually manifested through constant shifts between high and low angles. Both characters also diverge in the way they are styled. With her cropped bob hairstyle, black blouse, white lace leggings, and clunky patent leather black pumps, Able's pseudo-corporate look is quite a departure from the futuristic beach outfit Fitch sports in the *W* editorial spread.

In a Q&A with the artist, Trecartin explains that the fashion editorial was originally conceived as a script and the body as the platform to house that script. The images function as portraits reminiscent of the characterizations in his movies.[23] Yet, there exists a clearly distinct and separate vision portrayed between the images in the editorial fashion spread and the characterizations in his movies. If we consider *W* magazine's photo shoot as an extension of *Any Ever*, then we may wonder why new and seemingly unrelated characters were specifically created for the project, rather than re-creating popular ones from the videos in order to bridge the shoot with his movies. It is not uncommon nowadays to find actors and actresses posing in fashion shoots to promote their latest movies, sometimes styled and dressed in the same fashions they wear onscreen. However, if Trecartin had simply duplicated and transposed the protagonists from his videos into the glossy pages of *W* magazine, it would have implied that they are fixed. As previously indicated however, the artist understands his characters to be fluid subjects or "pluri-cultural subjects." It is precisely by shifting their appearance that Trecartin is able to link his philosophical outlook with the fluidity between the version of the characters in the magazine spread and those in his movies. Although they may appear discrete at first, the models in the spread are essentially unique manifestations of the same performers in his movies. Each is able to exist outside of the world of the videos.

Veronica Gelbaum is displayed on the second page in an equally complex pose. As "Crop Charity," Gelbaum shows off a white Dior calfskin tote encased inside a large plastic comforter bedding case. A water box labeled "BOXED WATER IS BETTER FOR THE VIEW" is detected on top of a pile of broken safety glass accumulated at the bottom of the plastic case. Above, a Dior handbag displays an attached Post-it, which reads "Hobby Lossless 143: 1AB." This play-on-words merges the tax code regulation "Hobby Loss Rule," which limits losses that can be deducted from income (from Internal Revenue Code Section 183), with "Lossless," a data compression term that signifies no quality was sacrificed during compression. According to Trecartin, "143" stands for "I love you," and "1AB" for "wannabe."[24] Unlike Fitch's character in Negative Beach, whose outfit consists of a mash-up of barely distinguishable garments, Gelbaum's attire consists primarily of a mix of luxury brand items in their original state. In her right hand, she carries a pair of Martin Margiela Money shoes, a Chopard palladium-finish, resin-and-lacquer pen is suspended from her belt, and a dozen Movado watches are linked together to form a necklace. The fully customized designer outfit is then further accessorized with a multitude of department store clothing price tags from Target, Ross, and Marshalls, hung about her torso.

Veronica Gelbaum's blasé socialite persona takes inspiration from the character she plays in *Temp Stop* (*Re'Search Wait'S*). In it, Gelbaum plays Y-Ready, a power-hungry executive manager. *Temp Stop* opens with an overhead shot of Y-Ready lying on the floor conducting sit-up exercises as she delivers a vituperative monologue to her subordinate workers.

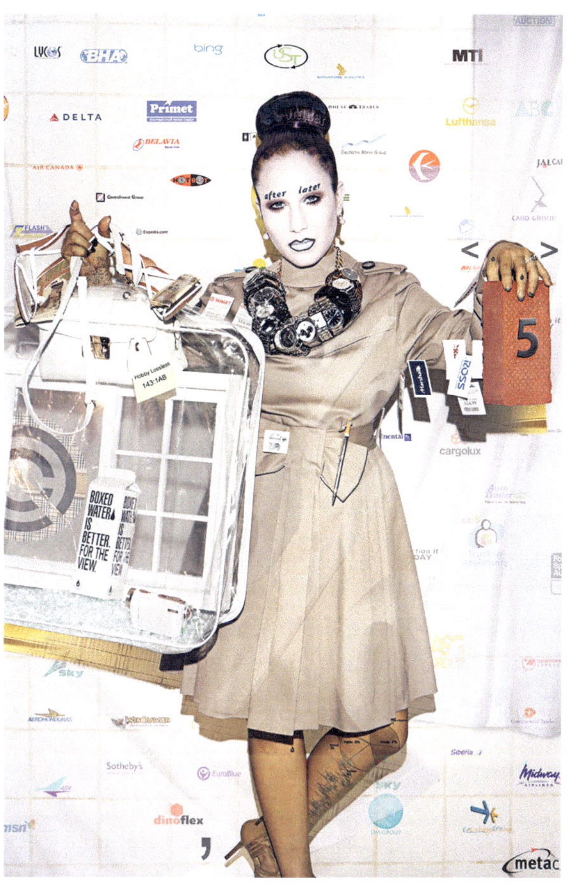

Figure 4.10
Crop Charity in *W* magazine, November 2010

> Each and every time you walk passed that door I need you to ask me what I want from you and even if I don't want anything, [...] but I don't want anything right now so you're just bugging the shit out of me actually [...] Has anybody told you to go fuck yourself? Don't ask me if I need your help unless I look at you, which I will never do because you are subservient.

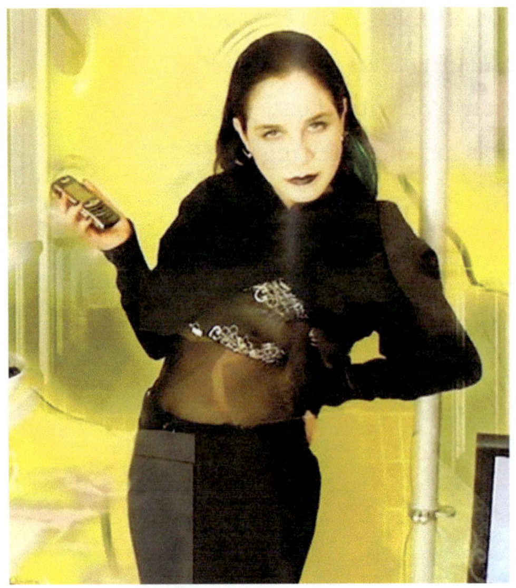

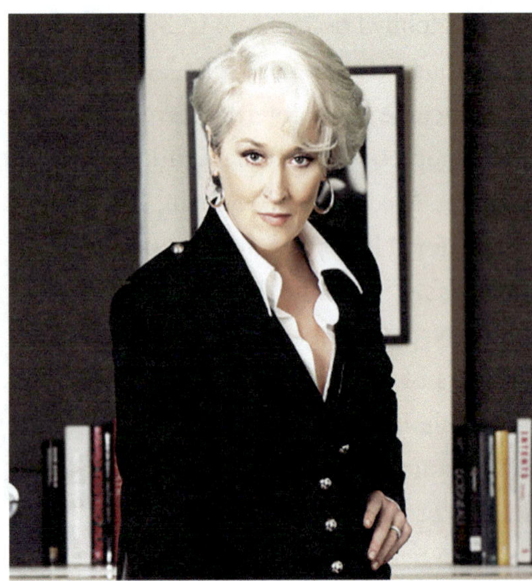

Figure 4.11 *Ready* (*Re'Search Wait'S*) (2010)

Figure 4.12 *The Devil Wears Prada* (2006)

Y-Ready's degrading commands recall those delivered by the almighty fashion editor, Miranda Priestly (Meryl Streep) in *The Devil Wears Prada* (2006): "Is there some reason that my coffee isn't here? Has she died or something?"[25] Both characters also sport similar outfits in dichromatic combinations of black and white. However, much like Miranda Priestly, Y-Ready puts on a tough exterior facade during office hours, however, in *P.opular S.ky* (*section ish*), she reveals her sensitive side. Sitting in a car's passenger side, Y-Ready flirts with someone off-screen. Her apparent shyness and awkwardness betray a sense of insecurity that was completely undetectable in previous scenes. Examining and contrasting *W*'s photo shoot with the videos in *Any Ever* enables us to understand how the protagonists negotiate their pluralistic identities. Trecartin comments on how he further expands on this theme, which he began exploring in *I BE Area*: "We're all networked and we're maintaining our own discrete networks of multiple selves."[26]

Later in the editorial shoot, fashion designer/performance artist turned model, Telfar Clemens, strikes a pose in his techno-inspired shoot, "General Control." In it, Clemens wears a sports bra with the recycle symbol printed on it. The bra is covered by a transparent cropped plastic bag designed by Clemens himself. Tags that read "NETWORK NEUTRALITY" hang from the handmade cropped top. An oversized zipper serves as a necklace that hangs from his neck wrapped in a thin layer of green bubble wrap with the logo "PROACTIVE SOLUTIONS" printed on it. A computer home icon is employed as a belly button ring. An iPad with a pony tail glued to its back stands in as a handheld mirror. One of his legs is propped up on top of a metallic carry-on suitcase to feature one of Trecartin's shoe creations: sandals made from flip-flops and wattle-firming neck pumpers.

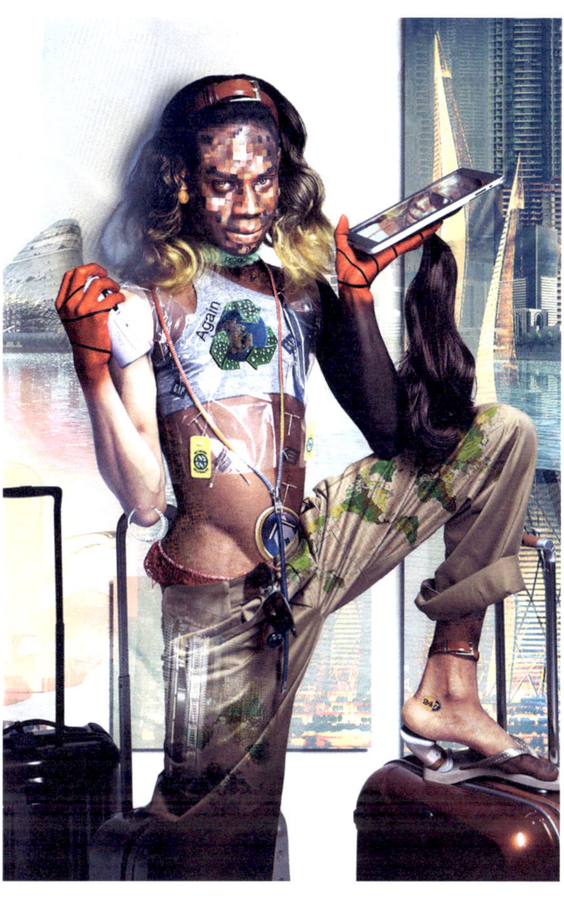

Figure 4.13 *General Control* in *W* magazine, November 2010

Finally, the last section of the story, "Anti-Virals," is modeled by Ashland Mines. Mines wears an Ed Hardy hat drenched in crusty Wite-Out. A bottle of the correction liquid is hooked to a belly chain, hanging off his hat. Trecartin creates what he calls a "belly button situation" by piercing the rim of the hat with a plastic button. One side is designed to look like an internet mail button and the other a computer power button.[27] Ankle-length microbraids seem to spring out of the back of the Ed hardy hat, cascade down, and drape over the character's right shoulder. Mines's body is manscaped in such a manner that produces what the artist calls "a very personalized idea of sexy chiseled body-hair: ultra clean and gross . . . yet weirdly pretty and sensitive."[28] The model also sports fingerless biker gloves, one green and one red, worn on top of surgical nitrile gloves. Trecartin explained that he wanted the hands to look like the thumbs up/thumbs down icons used as response tools in websites such as YouTube and Facebook.[29]

More recently, Ryan Trecartin and Lizzie Fitch were commissioned to art direct an editorial spread and cover for *W*'s 2016 Art Issue. Unlike their previous collaboration with the magazine, in this assignment, Fitch and Trecartin employ highly sought-after fashion models Gigi Hadid and Kendall Jenner, as well as a mutual friend, pop-star/stylist Lauren Devine. The artists incorporate their trademarked sense of aesthetics into what may

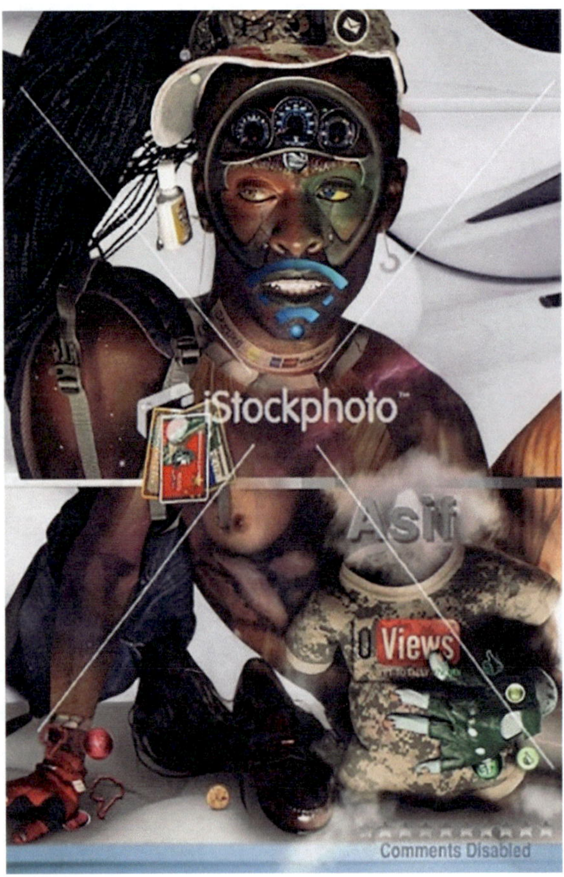

Figure 4.14 *Anti-Virals* in *W* magazine, November 2010

otherwise appear to be a high-fashion spread. The heavily Photoshopped images feature Hadid and Jenner transformed into what Trecartin calls friendly "alien humanoids," sporting prosthetic noses and furry animal ears resembling Snapchat animal lenses come to life.[30] According to the artist, "Placebo Pets," explores the intertwined relationships humans maintain with their domesticated pets and technology. The models-turned-characters are shown clinging to their technological devices—phone, handheld digital camera, and microphone—while simultaneously equally captivated by the presence of an adorable sleepy puppy. The artist observes that we have become conditioned to modify our language, gestures, and behavior in order to interact with digital telecommunication, the same way pets are domesticated to adapt to our language. He deliberately juxtaposes the zoomorphic models in conjunction with tech gadgets to illustrate the idea that pets, like technology, are domesticating us—training us to want them—by making themselves increasingly friendly.[31] We have thus become, in Trecartin and Fitch's words, "placebo pets."

As with any Trecartin movie, critical subtexts are woven into the content of the images. According to the artist, the idea for the project began with a simple question, "Who would survive if a superior alien humanoid species came to Earth?" The answer: "the friendliest."[32] Although Trecartin's inherent optimism is apparent in the models' cheerful poses, nested within green screens, a certain eeriness pervades the spread. In one image, Gigi Hadid is sitting on a camping stool, legs wide open, facing the camera, seemingly oblivious to the two three-dimensional aliens crouching behind her. In another instance, Hadid is photographed covering her face with her hand as if avoiding the camera's gaze. While the artist claims the editorial is about representing friendliness, it possesses the dark undercurrent of a survival game, one in which players' sole source of defense is predicated on how friendliness is tabulated or quantified through the number of likes garnered on selfies posted on their social media pages.

Most fashion editorials tell an alluring story in order to sell clothing. However, in this spread Hadid and Jenner are not simply exhibiting the latest trends in the name of commerce. Garments are not privileged, as many of the items photographed compete with and are actually overwhelmed by incongruous koala bears, inflatable mats, and binoculars, among other items, manifesting the styling philosophy of more is more. The aim is to convert the young celebrity models into designed characters straight out of his movies. In fact, Trecartin prepared a script, fed the models a few words, and encouraged them to repeat them over and over during the photo shoot, exactly as he directs performers in his films.[33]

It is evident that the artist's ultra-stylized photo shoots are intended to appeal to the primary sensory mode of consumer culture: visual display.[34] However, these images are not meant to be part of ad campaigns attempting to sell products under the guise of high art. While advertising seeks to add value to products by showcasing their design or functionality, thereby promoting a desirable lifestyle and creating a false sense of need in consumers, Trecartin's projects, conversely take objects out of context and create meaning beyond their function. In doing so, he calls attention to the fact that consumption is not a passive process but an active one in which, as David Howes remarks, "all sorts of meanings and uses for products are generated that the designers and marketers of those products never imagined."[35] Thus, iPads are turned into handheld mirrors, postage stamps into earrings, belts into headbands, and a brick into a 4G network cell phone. Similarly recontextualizing objects, at the end of *P.opular S.ky (section ish)*, the entire crew gathers outside by the swimming pool and transforms the garden into an obstacle course. Bed frames are turned upside down and converted into monkey bars, and white book shelves are lunged into the pool and fashioned as surfing boards.

According to the artist, displacing objects from their intended use enables him to open up different interpretations of what is on display while simultaneously allowing audiences to reevaluate the meaning of a product beyond its packaging.

> I think it's exciting to house content in a state that is removed yet poetically connected to the known realities of its existence so that one can feel the vibe or sensation of that content in a more direct and visceral way. When something is housed in its normal environment, I think we tend to see only the accumulation of its "text" or chatter, but not the root of its body, the thing that makes people say, "I get it."[36]

A new wave of artists are remapping the meaning of objects in their practice, including Jacolby Satterwhite whose three-dimensional animation work "inspires [him] to perform in a way that queers the meaning of the object, dissolving the political potential of the object in relationship to [his] body."[37] In his video *Country Ball 1989–2012* (2012), Satterwhite magnifies the size of three-dimensional cakes in order to make them look like skyscrapers. "Bondage contraptions" are installed on the roof where the artist can be found voguing. He explains that this visual representation is a way to highlight how society "pollutes objects' meanings with history, politics and social anxiety."[38]

Jacolby Satterwhite's use of the term *pollute* suggests that the process of recontextualization is an act of resistance against an established system of branding. For Trecartin, however, branding is just another useful tool to employ. The artists' divergent approaches lead us to interrogate the relationship between art and advertising and ask ourselves if the separation between both still holds true today. In her article, "What Does Nike Want?," Agatha Wara writes,

> Misunderstood by the critical art sector as the total corporate instrumentalization of human physiological responses, the field of advertising continues to be disavowed from having any "critical" potential. Yet in a world where the language of advertising is becoming evermore sophisticated and ubiquitous, it seems almost pathological for art to continue to disregard its presence. *Why should the emergent system of signs known as art escape the grasps of a more expansive material ontology?*[39]

Wara argues that although branding and art are types of coding that share a common goal in that they both seek to catch and hold attention, advertising has generally been looked down on by critics due to its obvious commercial aim.[40] While it is not within the scope of this book to answer such a broad and charged question as the one posed by Wara, her statement serves as an entry point to further examine artists as brands.

Ryan Trecartin's conception of branding can be further explored in an article posted on the DIS Magazine website, which details the artist's creative process for his 2010 *W* magazine spread. Amid the dozens of instructions carefully laid out by Trecartin in the article, one in particular appears to provide some clarity into his motivations. The directive stipulates that although the models in *W* magazine may have body parts in a state of transparency to blend with the background, the face and hair will always remain opaque.[41] The artist then reiterates that "Any transparent moments will be from the neck down."[42] We then understand that Trecartin aims for his characters to be distinguishable.

Indeed, we detect that much emphasis was placed on the facial styling of each of his models comprised of makeup and digital effects. Fitch is made to look like she received a "ton of well done surgeries, at too young of an age. So that she looks 46,"[43] utilizing contour makeup. Veronica Gelbaum's makeup is applied in postproduction to look professional and refined while having "a quality of financially substituted features . . . ;"[44] Clemens's face is painted on with a "digital blur make-up foundation" composed of many multishaded digital pixel effects that transmit the appearance of a censorship blurring effect.[45] Finally, a steering wheel is superimposed over Ashland Mines's physiognomy in order to give his forehead, cheek bones, and jaw line a "facial steering" look, "so that the face vaguely feels like a steering wheel or navigational device for long distance and memory."[46] What we are left with are characters wearing some sort of digital masks that aesthetically resemble the multicolor, asymmetrical, geometric-patterned makeup applied to the protagonists in his movies. Interestingly, cosmetic camouflage has become increasingly popular in recent years as a practice by which to subvert biometric detection from machines.[47]

It is clear that protagonists in *Any Ever* do not attempt to blend in nor hide from cameras. On the contrary, they constantly demand the camera's attention through direct modes of address. In fact, while their makeup may function as a sort of mask, they are very much recognizable. Even in the 2010 *W* photo shoot, each performer is easily identifiable despite the abundance of postproduction effects applied to their faces. So, if not to escape the camera's scrutiny, then, what is the purpose of such tawdry maquillage? I assert that Trecartin's eccentric characterizations do more than solely serve a stylistic function. They are indeed a major part of his trademark—a clearly recognizable visual hallmark rooted in his branding.

In their essay "Characters on Parade," Ginger Gregg Duggan and Judith Hoos Fox note that character design in both fashion and art is an ideal tool for branding as it "tap[s] into our consumer sensibilities [by] emphasizing spectacle."[48] Trecartin's unique characters have become such iconic emblems that they now independently trend on Instagram and post selfies of themselves backstage.[49] Much like fashion labels, the artist has managed to brand himself by creating and promoting a distinctive look. This is indicative of his desire to extend the visibility of his work beyond the art world into mainstream culture.

Ryan Trecartin's rising pop status was first noticed when *Vogue* magazine featured him in its February 2010 issue. A close-up of Trecartin portraying Shin from *A Family Finds Entertainment* spanned across two full pages introducing a feature article about his work titled "The Body Eccentric" by Dodie Kazanjian. The writer identified a new trend in contemporary art termed *eccentric figuration*, defined as artists' tendency to create grotesque and even disturbing figurative works.[50] Kazanjian's focus on form and style was consistent with the magazine's goal to relate art to fashion, keeping in mind its fashion-centric target audience.

As mentioned earlier in the chapter, art has increasingly been deployed to confer cultural meaning to fashion and luxury brands. Artists, in turn, may mutually benefit from this association as the publicity garnished through ad campaigns and fashion spreads could propel some to stardom. This alliance between fashion and art began with Pop Art in the late fifties and early sixties, with artists such as Richard Hamilton and Andy Warhol, whose works blurred the lines between what at that time were two distinct fields. Hamilton created the *Fashion Plate* collage series from 1969 to 1970, incorporating cutouts of magazine images and makeup. Then in 1969, Warhol, posed in the February/March issue of *L'Uomo Vogue*, modeling men's fashions intended to appeal to a mass audience. But most notably, he founded the widely circulated arts and fashion publication *Interview* magazine in 1974.[51]

More recently, contemporary artist Tracey Emin and painters Elizabeth Peyton appeared in British *Vogue* and *Purple Fashion*, respectively, adorned in luxury labels, Vivienne Westwood, Marc Jacobs, and Miu Miu.[52] These latest alliances highlight examples of the relationship between fashion and art, but they merely present the artists as models. Vanessa Beecroft and Takashi Murakami each partnered with the luxury brand Louis Vuitton, not as models but as commissioned artists. Beecroft, who is primarily known for setting up and directing large-scale installations with live models, staged a performance for the opening of the Louis Vuitton store on the Champs-Elysées in October 2005. She arranged models on the boutique's shelves among the brand's handbags. More recently, she has been working closely with Kanye West to orchestrate all of his Yeezy fashion shows.[53] In 2002, Marc Jacobs, who was then the creative director of Louis Vuitton, invited Murakami to collaborate on a handbag collection. Murakami reinterpreted the house's signature LV monogram by merging it with his unique Manga-inspired graphics, which was an immense commercial success.

Trecartin's involvement with the fashion industry is multifaceted, since he and his performers not only model, but he also directs the photo shoots, and creates one-of-a-kind fashion items that are incorporated into the styling of his projects for *W* magazine. As a result, the market pages in the back of the magazine detailing product and shopping information for goods used in editorial spreads, featured accessories from his own shoot, such as the sandals worn by Telfar Clemens on sale at dismagazine.com for $275.00.[54] Ryan Trecartin has also designed the sweatshirts with the WITNESS logo worn by performers in *Coma Boat* (2013) and replicated them for the group exhibition organized by the DIS Collective, titled *DISown: Not for Everyone*, where they were sold to the public. The show displayed affordable mass-market products that could be sold during the exhibit.[55] Blurring the boundaries between art and commerce, the exhibit also attempted to dispel the romantic myth that artists can sustain themselves without having to sell their work. As Lauren Boyle, cocurator and member of the DIS collective, astutely put it, "You actually do need money to live."[56]

Yet, paradoxically, we must not forget that Ryan Trecartin distributes the entirety of his videos freely online. How do we then reconcile the image of Trecartin as personal brand with his noncommercial approach to the distribution of his work? When asked to comment on his unrestricted modes of distribution and exhibition, he replied,

> I think the movies are native to a multiplicity of situations. [. . .] Also, artists who are inspired by a diverse range of cultural hubs and mentalities should share with the worlds that inspire them. I don't think art is outside or higher than other aspects of culture, but it is special, since it potentially has no boundaries and complete freedom. It's important to mix that into the world.[57]

Going mainstream for Trecartin does not carry the negative connotation often associated with art merging with mass culture, since he does not believe that "art is outside or higher than other aspects of culture." In fact, he is the first one to admit that his work is "part of something that is larger than the art world, something that includes advertising and TV shows and journalism."[58] Therefore, we cannot say that Trecartin has only recently become a pop figure, since he has always been one. Nor can his work be said to have made the transition from galleries and museums to the general public, since it was never conceived for such venues in the first place. Gaining visibility for him is not about achieving fame. For the artist, it is about reaching a wider audience and sharing back with the world that inspires him.

// 5 //

Priority Innfield

Interactive Gaming Simulation as Expanded Cinema

> The future and the past can be equally malleable; I don't think they go in opposite directions. Memory is more an act of memorizing than recalling: you're creatively constructing something that doesn't really exist behind you, it exists in the same place the future exists. In my videos the characters try to treat that idea as fact.[1]
>
> —Ryan Trecartin, *Frieze*, 2011

PRIORITY INNFIELD (2013) debuted at the 55th Venice Biennale as part of *The Encyclopedic Palace* exhibition. The cinematic installation invites us to anticipate the future while looking back at the past. Comprised primarily of four independent yet interrelated videos, *Junior War, Comma Boat, Center Jenny,* and *Item Falls,* this body of work permits us to reflect back on the artist's trajectory, from his senior year in high school to the present. The project was conceived as a gaming system in which characters range from human-like figures to raw data that travel from one game level to another. *Priority Innfield* explores the potential for an immersive cinematic experience that offers more navigational agency to the spectator than was possible in his prior works.

The artist erases the divide between the lens of his handheld camera and the world of his films by recording the action from a 360-degree perspective. He achieves this by placing his actors within large open spaces containing mobile walls that he moves accordingly in order to engage with the performers while simultaneously filming them. Spatial configuration is given special importance as it truly helps to advance the plot. The movies function as gaming systems in which game levels must be surpassed in order to gain experience.

Space is experienced rather than displayed. Trecartin no longer sees himself exclusively as a director but expands his role to that of animator/ programmer and merges these roles. Many of the postproduction effects he applies draw direct reference to recurring formal elements commonly found in digital animation: cel shading, shape-shifting three-dimensional models, morphing, datamoshing, and 360-degree camera pans.

Junior War, the first video in the series, consists of recovered footage that Trecartin filmed in 1999 while still in high school. He did not however edit the movie until he was invited to participate in the Venice Biennale. Inspired by *The Blair Witch Project* (1999), the entire video was shot in infrared with a Handycam to resemble footage viewed with night vision goggles.[2] The loose plot follows random acts of vandalism of a group of teenagers on a late night excursion in Ohio. "Fucking shit up" is the main mantra and recurring theme. The characters delight in smashing and banging things up, from television sets to metal mailboxes—an action that is replicated throughout Trecartin's body of work. The artist's signature fast-paced, in-your-face editing style is clearly recognizable in this pseudo-anthropological look at youth in rural America.

Noticeably different is the protagonists' relationship to the camera, which deviates drastically from that in later works. *Junior War* was filmed before the advent of social network and selfies. As such, the camera's presence was construed at the time as intrusive—a fact made evident by the teenagers' repeated demands, "Ryan, turn it off!" Conversely, certain scenes illustrate that they also wish to perform specifically for the camera, however awkward and uneasy that seemed. For instance, one of the artist's friends exclaims, "Let's fuck shit up!... that's the phrase right?" The filmmaker has expressed that looking back at this footage made him realize that "people's relationship to the camera used to be really primitive."[3]

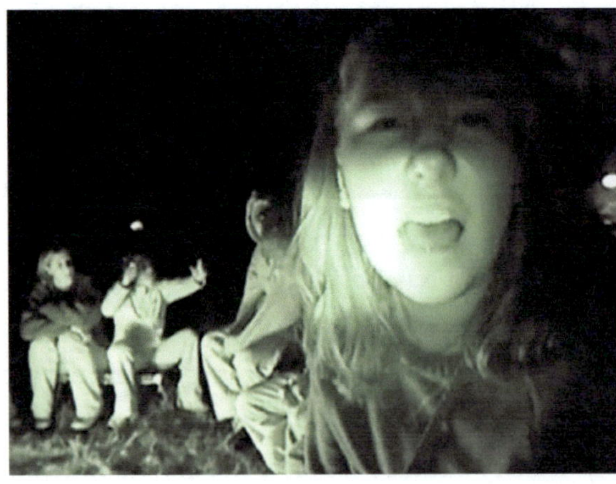

Figure 5.1 *Junior War* (2013)

In an interview, Trecartin revealed that *Junior War* inspired much of the rest of *Priority Innfield*'s content.[4] The artist chose to further explore the role of the camera in the other three distinct videos included in this body of work. Its presence, however, no longer inhibits its protagonists' performances but rather enhances it. Trecartin's latter characterizations have internalized and adapted to new technology to the point that their existence seems to only be validated if recorded in "real-time." The camera's function is elevated from entry-point into the world of film to that of a navigational device. This, in turn, simulates audience members' motion via Trecartin's newly rendered universe. *Priority Innfield* shifts the focus from a character-centered narrative point-of-view to a first-person experiential one.

In fact, the cinematography in the last three videos consists primarily of first-person subjective camera angles. In his essay, "Origins of the First-Person Shooter," Alexander Galloway argues that in this specific type of shot, which takes its cue from first-person shooter (FPS) video games, "The camera merges with the character both visually and subjectively [to] show the exact physiological or emotional qualities of what a character would see. [...] The subjective shot very precisely positions itself inside the skull of that character."[5] This aesthetic decision further illustrates the artist's focus toward a gamic mode of storytelling.

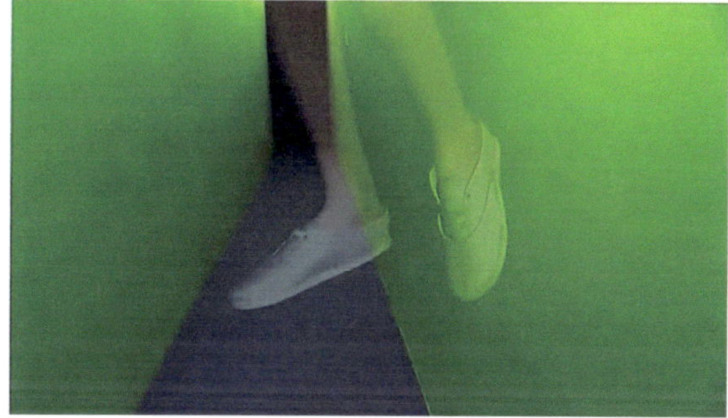

Figure 5.2
Center Jenny
(2013)

Center Jenny opens with a point-of-view shot of a long narrow corridor. The camera moves in unison with the character's footsteps in order to reinforce the feeling that we are simultaneously advancing as well. Making our way through the tight hallway is reminiscent of the effects of first-generation three-dimensional graphics FPS, such as *Wolfenstein 3D* (1992) or *Doom* (1993), which require gamers to maneuver through dark and constricted passages. This reference to nascent video games is further emphasized when a pair of translucent cropped three-dimensional legs appear to be moving

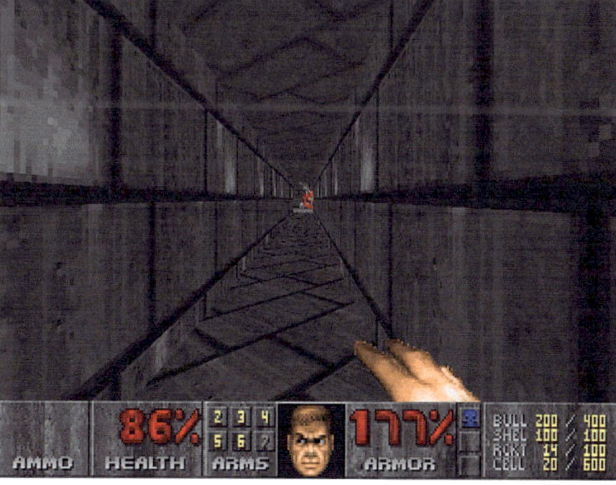

Figure 5.3
Doom
(1993)

across the screen, indicating that the first-person perspective is in fact that of a digital avatar.

Trecartin's visual reference to this pioneer generation of games is quite fitting, as this opening scene affirms the artist's theory that the past and future can exist simultaneously in the same space. Allusions to the past can also be observed through the off-screen voices that exclaim in the background, "What's a camera? What's a camera? Yeah, put it down!" These statements represent a direct replay of those made fifteen years earlier by the teenagers in *Junior War*, who repeatedly asked Ryan to turn his camera off when they were uncomfortable being filmed for fear they would not be portrayed in the best possible light. These extradiegetic voices help us understand the evolution of the role of the camera in his work, from his first foray into directing to his recent and more interactive videos.

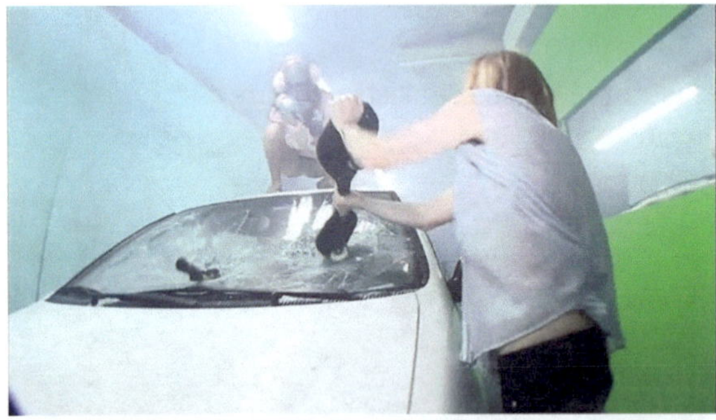

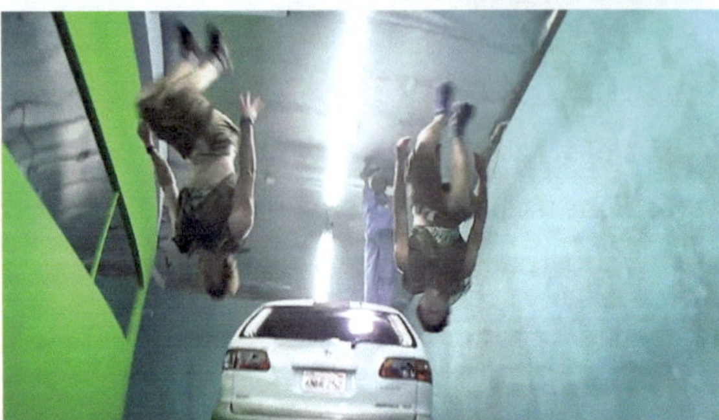

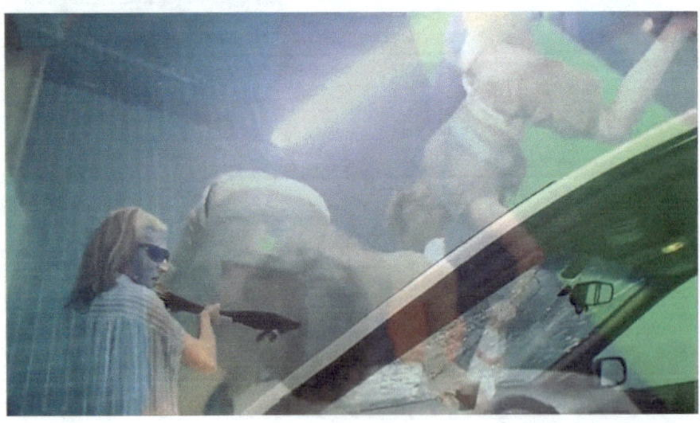

Figures 5.4, 5.5, and 5.6 *Center Jenny* (2013)

As the camera encroaches on the exit, the artist jump-cuts to what appears to be a war zone. The cut is accompanied by the sound of an explosion immediately proceeded by a loud alarm. We are suddenly witnesses to a group of young adults smashing car windows with hammers and skateboards. Simultaneously, several parkour athletes execute a series of dangerous acrobatic moves across the screen. This sense of high physicality is reinforced by dynamic crosscuts between diverse camera angles. Trecartin merges multiple perspectives into one by layering several shots on top of each other and decreasing their opacity, so that all are visible onscreen at the same time. This effect provides viewers with the impression that they are experiencing the action through a 360-degree perspective.

Although the editing here is as intricately layered as ever, the actual footage does not appear to be very digitally processed. Trecartin points out, "A lot more happens in real time in this project. Normally I shoot to create material for the editing process, not for the live performances."[6] Some critics have expressed disappointment with regard to the lack of media layering in *Priority Innfield* in comparison to his earlier work, claiming that

> It is as if Trecartin has [. . .] proudly abandoned writing—a temporal process bound up with the act of documenting history—for instantaneous recording. These shifts away from writing and editing not only have regrettable political consequences, but also result in a relatively homogenous temporal and visual palette that cannot sustain the animating tensions found in *I-Be Area* or "Any Ever."[7]

Trecartin's decision to preserve the raw footage in its purest form should not be seen as detrimental to his work, because in doing so he unleashes the linguistic potential of the camera. He no longer simply edits the footage with postproduction software but also crops and rearranges time and space in real time, propelled by the impetus of the filming.

For the artist, "holding the camera is itself a performance."[8] In fact, many of his camera operators actively engage in the action while simultaneously filming it. For instance, during the combat scene in *Center Jenny*, a crew member smashes a cement brick over the head of one of the characters while another is perched on the rooftop of a car recording the mayhem with his camera. The cameras not only serve as points of access for viewers, who are made to feel as if they are actively interfacing with the protagonists, but simultaneously become subjects on screen. This approach is indicative of Trecartin's desire to simulate a fully rendered actionable space accessible to spectators.

As we move into the next phase of the game level, we encounter a group of sorority girls partaking in an initiation ceremony. Each girl is framed through a tight close-up as they individually introduce themselves to the camera. One sorority sister, however, appears to be surprised by its presence. Unlike the other girls, this character (Rachel Lord) does not possess a name. "I don't have a name yet, we're not even on a level." She represents the simplest, most rudimentary incarnation possible in the gaming system and is referred to as "Basic Jenny." She is often shot from high angles to reinforce her subordinate status. Her white contact lenses make her appear to be blind—a potential impairment considering the movie's intensely graphic rendering. This apparent optic limitation is another indication of her lower status within the network.

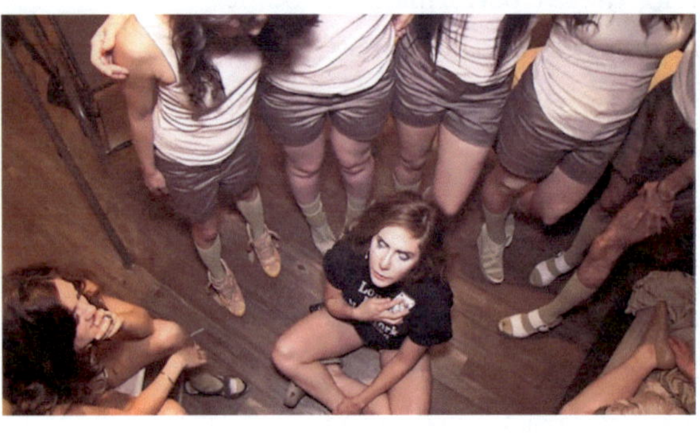
Figure 5.7
Center Jenny (2013)

Similar to avatars in role-playing games such as those in the Final Fantasy franchise, the protagonists in *Priority Innfield* gain experience points by advancing to higher levels. In doing so, they acquire more skills and attributes, including individual names. We are introduced to this concept in the opening scene of *Item Falls*, when a character points out, "This is first level, there are no names here. I am super simple. [. . .] My goal is to make it to Level Center." "Level Center" represents the ultimate rank all protagonists aspire to reach. But, before accessing it, one must successfully complete each task leading to it. Each of the six individual sororities represent a level that the protagonist, Basic Jenny, must ascend in order to evolve into a more advanced version of herself.

Like Ericka Beckman's digital game video *Hiatus* (1999), *Center Jenny* follows a female lead who comes into existence by overcoming obstacles and learning how to act within the virtual world she has ventured into. Both works place their respective protagonists in new environments as they advance levels. Each scene serves as a gradual stepping-stone toward the characters' main objective. However, unlike techno-normative gaming narratives, the main goal is not to win, but rather for the protagonist to attain the highest level of herself. The filmmaker thereby rejects hegemonic notions of progress, as he subverts the dominant gaming structure of winning versus losing. I argue that Trecartin expands upon what Edmond Y. Chang coins "queergaming" by queering a cinematic narrative whose premise is based on video games. The artist imagines a gameplay that does not abide by a strict binary system, instead emphasizing the heroine's queer experience as an outsider and nonconformist player.[9]

Center Jenny can be considered a cyberdrama, a form of digital storytelling that emphasizes "the enactment of the story in the particular fictional space of the computer."[10] *Center Jenny*'s plot is created much like a walk-through game in which the space serves as the container for the narrative similar to the platform game *Tomb Raider* (1996). Polygonal environments are created with semidefinite boundaries and function as outlines in which the action is carried out. In open-gaming systems, the setting may be less static and more dynamic, as it shifts according to the pathway the gamer decides to take. *Priority Innfield*'s sets are conceived as those in open-gaming systems wherein boundaries between inside, outside, on- and offstage, and audience are all blurred. Trecartin calls this type of open mise-en-scène a "continuous 360-degree situation."[11]

In order to simulate this sense of immersion, Trecartin set up cinematic installations at *The Encyclopedic Palace* exhibition that challenged conventions of spectatorship and modes of exhibition, and created an interactive and participatory experience of expanded cinema.[12] He achieved this partly through the addition of free-standing sculptural theaters that provided viewers with a feeling of active engagement within the expanded cinematic space. Trecartin's installation shares the scale and immersive quality of Cory Arcangel's *Various Self Playing Bowling Games* (2011), which submerges spectators within the pixelated worlds of actual video games he redesigns, sometimes in collaboration with other artists. However, even though Arcangel's immense projections are impressive in scale, they remain somewhat traditional as they consist primarily of large flat screens in front of which a single viewer may be able to participate. Ryan Trecartin in collaboration with Lizzie Fitch, on the other hand, constructs three-dimensional environments in which spectators stand, walk around, and interact, as they watch the videos projected within them. This mode of exhibition offers a dimension of collective reception in addition to a singular viewer experience.

The artist had already expressed a desire to create fully interactive projects anticipating *Priority Innfield*, as he mentions in 2010, "I'd like to make a surround movie with multiple screens that is an actual experience that you can walk into and use technology that allows the direction of the movies to change in relation to the audience's response."[13] The idea that one can literally walk into a viewing experience suggests that the artist has taken into account the structural representation of his narrative. Sophia Psarra writes in *Architecture and Narrative*,

> Narrative enters architecture in many ways, from the conceptual "messages" it is made to stand for to the illustration of a design through models, drawings and other representational forms. This aspect of architectural expression, what the design *speaks of*, is relevant to narrative as representation. It concerns the semantic meanings of buildings and places, and the contribution of architecture to the expression of social and cultural messages.[14]

Whether it pertains to exhibition venues or his mise-en-scène, space plays a crucial role in Trecartin's coded narratives. The soundstage used in *Center Jenny*, for example, was actually constructed by professional Hollywood set builders and designed to adapt and modulate as the storyline progressed. The spatial configuration of the set thus functions much like an algorithmic decision tree designed to determine outcomes and advance the plot.

Space also shares a relationship to language. In software design, for example, three-dimensional structures are simply visual translations of software codes written in a particular computer language such as Java or C++. Commands in Java 3D API, such as the one shown below, create three-dimensional nodes that are then added to a scene graph, which serves as the outline of the actionable space.

```
TransformGroup objTrans = new TransformGroup();

objTrans.setCapability(TransformGroup.
ALLOW_TRANSFORM_WRITE);

objRoot.addChild(objTrans);

objTrans.addChild(new ColorCube().getShape());
```

Similarly, Trecartin conceives of speech as an architectural form. In an interview for *Frieze* magazine, he explained that

> The characters are constantly negotiating ideas that I conceive of as architectures: their reality as an architecture, their being as an architecture. The space surrounding these structures is

> speech; reciprocally, articulation creates space. So, the characters are in the space of speech. Space is a translation of language, of information.[15]

This idea is best illustrated in *Comma Boat*, in which the artist plays an aggressive director/animator who controls and orders performers around the set. He announces the transformation of the set to the crew, "This stage is officially a tranny! [. . .] Now come the fuck down stage!"

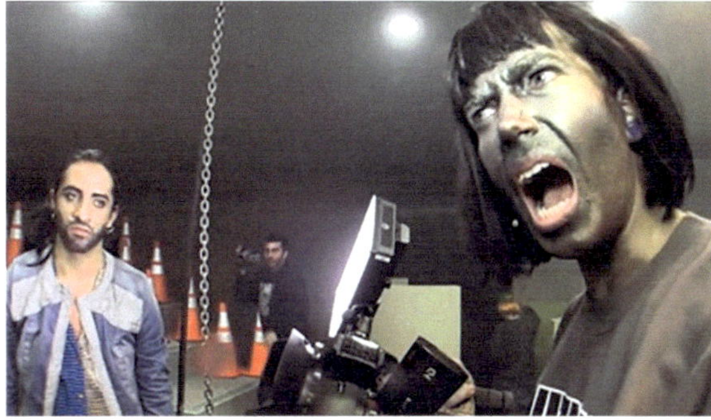

Figure 5.8
Comma Boat
(2013)

The director/protagonist (Trecartin) commences contorting to rock music as a massive circular platform suspended from the ceiling slowly descends to the ground in front of him. He reorganizes the spatial arrangement of the set much in the same manner that he directs the actors in the movie within the movie. The set morphs according to the multifunctional character's verbal commands. The director/character is able to manipulate his surroundings as if controlling a graphic user interface in runtime.[16] Not only does he act, direct the performers, and control the set transformation, but he also selects camera angles, all simultaneously on-camera during the filming. It is as if the writing, filming, and editing all occur live within the film.[17] *Comma Boat*, like *Center Jenny*, offers viewers a variety of perspectives by employing several cameras that encircle the performers at all times.

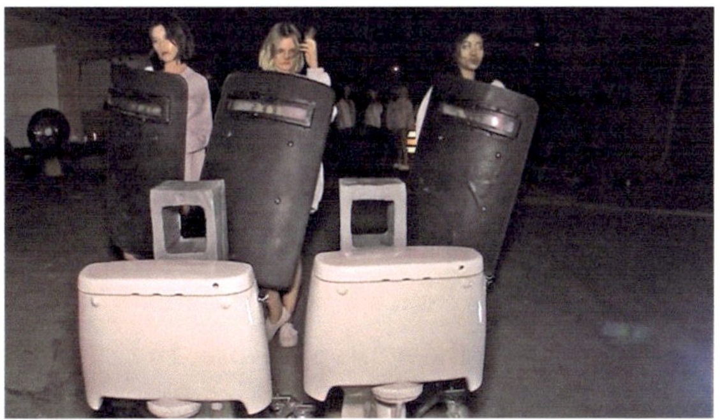

Figure 5.9
Center Jenny
(2013)

The director/animator character in *Comma Boat* may be interpreted as a stand-in for Ryan Trecartin himself. However, each individually possesses quite disparate directing styles. Trecartin seeks to assign actors a sense of autonomy and freedom while also allowing them to generate their own content. The artist empowers his group of performers to collaboratively and interactively film various versions of the action occurring within the mise-en-scène. The protagonist in *Comma Boat*, on the other hand, dictates the performers' every move and appears to relish torturing them.

An overall sense of hostility seems to permeate *Priority Innfield*. A combative undercurrent conveys the kind of atmosphere simulated in many violent video games. Gaming systems set in place structures that include winners and losers. As such, they often require players to defeat other opponents in order to declare a victor. Similarly, performers in the series compete against each other in order to reach Level Center. They not only demolish their environments, but also attempt to destroy one another in the process. Characters throw faux cement bricks at each other, and red cups explode and shatter across their faces. Actors, such as Telfar Clemens, even guard themselves behind massive shields as if preparing for battle and refer to each other as adversaries: "I will fucking weaponize your territory on the enemy!" Others make direct reference to combat. One sorority girl declares, "I sense a rainstorm coming from the north." A girl sitting next to her suddenly interjects, "How can you tell which way is north?," and she replies, "Because my ancestors outlived the war." It is unclear this early in the narrative if the war is over or if it is underway. However, several references to martial law and the omnipresence of props such as pink earmuffs stuffed with razor blades suggest that perhaps they are still in the midst of a battle.

It is apparent that the artist's Gesamtkunstwerk possesses an underlying dark mood. Characters are not only antagonistic but also surveil and exert control over others. The omnipresent cameras transmit this sense of surveillance—an overarching theme in *Priority Innfield*. Its pervasiveness is also specifically evoked through the presence of characters wearing sweatshirts with the words "WITNESS 360," printed on them, who pride themselves on their ability to observe everything. These intrusive denizens scrutinize others in an attempt to block them from advancing through the levels. At the top of this oppressive futuristic caste system is Sara Source (Renee Plaza), the most "advanced" character, charged with overseeing the entire network. In order to remain in power, she sets in place a very restrictive linear network. In it, the only way to reach Level Center is by progressively ascending predefined levels. Skipping steps is considered a crime and any deviation from this preestablished path is subject to punishment. Basic Jenny wishes to liberate herself from such a predetermined course to freely travel across levels regardless of her rank within the network. However, her journey will be replete with hurdles and difficulties as Sara Source scrutinizes her every move.

After repeated failed attempts at infiltrating advanced-level cliques, the heroine stumbles on an underground group called Left-of-Center. Dissimilar to the other sororities, members of this club do not strive to attain Level Center, instead priding themselves on being different. Each one sports a unique look and possesses an individual name. These Left-of-Center characters welcome Basic Jenny into their community and immediately accept her as one of their own. The protagonist addresses the camera directly and declares her new self-assigned name for the first time, "Hi my name is Athens Ornamental and I'm a regular." The ingenue has upgraded from a basic version to a regular one, bypassing the next level, thereby violating the rules of the system.

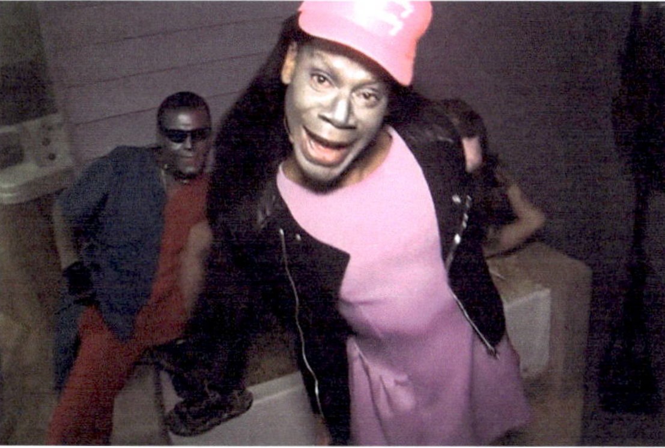

Figure 5.10 *Center Jenny* (2013)

The director suddenly cuts to a new scene in which an advanced Jenny (Jena Malone) humiliates Basic Jenny for her defiance. The bully pulls her hair while confronting the camera, and shouts,

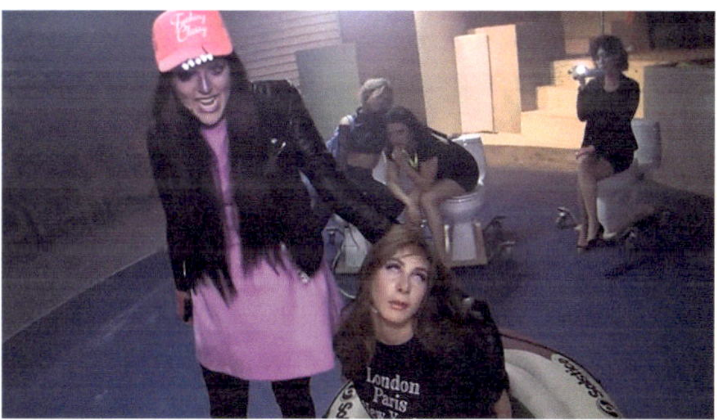

Figure 5.11 *Center Jenny* (2013)

> This is one of my many intern protégé bullshit [. . .] Don't look at me Basic Jenny! [. . .] She's a first-level dummy [. . .] She's stupid! You are left of center, do you fucking understand me? [. . .] No one wants to stay in your world. [. . .] You're a redundant ass and you might be respected on secondary levels but you will never graduate emotionally because your chip sucks. Stay here, we don't want you there.

As we delve further into the plot, it becomes apparent that the more advanced characters are in fact the most primitive and barbaric ones. These higher-level sorority girls find great pleasure in binge drinking and physically assaulting each other. Sara Source declares directly into the camera, "I think the only thing I'll ever study is the human-era hazing and how significant and awesome it is. [. . .] The humans were so cool."

Characters talk about their human ancestors as if they were mythological figures. A university professor (Lee Kyle), for example, makes bombastic declaratives about world history to his students. "Back in the human era, dinosaurs evolved into chickens. This is a fact. [. . .] We have evolved from animations, those are our ancestors." His students react with hostility and have difficulty grasping these concepts. One Jenny bluntly replies, "Like, the further we all move away from humanity, sexism just becomes, like, the coolest style." The characters' nonsensical rants betray their ignorance. Trecartin makes it clear that humanity has been relegated to a thing of the past. In their apocalyptic humanoid future, humans have simply become irrelevant. *Junior War* footage suddenly seems like an artifact from an ancient era.

The artist's animated cyborgs believe they have ascended to a higher existential plane, yet, their existence is utterly reliant on technology, particularly cell phone usage. Sara Source acrimoniously blurts out, "If anyone brings their phone in here, they're not gonna have a tracking system and they're gonna fucking die!" *I-BE Area*'s high-tech utopia celebrated the promises of unlimited freedom afforded by technology, while the dismal world of *Priority Innfield*, envisions it as a means of entrapment much in the same vein as dystopian sci-fi films like *Blade Runner* (1982) or *The Matrix* (1999). The artist's bleak vision should not merely be relegated to the realm of popular fiction, as academics have recently begun to share concern over the effects of digital culture. Jonathan Zittrain, professor of internet law and computer science at Harvard University, comments,

> Internet users are again embracing a range of "tethered appliances," reflecting a resurgence of the initial model of bundled hardware and software that is created and controlled by one company. This will affect how readily behavior on the Internet can be regulated, which in turn will determine the extent that regulators and commercial incumbents can constrain amateur

> innovation, which has been responsible for much of what we now consider precious about the Internet.[18]

Zittrain's observation is consistent with Trecartin's thoughts about the impact of the internet on our basic rights and freedoms. However, this is not to say that the artist has become antitechnology. His commentary does not really denounce technology as an entity but rather problematizes the ways it is being utilized. The protagonists in *Center Jenny* are so consumed by the magnetizing power of their handheld cameras and touch-screen cell phones that they have become completely alienated from each other and their past. They increasingly contact each other, but have strangely become more alienated because interactions are primarily mediated through the use of devices.

Basic Jenny is the only character who wishes to experience intimate interaction. *Priority Innfield* may be set in a futuristic cyberworld, but on deeper probing, we find that at the core of its storyline are themes that emphasize humanistic values—belonging, self-discovery, and freedom. Indeed, the artist has expressed,

> I'm actually trying to think past technology at this point and more about creative desire. People want to feel situated and located, but they don't want to feel like they're a slave to anything. To deal with limitations of place, characters in the movie make "fourth-wall generators," "fifth-wall randomizers," "location situators" and "consciousness expanders," forcing old forms of exchange into scenarios that allow something to be broken. I'm interested in establishing a structure of obedient behaviors so that obedience can trigger destructive impulses.[19]

Basic Jenny triggers a response of disobedience within the linear structure of the gameplay mechanics. It is through her that others will converge and reconnect to find the strength to rebel against the oppressive world they inhabit.

This phenomenon occurs in the video's final scene. Multiple sororities gather around the heroine and begin scribbling directly onto her

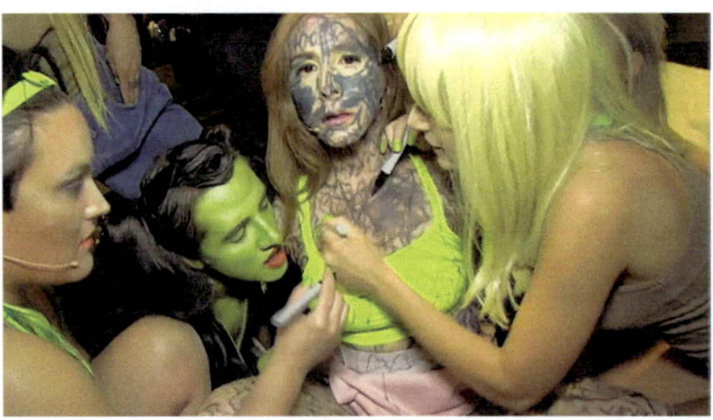

Figure 5.12
Center Jenny
(2013)

body with markers. The seemingly degrading act seems like another sorority observance, at first. However, the protagonist reveals that she finds the experience empowering. She faces the camera, and declares, "I'm really into call and response." The other characters yell back, "Call and response!" Call and response typically constitutes a form of verbal and nonverbal communication that stimulates participation between speakers and listeners. In this case however, the exchange assists in undermining *Center Jenny*'s despotic hierarchical regime. It is thanks to this egalitarian interaction that Basic Jenny finds the courage to revolt against the omnipotent Sara Source who controls the entire network: "That source is a fucking valet spot! I need to rehabilitate my think tank and recalibrate [. . .]." The protagonist's sudden insurgence leads other sorority members to challenge authority as well. One higher-level Jenny proclaims, "I hate that government!" Trecartin cuts to a reaction shot of the Left-of-Center clan members filmed behind the bars of a wrought iron bedframe. The parallel vertical lines—perhaps a nod to Alfred Hitchcock's well-establish visual motif—symbolizes the characters' entrapment within the frame but also within Sara Source's restrictive gaming system itself. One character brandishes a cement brick intended for Sara Source and shouts, "I'm gonna own you Sara Source! I'm gonna destroy you!" Sara Source retaliates,

> I might be some privileged bitch but I'm gonna fuck you up, 'cause I'm a privileged bitch that knows how to do that shit! And I might throw a fucking brick at your face 'cause you don't know, we might be friends or we might not, but whatever, I'm the only one that knows.

Sara Source is then presented alone lying on a hammock sulking while the other avatars rejoice. She delivers her last riposte, framed through a medium shot, ". . . Wha' . . . whatever, I'm the only one that knows . . ." The sudden shift in her tone of voice betrays her uncertainty, as if doubting her own authority. Her reiteration does not reinforce her dominance but rather reveals her insecurity as she attempts to convince herself of her self-proclaimed superiority over the other avatars.

The video ends with a shot of Sara Source appearing unsure of her fate. Basic Jenny seems to have succeeded in overthrowing the established oppressive system. In the process, she has regained control of her destiny and is free to create her own future, regardless of her original rank within the network. As we have come to expect from Trecartin videos, *Center Jenny*'s finale leaves us with unanswered questions. Will Basic Jenny ever reach a higher existential level? Or does the collapse of the network imply that she will be stuck in her basic state forever?

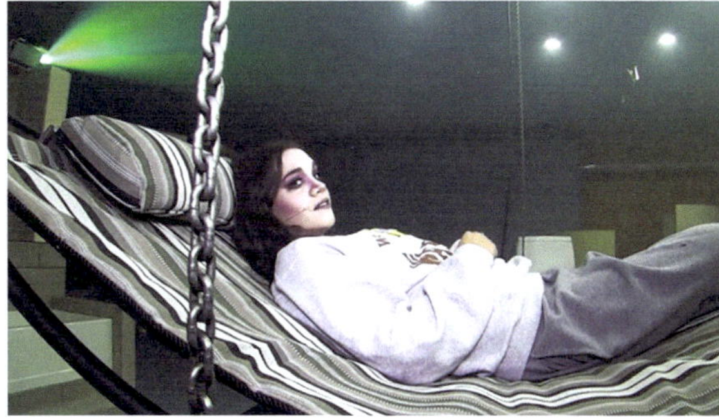

Figure 5.13 *Center Jenny* (2013)

Some of our queries find answers in *Item Falls*, which I consider the final movie in the series. The narrative takes place during the aftermath of the revolution that occurred in *Center Jenny*. The general mood is more cheerful and evokes the playfulness of *A Family Finds Entertainment*. The action is set once again in a constructed set resembling an all-American sorority house inhabited by a pack of rambunctious animated characters. Among them, we recognize Basic Jenny, now renamed "Elegant Audition Chick Line Item," who prides herself on having the capacity to exert her free will. Characters have at this point all reached a much higher existential level that is visually manifested by their ability to meld into digital animations of themselves. Trecartin also returns to the practice of extensive image processing and media layering.

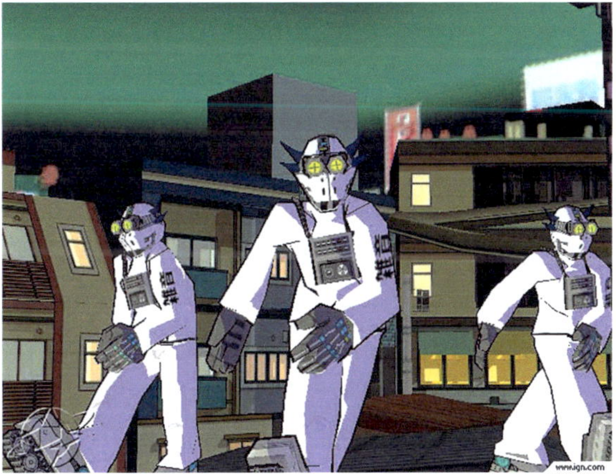

Figure 5.14 *Jet Set Radio* (2000)

The artist augments his already broad palette by using After Effects Trapcode Particular plug-in, which generates cel shading, a non-photorealistic technique that renders three-dimensional images into artwork with a hand-drawn flat graphic appearance. The results display sophisticated digital masks that truly give the impression we are no longer watching humans,

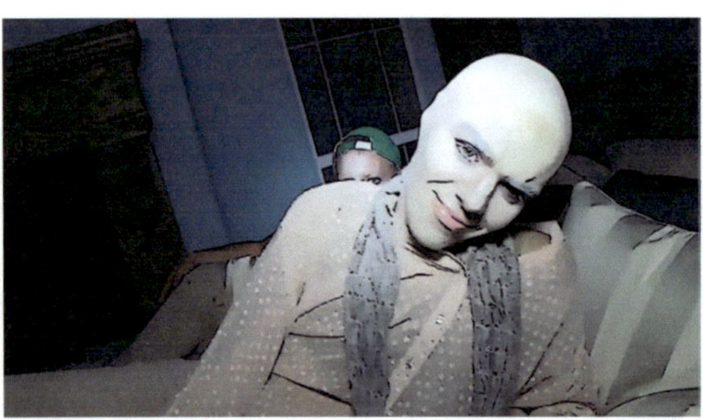

Figure 5.15
Item Falls
(2013)

but rather animations. The complex process first emerged in video games, most notably in Sega Dreamcast's *Jet Set Radio* (2000). In addition, Trecartin applies compression artifacts, a datamoshing tool that makes performers resemble glitches missing digital pixel information. The slew of effects the director incorporates renders subjects almost unnatural, creating the illusion that they are versions of polygonal video game characters. Ultimately, Trecartin embraces the entropic nature and productive failure of technology.

The lo-fi look adopted from glitch art bears semblance to the work of several artists, including Paper Rad, whose video art aestheticizes digital malfunctions by intentionally corrupting computational codes and data streams. In its video piece, *Super Mario Bros. Movie* (2005), produced in collaboration with Cory Arcangel, Paper Rad hacked Nintendo's *Mario Bros.* game and manipulated its sprites and narrative. This artistic practice was also implemented in the popular mainstream animated series, *Adventure Time* (2010–present), currently airing on Cartoon Network featuring a similar computer bug aesthetic in its episode, *A Glitch Is a Glitch* (2013), directed by filmmaker David O'Reilly. Art collective, Space Slave Trade, appropriates images found online and layers them on top of each other until the final image takes on the form of a complex and nebulous, yet poetic, graphic explosion. Although Space Slave Trade's art is deeply influenced by the visual culture of the internet, the stillness of their two-dimensional images fails to convey the ecstatic velocity of cyberspace. Other artists, such as Stelarc, have fused art with technology to create posthuman representations. In seeking to transcend the physical limitations of the body, he has customized his own with robotics. Although Stelarc has conducted experiments in human cyborgization, his work mainly entails physically remodeling his own body, while Trecartin aspires to digitally do away with bodies completely.

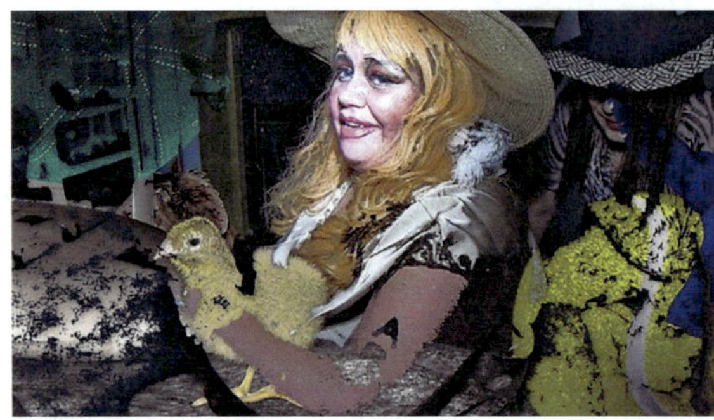

Figure 5.16
Item Falls
(2013)

In the final scene of *Item Falls*, the constructed set yields to a virtual environment modeled with Google's open source software SketchUP.[20] A three-dimensional replica of performer Alison Powell floats across the screen among dozens of three-dimensional chickens. The protagonists have been transformed into an advanced species as a result of their reconfiguration. This section may be read as the visual manifestation of the artist's conception of what he calls the "post-body" state. As he has expressed often, "it will someday be possible to truly liberate ourselves into a state where expression is existence and the accumulation of our situations become more of a catalogue of our identity rather than a written history."[21]

Previously, in *I-BE Area* Trecartin attempted to evince this state of transhumanism primarily through the use of makeup. This low-tech attempt was telling of his lofty goal but did not fully execute his vision. He appears to have achieved a greater level of success in *Item Falls*, as he concretizes this utopian vision in which bodies are transmutable data sets personified as three-dimensional figures. However, an ominous air permeates the ending of *Item Falls*. What initially seemed to be the apotheosis of the artist's ultimate fantasy, later reveals itself to be much more menacing. Multiple three-dimensional glitchy clones of Alison Powell wander aimlessly across the screen. An overwhelming number of images depicting chickens pop up, encircling the floating avatars and inundating the sorority house in flames. Trecartin abruptly ends *Item Falls* with a screen-within-a-screen image of actual chickens inside a bird coop. A night-vision camera inspects the brood confined within the narrow enclosure. This cut to an unmanipulated realistic shot of the animals awakens us to ponder whether we are not also being contained and monitored daily by security cameras, highway surveillance, mobile phone tapping, and even social media.

The jarring scene provides us with much insight into the internal conflict Trecartin feels regarding the availability of technology. He visually represents the tension existing between the independence and limitations it affords. While he embraces the internet's inherent potential to foster creativity, he feels some ambivalence regarding its use. This hesitation or conflict is primarily based on what he considers the danger concerned with its regulation. The artist takes the following stance on the subject:

I generally feel very positive, but pretty soon I think there are going to be basic freedoms and rights that we're going to have to fight for. All my movies have addressed that tipping point where one freedom replaces another. This has a lot to do with surveillance—not video camera surveillance, but the surveillance of people's activities, and the creation of algorithms that allow programs, companies or governments to understand what you like, buy or own. I think this is exciting and scary. [. . .] Once technology makes it possible to alter our brains, we're going to. Not everyone will. There will be more than one species of what are now humans. That split might follow class lines.[22]

Conclusion

SITE VISIT and Closing Remarks

CONCEIVED AS A SCULPTURAL cinematic installation, *SITE VISIT*, exhibited at the KW Institute for Contemporary Art in Berlin in 2014, generates a synesthetic experience intended to enhance viewer engagement.[1] Ryan Trecartin and Lizzie Fitch designed a built environment consisting of extendable lounge chairs and camping paraphernalia, among other sculptural elements, that parallels the sets in the *SITE VISIT* movie, thus blurring the line between the museum's exhibition space and the action that occurs onscreen. *SITE VISIT*'s immersive environment is enhanced by a thirty-channel Dolby surround-sound system. The addition of an all-encompassing soundtrack offers audiences an additional mode of entry into the work not present in previous pieces. The three-dimensional soundscape envelops visitors as they wander through the corridors of the exhibition space, which leads to the central hall. Adjacent rooms devoid of screens but furnished with home theater furniture, including seats equipped with audio transducers, allow audience members to feel the reverberation of the sound of the action. The public can thus sense the distant movie before actually viewing the six video projections inside. No matter where one may stand in the main exhibition space, it is nearly impossible to absorb the narrative in its entirety. The multidimensional projections overwhelmingly invoke the feeling of surfing the web. Participants are assaulted by unfettered, seemingly random continuous content, making it difficult to digest the piece all at once. The omnipresent audiovisual sensations break down established barriers between viewers and movie and computer screens. Ryan Trecartin states,

> We wanted to make a movie experience function more as a location or a space, rather than a meeting point between a single screen and a stationary audience. [. . .] A 360 degree movie that visually surrounds the viewer by extending the space of the movie screen through an audio logic—while also expanding the space of

> approach that inevitably foretells arriving at a screen. The tendency of sound to bleed is treated as an opportunity to create a continuity to journey through, so that the movie functions in the space like a destination site in a national park—it's continuous with the hike necessary to arrive at the view.[2]

Integrated into this web of images, surround sound, vibrations, sculptures, and furniture, the installation offers visitors an opportunity to experience an amplified dimension of our world while becoming more aware of their presence within it through sensorial stimulus. With *SITE VISIT*, Ryan Trecartin demonstrates that his artistic investment goes beyond the physical, material, and even narrative; it is about creating an experience, a journey.

The movie exhibited in *SITE VISIT* takes place primarily in an abandoned Masonic temple on Wilshire Boulevard in Los Angeles.[3] Its loose plot follows groups of participants who spend the night in the vacant shrine. They are arranged into teams identifiable through their idiosyncratic costumes consisting of some Jurassic Park T-shirts and camping expedition outfits, gear, and guns. The director explains, "The movies themselves are the interiors of educational gaming systems, ideological recollection centers, real-time diversity spots, and relativity parks that have been repurposed for off-label modes of recreational existence and observation."[4] Each team is charged with a mission. A group of college students, for instance, wants to enact the script of a horror/adventure movie inside the deserted building; other friends are paid to remain overnight as an experiment; and another group roams the hallways with their mini-digicams in search of potential subjects for their low-budget documentary.

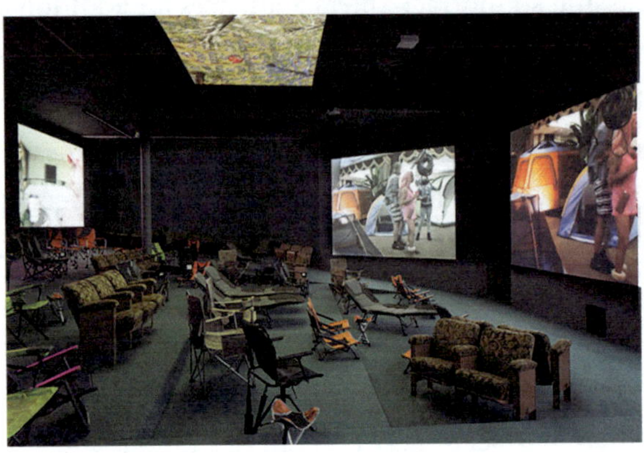

Figure C.1 *SITE VISIT* (2014)

Similar to survival horror games such as *Resident Evil* (Capcom, 1996), the protagonists venture into a haunted house populated by menacing creatures and ghosts. They gather at the entrance hall of the abandoned mansion, each one commenting on the immensity of the space—a déjà vu for connoisseurs of Playstation's cult video game. The threatening ambience pervading the opening scene quickly leads way to a much lighter mood. Trecartin infuses some crass comic relief with dialogue concerning getting inebriated and defecating in the toilet. Meanwhile, the artist films the entire scene through various vantage points to suggest that the protagonists are being surveilled. It is at times difficult to determine whether we are watching a horror film, comedy, or both, as the tone continuously shifts from sinister to comical, much like the movie's cameras alternate between shots. The editing in *SITE VISIT* is taken to a new extreme—it constitutes an assaultive collage of clashing images.

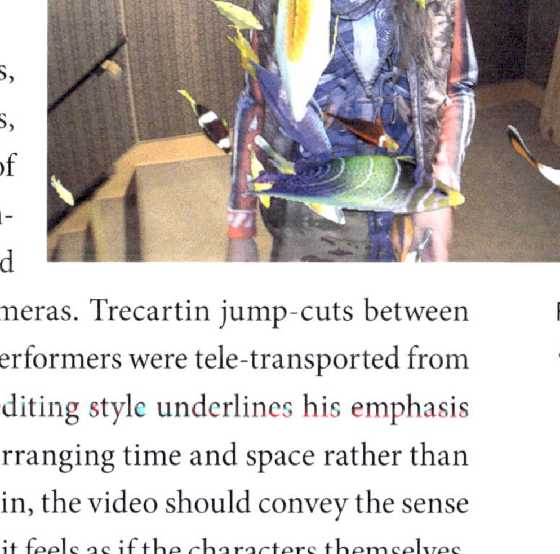

Figure C.2 *SITE VISIT* (2014)

SITE VISIT's multilinear plots, presented through six video channels, converge and collide at the speed of light. Aesthetically, this piece resembles earlier fast-paced, highly processed work shot with jittery handheld cameras. Trecartin jump-cuts between different unrelated scenes, as if the performers were tele-transported from one space to another. This radical editing style underlines his emphasis in *SITE VISIT* on "cropping and rearranging time and space rather than footage." According to Ryan Trecartin, the video should convey the sense that "real time can be altered, so that it feels as if the characters themselves, or the building itself, have edited it."[5] Performers address each other as if they occupy the same time and space, but the constant crosscutting makes it clear that each inhabits different zones. They may enter through the same door but end up in different environments, while others appear to be physically located within the same area but never acknowledge each other's presence.

The importance given to the enveloping experience is also substantiated by the performers who are charged with recording footage with mobile phones, digicams, and GoPro cameras strapped to their bodies. Trecartin cuts back and forth between the characters' perspectives and that of the hidden cameras flying above on drones. He employs up to fourteen different cameras to record individual scenes, thus creating multiple viewpoints and angles, which he describes as "mapping in 360 degrees."[6]

Some reviewers have criticized the videos in *SITE VISIT* for not being narrative-driven and lacking the character development of his earlier movies.[7] It is true that the proxies (Trecartin's moniker for the characters in *SITE VISIT*) lack some of the depth of characterizations in prior works, primarily due to the fact that the movie was not conceived with a script in mind. Instead, *SITE VISIT* was compiled from lists of moods and atmospheres as sources of inspiration for individual scenes. This fundamental shift partially explains why, according to the artist, viewers should "perceive the whole thing more via the space, the environment, than via character development."[8]

Critics of the film, however, fail to recognize not only that the temple is the main protagonist but that it is instrumental in propelling the plot forward. Trecartin emphasizes the significance of the building-as-character by continuously reconfiguring the space and altering its decor. The dialogue also reflects its prominence: "Some of these corners are not the way I'm used to them being," and "Guys I've never seen anything like that!" The director immediately accentuates the architecturally complex temple by opening with a panning shot of a three-dimensional rendering of the main entry hall. The proxies are recorded exploring the temple, wandering in and out of its rooms and hallways as if being transported while surfing the web from one unrelated web page to another, catapulted by mouse clicks. They function as data retrieval units or URL links connecting the web of plots together. In my 2014 interview with the artist, he explained,

> With *Priority Innfield* it's like a first-person shooter style, and with KW [*SITE VISIT*] it's like the space is the perspective and [. . .] personalities are accessed as a utensil, or like a tool, or a device to like navigate the actual content, whereas in *Any Ever*, personalities were an inventive free space to articulate meaning.[9]

While Trecartin's characters have been described as avatars in previous projects, CGI representations for singular modalities, here, they function as vehicles for collective consciousness. Ellen Blumenstein suggests that *SITE VISIT*'s protagonists have "abandoned all ambition."[10] Yet, while they may appear at first as aimless wanderers, by the end of the video the adventurers rebel against the oppressiveness of the building, climbing walls and riding zip lines across the amphitheater, smashing and destroying their surroundings as a way to gain some agency.

It is unclear whether they will ever exit the temple, as the ending does not provide any sense of closure or resolution. Trecartin has stated that the footage in *SITE VISIT* only consists of a small fraction of the material shot in the Masonic temple.[11] As such, we may understand the ending "to be continued..." What is understood, however, is the relationship between proxies and building. By the end of the movie, a proxy directly addresses the camera in order to confront the graphic designers that animated his face for not making it perfectly smooth. This telling scene divulges that the characters are aware of their status as animated proxies who are not simply outsiders conducting a site visit. They are indeed an integral component of the environment (building), since proxies by definition must be hosted. Therefore, they exist because the building exists. Trecartin further represents this by applying a transparency filter to the last scenes, thus superimposing the proxies within their three-dimensional surroundings. This revelation helps viewers understand the role of the building as a complex interconnected network hosting proxies, akin to the internet. They do not simply interact with the web. They inhabit it.

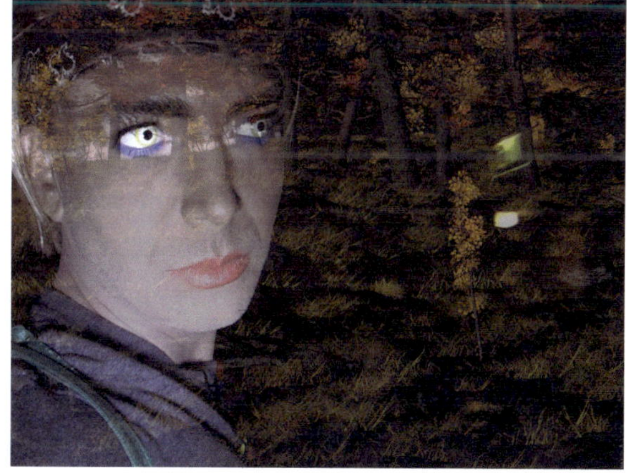

Figure C.3
SITE VISIT
(2014)

Closing Remarks

> I hope it will someday be possible to truly liberate ourselves into a state where expression is existence and the accumulation of our situations become more of a catalogue of our identity rather than a written history. Maybe our personalities can be the location rather than our bodies. It would be great if the body could be utterly neutral and malleable.[12]
>
> —Ryan Trecartin, *Fillip*, 2011

Trecartin's quote is emblematic of his outright rejection of essentialism and willingness to embrace change. As we have seen, the vertiginous pace of his montage, hybrid characters, and ever-shifting narratives do not conceal an underlying fear but rather an optimism toward the future. His work, which at first may appear jarring, actually reveals itself to be positive and empowering, transporting viewers into a journey of perpetual transformation. In all of his narratives, the protagonists fight to establish their agency in order to claim ownership over their destiny and more fully realize their humanity. This recurring theme in the work parallels the artist's unquenchable desire for infinite freedom, best exemplified through his distinctive visual language.

Feedback posted on his YouTube channel—such as ioana dobroiu's, "it's like i've already died and get to see a new behavioural perception of reality... gummy gum... it't [*sic*] something something... great"[13] or Joshlikestea's, "Your videos are the best thing that's ever happened to me"—corroborate that his work amounts to more than a critical observation of his own contemporaneity. His mass appeal is evident and the accessibility of the work has broad implications.

When contemplating his body of work, we recall that in *Early Baggage*, he had already established his idiosyncratic practice, consisting of appropriations of earlier experimental filmmaking and television techniques, which he revamped utilizing contemporary postproduction software. In *A Family Finds Entertainment*, he playfully remixed the cinematic tropes of the family melodrama, and further developed his vocabulary by introducing what would become his signature motif—the multiple screens. This work is followed by *I-BE Area*, where the artist blurs the lines between cyberspace and physical space by incorporating the web aesthetic into his visual style. Characteristic formal elements remained present—fast-paced editing, grotesque montage, superimposition, oblique camera angles, repetition, fragmented shots, and discontinuity—but there is definitely a leap toward a more technocentric approach. Computer desktop wallpapers, monitors, three-dimensional special effects, digital pictograms, and graphic user interface-inspired designs are interspersed throughout. *I-BE Area* was a significant turning point in Trecartin's career, as it firmly grounds his engagement with technology.

During the creation of the epic work *Any Ever*, the artist elevated the practice of multimedia layering to extreme heights by applying an abundance of two- and three-dimensional special effects to almost every shot of the seven individual videos concerned with branding and consumption. With *Priority Innfield*, Trecartin further disturbed the boundaries between technology and humanity. It is also with this work that he explored the possibilities of the postbody state rendering his protagonists' gravity-defying three-dimensional extensions of themselves using SketchUp and transparency filters. Although not completely "realistic," these three-dimensional animations do not appear unfamiliar. This process of cyborgization feels completely natural in the evolution of his work. It is as if we had expected this all along. Perhaps because Trecartin slowly prepared us for it, or perhaps because we have come to understand that existing in the world is now intrinsically connected with interacting with technology. Ryan Trecartin hopes to develop software to make his videos even more interactive and potentially reach a sense of enhanced physical connection. In an interview for *Dazed Digital*, he observed that he would like to create an app that would allow viewers to navigate his movies by typing key words linked to sequences.[14]

In February 2015, "Surround Audience," the New Museum of Contemporary Art triennial, co-curated by Ryan Trecartin and Lauren Cornell, opened to the public. The survey of contemporary art examined various modes of hypermediated cultural production and their effect on our understanding of selfhood and identity. The New Museum also inaugurated its first creative incubator, New Inc., located next door on the Bowery. Designed as a live/work environment, the space invites visual artists, architects, and scientists working with technology in experimental ways to collaborate on innovative interdisciplinary projects. Later in 2015, *Yielders Path* marked the first presentation of a Fitch/Trecartin work at Andrea Rosen Gallery. The sculptural installation featured a single-channel digital video with sound, large upholstered forms, pillows, sleeping bags, seating, artificial trees, logs, carpet, paint, low-frequency tactile transducers, drop ceiling with display screen, and lighting.

One year later, Ryan Trecartin and Lizzie Fitch's first solo exhibition at Andrea Rosen Gallery opened in March 2016.[15] For the occasion, the artists transformed the gallery space into a maze of passageways leading visitors to four distinct sculptural theaters each screening new movies, *Temple Time* (2016), *Mark Trade* (2016), *Stunt Tank* (2016), and *Permission Streak* (2016). Location shooting took place in the desert, canyons, forest, and lakes to convey the prevailing thematic subtext of nature replicated in the gallery with sculptural elements interspersed throughout the installations which included custom seats carved out of foam to resemble rocks, hot coal bins, park grills, and artificial trees.

The immersive environments featured projected movies that bled into the physical space in a manner that recalled *SITE VISIT*'s all-encompassing spatial composition and its remix of archival footage from the interior of the Masonic Temple. Yet, one cannot deny the striking stylistic departure of utilizing available lighting during location shooting, the almost complete absence of any special effects, and a preponderance of long takes in these films.

Characters are visibly mesmerized and bewildered by their natural surroundings, as if experiencing nonvirtual life for the first time. The all-pervasive soundtrack promotes an overall ominous feeling echoing *SITE VISIT*'s haunted mansion theme and Resident Evil's mood. The creation of this series, much like *SITE VISIT*, was primarily influenced by video gaming.[16] The characters-turned-avatars explore environments as if they were levels, acquiring objects along their seemingly endless quest. By emulating a gamic mode of exploration Fitch and Trecartin offer participants, like onscreen protagonists an opportunity to explore.

The investigation of the intersections between new technology and the world we live in has become a major focus in contemporary art. The importance given to spatial configuration in relation to technology in

Trecartin's *Priority Innfield* and *SITE VISIT* points to the fact that cyberspace is no longer viewed as an intangible software entity or space *outside* our physical reality, but as a pervasive presence imbedded within our DNA. Cyberspace can no longer be seen as *cyber* but simply as *space*. The online/offline binary divide is becoming increasingly obsolete, as wireless technology and Ethernet networks no longer need a switch button to transmit data.

Many contemporary artists have labeled their artistic practice "postinternet," in order to articulate this cultural shift. Michael Connor, curator and editor at Rhizome, further expands on the subject.

> It no longer makes sense for artists to attempt to come to terms with "internet culture," because now "internet culture" is increasingly just "culture." In other words, the term "post-internet" suggests that the focus of a good deal of artistic and critical discourse has shifted from "internet culture" as a discrete entity to an awareness that all culture has been reconfigured by the internet, or by internet-enabled neoliberal capitalism.[17]

Yet, the term *postinternet* is still problematic as it suggests a distance or break from the internet. Whether the artwork is directly created online or is simply influenced by the web, it remains in direct conversation with technological mediation. Lauren Cornell also points to the term's limitations when she remarks that "the term 'Post-internet' needs to be broken down, since it encompasses so many diverse practices."[18]

Trecartin's art cannot be categorized as "postinternet," nor can it be called internet art, since it is located in-between analog and virtual space. The artist understands that the internet is not comprised of hardware but software. That is to say, the World Wide Web, as its name suggests, is a hyperobject, an entity massively distributed that surpasses spatiotemporal specificity.[19] The internet, and more broadly, digital culture, is much more than a medium, as it extends into every aspect of our lives. Trecartin's work can be situated online but also exists within art institutions, movie theaters, and galleries. It successfully manages to extend the digital realm beyond the limitations of the subject, the screen, and the internal logic of machinery into our familiar physical world. When experiencing a Trecartin work, whether it is set up as a multichannel installation or displayed on a singular computer monitor, we come to understand, intrinsically and viscerally, that what we are witnessing is in fact an acute visual manifestation of the integrated networked manner in which we engage with the world today.

In an interview with Calvin Tomkins in the *New Yorker*, the artist expressed his own understanding of how his work functions.

> Everything we do is going to be captured and archived in an accessible form, whether you want it or not. It's going to change all of our lives. We are a species that can no longer assume a sense of privacy. It's not an individual decision, and I feel that's exciting to explore—or something. There's a lot of cultural content being generated right now that sees itself as post-human, but it's assuming the twentieth century as its audience. It leans on structures that we already understand, but that we're moving away from. My work is about humanity, and about the time I'm making it.[20]

The significance of Trecartin's art is in part due to how it addresses a major societal shift in the consumption and dissemination of culture. His idiosyncratic practice, characterized by multilinearity, multimediality, interactivity, and the grotesque montage, furthers our understanding of technology's potentially liberating power while also acknowledging its shortcomings. The work proposes new modes of existing in the world and ways of thinking about identity, time, and space.

Many art critics have claimed that Trecartin's movies are bewilderingly accelerated, so much so that it is almost impossible to concentrate on the narrative or remember any of the characters. Yet, if one spends time with the work, it becomes evident that although the videos are fast-paced, their speed is in fact representative of the momentum of contemporary life. The artist amplifies our level of awareness by questioning and challenging what it means to be human in our globally connected mediascape. However, Ryan Trecartin does not attempt to provide any definitive answer. He, too, is in the midst of an ongoing process of self-realization. We are, therefore, left to our own devices, navigating and exploring the cyberworld's gigantic sea of content—an experience that is as daunting as it is freeing.

Notes

Introduction

1. Peter Schjeldahl, Party On: Ryan Trecartin at P.S. 1," *New Yorker*, June 27, 2011, 84.
2. Roberta Smith, "Like Living, Only More So," *New York Times*, June 24, 2011, Arts and Entertainment, C25.
3. Ibid.
4. Ibid.
5. Jeffrey Deitch, "The Post-Reality Show," in *Any Ever: Ryan Trecartin* (New York: Skira Rizzoli Publications in association with Elizabeth Dee, 2011), p. 7.
6. Ibid.
7. Dennis Cooper, "First Take, Dennis Cooper on Ryan Trecartin," *Artforum*, January 2006.
8. Ryan Trecartin, (*Tommy-Chat Just E-mailed Me*), http://www.eai.org/titleOrderingFees.htm?id=12462 (2006).
9. Omar Kholeif, *Moving Image* (Cambridge, Mass.: MIT Press, 2015), p. 137.
10. Ryan Trecartin views the body as a blank canvas onto which "personalities" are projected and articulated. In an interview with Arthur Lubow, he was quoted as saying, "I see people as being what their personality is at the moment of expression. I feel genitals hold us back a lot. They keep us connected to our older ideals of humanity [. . .] I think it's really interesting that there are a lot of trannies now who are in transition and want to be in transition—they don't want to be a man or a woman [. . .] The more nuanced we get, the more things people want to be."
11. Chris Wiley, "We Have a Situation," *Frieze* 142 (October 2011).
12. Quote taken from *K-CoreaINC.K* (*Section a*) (2010).
13. Roberta Smith, "Like Living, Only More So," *New York Times*, June 24, 2011, Arts and Entertainment, C25.
14. Lev Manovich, "What Is Digital Cinema?" in *Critical Visions in Film Theory: Classic and Contemporary Readings*, ed. Timothy Corrigan, Patricia White, and Meta Mazaj (Boston: Bedford/St. Martin's, 2011), pp. 1060–70.

15. Jon Silber, "Interview with Ryan Trecartin, Video Artist, 'Any Ever,'" http://www.creativeplanetnetwork.com/dv/feature/interview-ryan-trecartin-video-artist-any-ever/16738 (2011).

16. Trecartin, interview with Kristina Lee Podesva, "When the Time Comes You Won't Understand the Battlefield," *Fillip* 13 (Spring 2011): 103.

17. Mary Jordan, interview with George Kuchar, from *Jack Smith and the Destruction of Atlantis*. Film. Directed by Mary Jordan (Brooklyn, NY: Tongue Press), 2006.

18. The term *butch queen* is used to describe masculine-looking drag queens. The term *vogue femme* is employed to describe female impersonators with exaggerated feminine movements influenced by ballet. The term *girlfag* is used to describe female-born individuals who feel a strong attraction to gay and bisexual men, and gay male culture. The term *guydyke* is used to describe male-born individuals attracted to lesbians, bisexual women, and lesbian culture.

19. Julia Stoschek, and Julia Stoschek Foundation, *Collection Number Six: Flaming Creatures* [in parallel text in English and German], vol. 1 (Deutschland: Hatje Cantz, 2013).

20. Ibid.

21. Richard Dyer, *Now You See It: Studies on Lesbian and Gay Film*, 2nd ed. (London; New York: Routledge, 2003), p. 149.

22. P. Adams Sitney, *Visionary Film: The American Avant-Garde, 1943–2000*, 3rd ed. (Oxford; New York: Oxford University Press, 2002), p. 349.

23. Chris Meigh-Andrews, *A History of Video Art: The Development of Form and Function* (Oxford; New York: Berg, 2006), p. 13.

24. Ibid.

25. Ibid., 9.

26. Ibid., 8.

27. Tracey Warr, and Amelia Jones. *The Artist's Body* (London; New York: Phaidon, 2012), p. 92.

28. Ryan Trecartin et al., *Any Ever: Ryan Trecartin* (New York: Skira Rizzoli Publications in association with Elizabeth Dee, 2011), p. 144.

29. Quote taken from *Junior War* (2013).

30. Glenn Phillips and J. Paul Getty Museum, *California Video: Artists and Histories* (Los Angeles: Getty Research Institute and the J. Paul Getty Museum, 2008), p. 12.

31. John Fiske, *Television Culture* (London; New York: Methuen, 1987), p. 99.

32. Goldberg, RoseLee, *Performance Art: From Futurism to the Present*, 3rd ed. (New York: Thames & Hudson, 2011), p. 9.

33. Judith Halberstam, *In a Queer Time and Place: Transgender Bodies, Subcultural Lives* (New York: New York University Press, 2005), p. 6.

34. Ibid.

35. Terry Smith, *What Is Contemporary Art?* (Chicago: University of Chicago Press, 2009), pp. 243–71.

36. Ibid., 241.

37. Ibid., 4.

38. Ibid., 6.

39. Katie Kitamura and Hari Kunzru, "Ryan Trecartin: In Conversation," *Frieze* 142 (October 2011).

40. Nicolas Bourriaud and Tate Britain, *Altermodern: Tate Triennial* (London: Tate Publishing, 2009), p. 18.

41. Elizabeth Freeman, *Time Binds: Queer Temporalities, Queer Histories* (Durham, N.C.: Duke University Press, 2010), p. 11.

42. Ibid., 23.

43. Nicolas Bourriaud and Tate Britain, *Altermodern: Tate Triennial* (London: Tate Publishing, 2009), p. 13.

44. Ibid., 20.

45. Ryan Trecartin et al., *Any Ever: Ryan Trecartin* (New York: Skira Rizzoli Publications in association with Elizabeth Dee, 2011), p. 144.

46. Whitney Ford, "The Q&A: Ryan Trecartin, Video Artist," http://moreintelligentlife.com/blog/whitney-ford/qa-ryan-trecartin (2010).

47. Judith Halberstam, *In a Queer Time and Place: Transgender Bodies, Subcultural Lives* (New York: New York University Press, 2005), p. 1.

48. Ibid.

49. Ibid.

50. Nicolas Bourriaud and Tate Britain, *Altermodern: Tate Triennial* (London: Tate Publishing, 2009), p. 22.

51. José Esteban Muñoz, *Disidentifications: Queers of Color and the Performance of Politics* (Minneapolis: University of Minnesota Press, 1999), p. 31.

52. Ibid., 11–12.

53. Ibid.

54. Ibid., 32.

55. Ibid., 161.

56. Ibid., 165.

57. Kevin McGarry, "Ryan," *V Magazine*, February 2015.

58. Alexander Doty, *Flaming Classics: Queering the Film Canon* (New York: Routledge, 2000), p. 6.

59. Ibid., 7.

60. Ibid.

61. Jodie Taylor, *Playing It Queer: Popular Music, Identity and Queer World-Making* (Bern: Peter Lang, 2012), p. 100.

62. Whitney Ford, "The Q&A: Ryan Trecartin, Video Artist," http://moreintelligentlife.com/blog/whitney-ford/qa-ryan-trecartin (2010).

63. Mikhail Bakhtin,. *Rabelais and His World* (Cambridge, Mass.: MIT Press, 1968), p. 317.

64. Ibid.

65. Ibid., 320.

66. Ibid., 10.

67. Julia Kristeva, *Powers of Horror: An Essay on Abjection*. European Perspectives (New York: Columbia University Press, 1982), p. 4.

68. Ibid.

69. Victor Turner, "Carnival in Rio: Dionysian Drama in an Industrialized Society," in *The Anthropology of Performance* (New York: PAJ Publications, 1986), p. 105.

70. Ibid., 104.

71. Ibid., 118.

72. Ryan Trecartin et al., *Any Ever: Ryan Trecartin* (New York: Skira Rizzoli Publications in association with Elizabeth Dee, 2011), p. 143.

73. Robert Stam, *Subversive Pleasures: Bakhtin, Cultural Criticism, and Film* (Baltimore, Md.: Johns Hopkins University Press, 1989), p. 86.

74. Ibid., 110.

75. Ibid., 110–11.

76. Ibid., 115.

77. Francesco Bonami, "The Good, the Bad, and the Ugly." *Frieze* 141 (September 2011).

78. Trecartin, interview with Kristina Lee Podesva, "When the Time Comes You Won't Understand the Battlefield," *Fillip* 13 (Spring 2011): 103.

79. Caryl Flinn, "The Deaths of Camp," in *Camp: Queer Aesthetics and the Performing Subject: A Reader* ed. Fabio Cleto (Ann Arbor: University of Michigan Press, 1999), p. 447.

80. Susan Sontag, "Notes on 'Camp,'" in *Camp: Queer Aesthetics and the Performing Subject: A Reader*, ed. Fabio Cleto (Ann Arbor: University of Michigan Press, 1999), pp. 64–65.

81. Jack Babuscio, "The Cinema of Camp," in *Camp: Queer Aesthetics and the Performing Subject: A Reader*, ed. Fabio Cleto (Ann Arbor: University of Michigan Press, 1999), p. 118.

82. Ibid.

83. Aymar Jean Christian, "Camp 2.0: A Queer Performance of the Personal," *Communication, Culture, & Critique* 3, no. 3 (2010): 352–76.

84. Ibid.

85. Jonathan T. D. Neil, "Ryan Trecartin: Taking the Real World to Another Planet," *Art Review*, September 2010.

86. Jon Silber, "Interview with Ryan Trecartin, Video Artist, 'Any Ever,'" http://www.creativeplanetnetwork.com/dv/feature/interview-ryan-trecartin-video-artist-any-ever/16738 (2011).

87. Douglas Davis, "The Work of Art in the Age of Digital Reproduction (An Evolving Thesis: 1991–1995)," *Leonardo* 28, no. 5, Third Annual New York Digital Salon (1995): 381–86.

88. Trecartin, interview with Kristina Lee Podesva, "When the Time Comes You Won't Understand the Battlefield," *Fillip* 13 (Spring 2011): 103.

89. Nicolas Bourriaud, *Relational Aesthetics* (Dijon: Les Presses du réel, 2002), pp. 17–18.

90. Ibid., 61.

91. Ryan Trecartin et al., *Any Ever: Ryan Trecartin* (New York: Skira Rizzoli Publications in association with Elizabeth Dee, 2011).

92. Ryan Trecartin and Lizzie Fitch also work collaboratively as "Fitch/Trecartin" primarily creating sculptures and installations.

93. Calvin Tomkins, "Experimental People," *New Yorker*, March 24, 2014.

94. John Roberts, *The Intangibilities of Form: Skill and Deskilling in Art after the Readymade* (London; New York: Verso, 2007), p. 181.

95. Ryan Trecartin et al., *Any Ever: Ryan Trecartin* (New York: Skira Rizzoli Publications in association with Elizabeth Dee, 2011), p. 146.

96. Francesco Bonami, "The Good, the Bad, and the Ugly," in *Frieze* 141 (September 2011).

Chapter 1

1. Randy Kennedy, "His Nonlinear Reality, and Welcome to It," *New York Times*, February 1, 2009, Arts and Entertainment, p. 1(L).

2. Linda Norden, "When the Rainbow Is an Option," in *Any Ever: Ryan Trecartin* (New York: Skira Rizzoli Publications in association with Elizabeth Dee, 2011), p. 12.

3. Ibid.

4. Ryan Trecartin and James Franco, "All-American Golden Boy," *Another Man*, November 2010.

5. Trecartin uses the term *personality* specifically because according to him, "personality [. . .] can be changed or reworked at will, while not being classified or grouped very easily." Quoted from "The Q&A: Ryan Trecartin, Video Artist," by Whitney Ford, http://moreintelligentlife.com/blog/whitney-ford/qa-ryan-trecartin (2010).

6. From the BAMcinématek press release for the fifth annual Migrating Forms film festival.

7. Susan Sontag, "Notes on 'Camp,' " in *Camp: Queer Aesthetics and the Performing Subject: A Reader*, ed. Fabio Cleto (Ann Arbor: University of Michigan Press, 1999), p. 54.

8. Jack Babuscio, "The Cinema of Camp," in *Camp: Queer Aesthetics and the Performing Subject: A Reader*, ed. Fabio Cleto. (University of Michigan Press, 1999), p. 122.

9. Ryan Trecartin and James Franco, "All-American Golden Boy," in *Another Man*, November 2010.

10. Amelia Jones, Self/Image: Technology, Representation, and the Contemporary Subject (London; New York: Routledge, 2006), p. 234.

11. Robert Stam, *Subversive Pleasures: Bakhtin, Cultural Criticism, and Film* (Baltimore, Md.: Johns Hopkins University Press, 1989), p. 86.

12. Mikhail Bakhtin, *Rabelais and His World* (Cambridge, Mass.: MIT Press, 1968), p. 11.

13. Ibid., 317.

14. Julia Kristeva, *Powers of Horror: An Essay on Abjection*. European Perspectives (New York: Columbia University Press, 1982), p. 4.

15. Ajay RS Hothi and Christabel Stewart, "Pop Eats Itself," *Tank Magazine* 53 (May 2011).

16. J. Hoberman, *Jack Smith and His Secret Flix*, Program Notes for the American Museum of the Moving Image, January 5, 1998.

17. Wayne Koestenbaum, "Situation Hacker," *Artforum* 47, no. 10, Summer 2009.

18. Ryan Trecartin and James Franco, "All-American Golden Boy," *Another Man*, November 2010.

19. Comment can be found at http://www.youtube.com/user/WianTreetin/discussion (2007).

20. Carol Vernallis, *Experiencing Music Video: Aesthetics and Cultural Context* (Columbia University Press, 2004), p. 3.

21. Ryan Trecartin and James Franco, "All-American Golden Boy," in *Another Man*, November 2010.

22. Jessica Helfand, *Screen: Essays on Graphic Design, New Media, and Visual Culture* (New York: Princeton Architectural Press, 2001), p. 125.

23. Jeremy G. Butler, *Television: Critical Methods and Applications*, 4th ed. (New York: Routledge, 2012), p. 12.

24. Karen Brooks, "Nothing Sells Like Teen Spirit: The Commodification of Youth Culture in *Youth Cultures: Texts, Images, and Identities*, ed. Kerry Mallan and Sharyn Pearce (Westport, Conn.: Praeger, 2003), pp. 3, 13.

25. Jeremy G. Butler, *Television: Critical Methods and Applications*, 4th ed. (New York: Routledge, 2012), p. 44.

26. Brooke E. Duffy, Tara Liss-Marino, and Katherine Sender, "Reflexivity in Television Depictions of Media Industries: Peeking Behind the Gilt Curtain," *Communication, Culture & Critique* 4, no. 3 (September 2011): 296–313.

27. Robert Stam, *Reflexivity in Film and Literature: From Don Quixote to Jean-Luc Godard* (Ann Arbor, MI: UMI Research Press, 1985), p. 16.

28. Karen Brooks, "Nothing Sells Like Teen Spirit: The Commodification of Youth Culture," in *Youth Cultures: Texts, Images, and Identities*, ed. Kerry Mallan and Sharyn Pearce (Westport, Conn.: Praeger, 2003), p. 14.

29. Quote by Ryan Trecartin found at http://www.saatchigallery.com/artists/ryan_trecartin.htm.

30. Mikhail Bakhtin, *Rabelais and His World* (Cambridge, Mass.: MIT Press, 1968), p. 317.

31. Judith Butler, *Gender Trouble: Feminism and the Subversion of Identity* (New York: Routledge, 1999), pp. 169–70.

32. Arthur Lubow, "Ryan's Web," *W* 11, 2010, 138.

33. Karen Brooks, "Nothing Sells Like Teen Spirit: The Commodification of Youth Culture," in *Youth Cultures: Texts, Images, and Identities*, ed. Kerry Mallan and Sharyn Pearce (Westport, Conn.: Praeger, 2003), p. 1.

34. David Oswell, "A Question of Belonging: Television, Youth and the Domestic," in *Cool Places: Geographies of Youth Cultures*, ed. Tracey Skelton and Gill Valentine (London: Routledge, 1998), pp. 35–49.

35. Kevin McGarry, "Worlds Apart," in *Any Ever: Ryan Trecartin* (New York: Skira Rizzoli Publications in association with Elizabeth Dee, 2011).

Chapter 2

1. Dennis Cooper, "First Take, Dennis Cooper on Ryan Trecartin," *Artforum*, January 2006.

2. Ibid.

3. Thomas Schatz, *Hollywood Genres: Formulas, Filmmaking, and the Studio System* (Philadelphia: Temple University Press, 1981), p. 221.

4. Term coined by Thomas Elsaesser in "Tales of Sound and Fury: Observations on the Family Melodrama," first published in *Monogram* 4 (1972): 2–15.

5. Thomas, Schatz, *Hollywood Genres: Formulas, Filmmaking, and the Studio System* (Philadelphia: Temple University Press, 1981), p. 224.

6. John Mercer, and Martin Shingler. *Melodrama: Genre, Style, Sensibility* (London; New York: Wallflower, 2004), p. 1.

7. Randy Kennedy, "His Non-Linear Reality, and Welcome to It," *New York Times*, February 1, 2009, AR1.

8. Stefan Sonvilla-Weiss, *Mashup Cultures* (Vienna; New York: Springer-Verlag, 2010), p. 9.

9. Judith Halberstam, *In a Queer Time and Place: Transgender Bodies, Subcultural Lives.* Sexual Cultures (New York: New York University Press, 2005), p. 4.

10. Jane Shattuc, *Television, Tabloids, and Tears Fassbinder and Popular Culture*, (Minneapolis: University of Minnesota Press, 1994), p. 101.

11. Elizabeth Grosz, "Bodies and Pleasures in Queer Theory," *Who Can Speak? Authority and Critical Identity*, ed. Judith Roof and Robyn Wiegman (Urbana: University of Illinois Press, 1995), p. 223.

12. Richard Troiden's queer identity development model in *Sexual Orientation in Child and Adolescent Health Care* by Ellen C. Perrin (New York: Kluwer Academic, 2002), p. 74.

13. Calvin Tomkins, "Experimental People," *New Yorker*, March 24, 2014.

14. Roberta Smith, "Like Living, Only More So," *New York Times*, June 24, 2011, Arts and Entertainment, C25.

15. Calvin Tomkins, "Experimental People," *New Yorker*, March 24, 2014.

16. Barbara Klinger, *Melodrama and Meaning: History, Culture, and the Films of Douglas Sirk* (Bloomington: Indiana University Press, 1994), p. 143.

17. Eve Kosofsky Sedgwick, *Epistemology of the Closet* (Berkeley, Calif.: University of California Press, 2008).

18. Ibid., p. 3.

19. Thomas Elsaesser, "Tales of Sound and Fury: Observations on the Family Melodrama," in *Home Is Where the Heart Is: Studies in Melodrama and the Woman's Film*, ed. C. Gledhill (London: British Film Institute, 1987), p. 61.

20. Joe Swanberg, "*A Family Finds Entertainment*: An Ongoing Discussion with Ryan Trecartin," http://www.filmbrats.com/editorials/ryantrecartin.html.

21. Arthur Lubow, "Ryan's Web," *W* 11, 2010, 138.

22. John Mercer, and Martin Shingler, *Melodrama: Genre, Style, Sensibility* (London; New York: Wallflower, 2004), p. 54.

23. Ibid., 13.

24. Arthur Lubow, "Ryan's Web," *W* 11, 2010, 138.

25. Ibid.

26. Ibid.

27. John Mercer and Martin Shingler, *Melodrama: Genre, Style, Sensibility* (London; New York: Wallflower, 2004), p. 13.

28. Calvin Tomkins, "Experimental People," *New Yorker*, March 24, 2014.

29. Barbara Klinger, *Melodrama and Meaning: History, Culture, and the Films of Douglas Sirk* (Bloomington: Indiana University Press, 1994), p. 142.

30. Steele, Bruce C. "Justifying Our Love: Pedro Zamora," in *Advocate*, November 12, 2012, p. 80.

31. Bruce Handy, "He Called Me Ellen Degenerate?" *Time* (April 13, 1997).

32. Darryl Littleton, and Tuezdae Littleton, *Comediennes: Laugh Be a Lady* (Milwaukee, Wis.: Applause Theatre & Cinema Books, 2012).

33. Ivan Petrella, "Queer Eye for the Straight Guy: The Making Over of Liberation Theology, A Queer Discursive Approach," in *Liberation Theology and Sexuality*, ed. Marcella Althaus-Reid (England; Burlington, Vt.: Ashgate, 2006), p. 33.

34. Steve Neale, "Melodrama and Tears," in *Screen* 27, no. 6 (1986): 6–22.

35. *Ze*. Gender-neutral third-person singular subject pronoun. In *Language and Gender* by Penelope Eckert and Sally McConnell-Ginet (Cambridge, U.K.; New York: Cambridge University Press, 2013), p. 217.

36. Lubow, Arthur. "Ryan's Web," *W* 11, 2010, 138.

37. *Zir*. Gender-neutral third-person singular subject pronoun. In *Language and Gender* by Penelope Eckert and Sally McConnell-Ginet (Cambridge, U.K.; New York: Cambridge University Press, 2013), p. 217.

38. John H. Haig, and Andrew Nathaniel. *The New Nelson Japanese-English Character Dictionary* (Rutland, Vt.; Tokyo: C. E. Tuttle Co., 1997), p. 1083.

39. Thomas Elsaesser, "Tales of Sound and Fury: Observations on the Family Melodrama," in *Home Is Where the Heart Is: Studies in Melodrama and the Woman's Film*, ed. C. Gledhill (London: British Film Institute, 1987), p. 59.

40. Arthur Lubow, "Ryan's Web," *W* 11, 2010, 138.

41. John, Mercer, and Martin Shingler, *Melodrama: Genre, Style, Sensibility* (London; New York: Wallflower, 2004), p. 60.

Chapter 3

1. Smith, Terry. *What Is Contemporary Art*? (Chicago: University of Chicago Press, 2009), p. 4.

2. Nell Tenhaaf, "Mysteries of the Bioapparatus," in *Immersed in Technology: Art and Virtual Environments*, ed. Mary Anne Moser and Douglas MacLeod (Cambridge, Mass.: MIT Press, 1996), p. 52.

3. Matilda Tudor, *Cyberqueer Techno-Practices: Digital Space-Making and Networking Among Swedish Gay Men* (MA thesis, Stockholm University, 2012), p. 7.

4. Nina Wakeford, "Cyberqueer," in *Sexualities: Critical Concepts in Sociology*, ed. Kenneth Plummer (Routledge, 2002), p. 352.

5. Ibid.

6. Pramod K. Nayar, *An Introduction to New Media and Cybercultures* (Chichester, West Sussex, U.K.; Malden, MA: Wiley-Blackwell, 2010), p. 133.

7. Nicolas Bourriaud, "Altermodern Manifesto: Postmodernism Is Dead," http://www.tate.org.uk/whats-on/tate-britain/exhibition/altermodern/explain-altermodern/altermodern-explainedmanifesto (2009).

8. Ibid.

9. Nicolas Bourriaud and Tate Britain, *Altermodern: Tate Triennial* (London: Tate Publishing, 2009), p. 13.

10. Ryan Trecartin et al., *Any Ever: Ryan Trecartin* (New York: Skira Rizzoli Publications in association with Elizabeth Dee, 2011), p. 143.

11. Jennifer Lange, "interview with Director Ryan Trecartin," http://wexarts.org/blog/interview-director-ryan-trecartin (2008).

12. Natalie Kessel. "Ryan Trecartin in conversation with LP studio," http://www.youtube.com/watch?v=u2uUq91FVjU (2011).

13. Patricia R. Zimmermann, "An Amateurized Media Universe," *Jump Cut* 55 (Fall 2013).

14. Massimiliano Gioni, "We Are Too Many," in *Younger Than Jesus: The Generation Book*, ed. by Lauren Cornell and New Museum of Contemporary Art (New York: New Museum; Göttingen: Steidl, 2009), p. 38.

15. Ibid.

16. Lisa Phillips, "Director's Foreword," in *Younger Than Jesus: The Generation Book*, ed. Lauren Cornell and New Museum of Contemporary Art (New York: New Museum; Göttingen: Steidl, 2009), p. 7.

17. Lauren Cornell, "New Age Thinking," in *Younger Than Jesus: The Generation Book*, ed. Lauren Cornell and New Museum of Contemporary Art (New York: New Museum; Göttingen: Steidl, 2009), p. 19.

18. Laura Hoptman, "Them," in *Younger Than Jesus: The Generation Book*, ed. Lauren Cornell and New Museum of Contemporary Art (New York: New Museum; Göttingen: Steidl, 2009), p. 45.

19. Joel Stein. "Millennials: The Me Me Me Generation," http://time.com/247/millennials-the-me-me-me-generation/ (May 20, 2013)

20. Natalie Kessel. "Ryan Trecartin in conversation with LP studio," http://www.youtube.com/watch?v=u2uUq91FVjU (2011).

21. Massimiliano Gioni, "We Are Too Many," in *Younger Than Jesus: The Generation Book*, ed. Lauren Cornell and New Museum of Contemporary Art (New York: New Museum; Göttingen: Steidl, 2009), p. 34.

22. Comment can be found at http://www.youtube.com/user/WianTreetin/discussion (2008).

23. Terry Smith, *What Is Contemporary Art?* (Chicago: University of Chicago Press, 2009), p. 262.

24. Ryan Trecartin and David Karp for Rhizome's "Seven on Seven Technology and Art Conference," 2010.

25. Sam Pulitzer, "Ryan Trecartin," *Artforum*, September, 2011.

26. Kevin McGarry, *Ryan Trecartin*, Hammer Projects Catalogue (Los Angeles: Hammer Museum, 2008).

27. James Bridle, "#Hackyourfuture: Hack the word!," http://www.dazeddigital.com/artsandculture/ article/16298/1/hackyourfuture-hack-the-word, (July 2013).

28. Arthur Lubow, "Ryan's Web," *W* 11, 2010, 138.

29. YouTube Statistics at http://www.youtube.com/yt/press/statistics.html.

30. Hal Niedzviecki, *The Peep Diaries: How We're Learning to Love Watching Ourselves and Our Neighbors* (San Francisco, CA: City Lights Books, 2009), p. 27.

31. Lisa Nakamura, *Cybertypes: Race, Ethnicity, and Identity on the Internet* (New York: Routledge, 2002), p. 35.

32. Description of Jeffree avatar at https://marketplace.secondlife.com/p/JEFFREE-full-drag-queen-avatar-included-AO/2832962.

33. Ibid.

34. A reference to Linda Montano's performance piece *Seven Years of Living Art* (1984–1991) in which she lived in a monochromatic room wearing color-matched outfits for one year at a time, expressing a different personality for each cycle.

35. Kevin McGarry, *Ryan Trecartin*, Hammer Projects Catalogue (Los Angeles: Hammer Museum, 2008).

36. Ibid.

37. Judith Halberstam, *In a Queer Time and Place: Transgender Bodies, Subcultural Lives* (New York: New York University Press, 2005), p. 174.

38. Ibid.

39. Ibid., 1–2.

40. Ibid.

41. Amelia Jones, *Self/Image: Technology, Representation, and the Contemporary Subject* (London; New York: Routledge, 2006), p. 87.

42. Tom Boellstorff, "Virtuality: Placing the Virtual Body: Avatar, Chora, Cypherg," in *A Companion to the Anthropology of the Body and Embodiment*, ed. Frances E. Mascia-Lees (Chichester, West Sussex, U.K.; Malden, MA: Wiley-Blackwell, 2011), p. 506.

43. Judith Halberstam, *In a Queer Time and Place: Transgender Bodies, Subcultural Lives* (New York: New York University Press, 2005), pp. 15, 36.

44. Ibid.

45. Steve Silberman, "We're Teen, We're Queer, and We've Got E-mail," in *The Columbia Reader on Lesbians and Gay Men in Media, Society, and Politics*, ed. Larry P. Gross and James D. Woods (New York: Columbia University Press, 1999), p. 537.

46. Nicolas Bourriaud and Tate Britain, *Altermodern: Tate Triennial* (London: Tate Publishing, 2009), p. 22.

47. http://wiki.secondlife.com/wiki/The_Corn_Field.

48. Rachel Falconer, "Rebooting the Relationship between Art and Tech," http://www.theguardian.com/technology/2014/jan/29/rebooting-the-relationship-between-art-and-tech (January 29, 2014).

49. Ibid.

50. Kevin McGarry, "Ryan Trecartin," Hammer Projects Catalogue (Los Angeles: Hammer Museum, 2008).

51. From the BAMcinématek press release for the fifth annual Migrating Forms film festival.

52. Kevin McGarry, "Worlds Apart," in *Any Ever: Ryan Trecartin* (New York: Skira Rizzoli Publications in association with Elizabeth Dee, 2011), p. 111.

53. Calvin Tomkins, "Experimental People," *New Yorker*, March 24, 2014.

54. Ryan Trecartin and James Franco, "All-American Golden Boy," *Another Man*, November 2010.

Chapter 4

1. Lauren Cornell, "Medium Living," in *Any Ever: Ryan Trecartin* (New York: Skira Rizzoli Publications in association with Elizabeth Dee, 2011), p. 55.
2. Randy Kennedy, "His Non-Linear Reality, and Welcome to It," *New York Times*, February 1, 2009.
3. Ibid.
4. Trecartin, interview with Kristina Lee Podesva, "When the Time Comes You Won't Understand the Battlefield," *Fillip* 13 (Spring 2011): 103.
5. Ibid.
6. Randy Kennedy, "His Non-Linear Reality, and Welcome to It," *New York Times*, February 1, 2009.
7. Diana Crane, *Fashion and Its Social Agendas: Class, Gender, and Identity in Clothing* (Chicago: University of Chicago Press, 2000), p. 134.
8. David Jacob Kramer, "Controlling the Chaos," *Paper*, June 17, 2011.
9. Lauren Cornell, "Medium Living," in *Any Ever: Ryan Trecartin* (New York: Skira Rizzoli Publications in association with Elizabeth Dee, 2011), p. 55.
10. Trecartin, interview with Kristina Lee Podesva, "When the Time Comes You Won't Understand the Battlefield," *Fillip* 13 (Spring 2011): 103.
11. Katie Kitamura and Hari Kunzru, "Ryan Trecartin: In Conversation," *Frieze* 142 (October 2011).
12. Theodor Adorno and Max Horkheimer, "The Culture Industry: Enlightenment as Mass Deception," in *Critical Visions in Film Theory: Classic and Contemporary Readings*, ed. Timothy Corrigan, Patricia White, and Meta Mazaj (Boston: Bedford/St. Martin's, 2011), p. 1016.
13. K-Hole, "Youth Mode: A Report on Freedom by K-Hole and Box 1824," available at http://khole.net/.
14. Joanne Entwistle, "Fashion and the Fleshy Body: Dress as Embodied Practice," in *Fashion Theory* 4, no. 3: 329 (2000).
15. Roland Barthes and Andy Stafford, *The Language of Fashion* (Oxford; New York: Berg, 2006), p. 13.

16. Joanne Entwistle, "Fashion and the Fleshy Body: Dress as Embodied Practice," in *Fashion Theory* 4, no. 3: 329 (2000).

17. Francesca Granata, "Decentering Fashion: Carnival Performance and the Grotesque Body," in *Not a Toy: Radical Character Design in Fashion and Costume* (Berlin: Pictoplasma, 2011), p. 21.

18. Patrizia Calefato. *The Clothed Body* (New York: Berg, 2004), p. 32.

19. Granata, Francesca. *Experimental Fashion: Performance Art, Carnival and the Grotesque Body* (I. B.Tauris, 2017), p. 1.

20. Mikhail Bakhtin, *Rabelais and His World* (Cambridge, Mass.: MIT Press, 1968), p. 26.

21. Francesca Granata, "Decentering Fashion: Carnival Performance and the Grotesque Body," in *Not a Toy: Radical Character Design in Fashion and Costume* (Berlin: Pictoplasma, 2011), p. 25.

22. Ryan Trecartin, "Ryan's Web 1.0," http://dismagazine.com/dysmor-phia/9844/ryan-trecartin-w-magazine/ (2010).

23. During a Q&A event at Florida International University as part of the Helen Venero Artist Lecture Series, Ryan Trecartin responded to Ricardo E. Zulueta's question regarding the artist's role in the *W* magazine shoot of November 2010 (November 19, 2014).

24. Ryan Trecartin, "Ryan's Web 1.0," http://dismagazine.com/dysmor phia/9844/ryan-trecartin-w-magazine/ (2010).

25. Quote from *The Devil Wears Prada*, film, directed by David Frankel, Twentieth Century Fox, 2006.

26. Katie Kitamuraand Hari Kunzru, "Ryan Trecartin: In Conversation," *Frieze* 142 (October 2011).

27. Ryan Trecartin, "Ryan's Web 1.0," http://dismagazine.com/dysmor phia/9844/ryan-trecartin-w-magazine/ (2010).

28. Ibid.

29. Ibid.

30. Solway, Diane. "Placebo Pets: How Kendall Jenner and Gigi Hadid Became Humanoid Creatures for W," in *W* magazine (October 20, 2016).

31. Ibid.

32. Ibid.

33. Ibid.

34. David Howes, *Empire of the Senses: The Sensual Culture Reader* (Oxford: Berg, 2005), p. 286.

35. Ibid., 294.

36. Trecartin, interview with Kristina Lee Podesva, "When the Time Comes You Won't Understand the Battlefield," *Fillip* 13 (Spring 2011): 103.

37. Lauren Cornell, "Techno-animism," *Mousse* 37 (February 2013).

38. Ibid.

39. Agatha Wara, "What Does Nike Want?" http://dismagazine.com/dystopia/evolved-lifestyles/32718/what-does-nike-want/ (May 24, 2012).

40. Ibid.

41. Ryan Trecartin, "Ryan's Web 1.0," at http://dismagazine.com/dysmorphia/9844/ryan-trecartin-w-magazine/ (2010).

42. Ibid.

43. Ibid.

44. Ibid.

45. Ibid.

46. Ibid.

47. Ana Cecilia Alvarez, "How to Hide from Big Brother," *Dazed Digital*, http://www.dazeddigital.com/artsandculture/article/19131/1/artists-writers-show-how-to-hide-from-big-brother-government-surveillance (March 2014).

48. Ginger Gregg Duggan and Judith Hoos Fox, "Characters on Parade: Contemporary Character Design Invades the Catwalk," in *Not a Toy: Radical Character Design in Fashion and Costume* (Berlin: Pictoplasma, 2011), p. 9.

49. http://dismagazine.com/blog/45870/behind-the-scenes-ryan-trecartins-new-movie/ (May 31, 2013).

50. Dodie Kazanjian, "The Body Eccentric," *Vogue*, February 2010.

51. Antje Krause-Wahl, "Between Studio and Catwalk—Artists in Fashion Magazines," *Fashion Theory* 13, no. 1: 16.

52. Ibid., p. 19.

53. Vanessa Beecroft has art directed Kanye West fashion shows: Yeezy season 1 (fall/winter 2015), season 2 (spring/summer 2016), season 3 (fall/winter 2016), and season 4 (spring/summer 2017).

54. *W* magazine, November 2010, 152.

55. Gabby Bess, "DISown Blows Away the Boundaries between Art and Commerce," in *Paper* magazine at http://www.papermag.com/2014/03/disown_art_show.php (March 11, 2014).

56. Ibid.

57. Trecartin, interview with Kristina Lee Podesva, "When the Time Comes You Won't Understand the Battlefield," *Fillip* 13 (Spring 2011): 103.

58. Dodie Kazanjian, "The Body Eccentric," *Vogue* February 2010, 192.

Chapter 5

1. Katie Kitamura and Hari Kunzru, "Ryan Trecartin: In Conversation," *Frieze* 142 (October 2011).
2. Sarah Lehrer-Graiwer, "In the Studio: Ryan Trecartin," *Art in America*, June 2013.
3. Ibid.
4. Ibid.
5. Alexander Galloway, "Origins of the First-Person Shooter," in *Critical Visions in Film Theory: Classic and Contemporary Readings*, ed. by Timothy Corrigan, Patricia White, and Meta Mazaj (Boston: Bedford/St. Martin's, 2011), pp. 1072–84.
6. Sarah Lehrer-Graiwer, "In the Studio: Ryan Trecartin," *Art in America*, June 2013.
7. Kareem Estefan, "A Cute Idea," http://thenewinquiry.com/essays/a-cute-idea/ (February 7, 2014).
8. Ryan Trecartin et al. *Any Ever: Ryan Trecartin* (New York: Skira Rizzoli Publications in association with Elizabeth Dee, 2011), p. 144.
9. Chang, Edmond Y., "Queergaming," in *Queer Game Studies*, ed. by Bonnie Ruberg, Adrienne Shaw, and Project Muse (Minneapolis: University of Minnesota Press, 2017), pp. 15-16.
10. Janet Horowitz Murray, *Hamlet on the Holodeck: The Future of Narrative in Cyberspace* (New York: Free Press, 1997), p. 4.
11. Sarah Lehrer-Graiwer, "In the Studio: Ryan Trecartin," *Art in America*, June 2013.
12. According to A. L. Rees, *expanded cinema*, a term originally coined by Gene Youngblood in 1970, has three main characteristics: "The first was to melt down all art forms, including film, into multimedia and live-action events. The second was to explore electronic technologies and the coming of cyberspace, as heralded by Marshall McLuhan. The third was to break down the barrier between artist and audience through new kinds

of participation. Each of these challenged existing notions of cinema as a commercialized regime of passive consumption and entertainment." From A. L. Rees, *Expanded Cinema: Art, Performance, Film* (London; New York: Tate Publishing; distributed in the United States and Canada by Abrams, 2011), p. 13.

13. Ryan Trecartin and James Franco, "All-American Golden Boy," in *Another Man*, November 2010.

14. Sophia Psarra, *Architecture and Narrative: The Formation of Space and Cultural Meaning* (Milton Park, Abingdon, Oxon; New York: Routledge, 2009), p. 2.

15. Katie Kitamura and Hari Kunzru, "Ryan Trecartin: In Conversation," *Frieze* 142 (October 2011).

16. This term is used in computer engineering to describe the process by which a virtual machine executes the instructions of a computer program.

17. Of course this is meant allegorically, since realistically editing takes place in postproduction.

18. Jonathan Zittrain, *The Future of the Internet and How to Stop It* (New Haven Conn.: Yale University Press, 2008), p. 9.

19. Sarah Lehrer-Graiwer, "In the Studio: Ryan Trecartin," *Art in America*, June 2013.

20. Kevin McGarry, "The Video: Center Jenny," http://www.vmagazine.com/site/content/1845/the-video-center-jenny (2013).

21. Trecartin, interview with Kristina Lee Podesva, "When the Time Comes You Won't Understand the Battlefield," *Fillip* 13 (Spring 2011): 103.

22. Sarah Lehrer-Graiwer, "In the Studio: Ryan Trecartin," *Art in America*, June 2013.

Conclusion

1. *SITE VISIT* was exhibited at the Kunst-Werke (KW) Institute for Contemporary Art in Berlin from September 14, 2014 to February 15, 2015.

2. Ellen Blumenstein, and Thomas Miessgang. "Walking in and Out of Clarity," in *Lizzie Fitch/Ryan Trecartin: SITE VISIT* (London: Koenig Books, 2014), p. 129.

3. Anna-Lena Werner, "Ryan Trecartin: *SITE VISIT*," http://www.artfridge.de/2014/10/ryan-trecartin-site-visit.html.

4. Kevin McGarry, "Ryan," *V Magazine*, February, 2015.

5. Ibid.

6. Beau Dent, "Reading Ryan Trecartin's *SITE VISIT* @ KW," at http://www.aqnb.com/2014/09/19/ryan-trecartins-site-visit-kw-reviewed/ (2014).

7. Christopher Knight, "Lizzie Fitch & Ryan Trecartin at Regen Projects," *Los Angeles* Times, November 10, 2014.

8. Ellen Blumenstein, and Thomas Miessgang. "Society's Idiots," in *Lizzie Fitch/Ryan Trecartin*: *SITE VISIT* (London: Koenig Books, 2014), p. 45.

9. Interview between Ryan Trecartin and Ricardo E. Zulueta at the Frost Museum of Art in Miami, Florida (November 19, 2014).

10. Ellen Blumenstein and Thomas Miessgang, "Society's Idiots," in *Lizzie Fitch/Ryan Trecartin*: *SITE VISIT* (London: Koenig Books, 2014), p. 44.

11. Kevin McGarry, "Ryan," *V Magazine*, February, 2015.

12. Trecartin, interview with Kristina Lee Podesva, "When the Time Comes You Won't Understand the Battlefield," *Fillip* 13 (Spring 2011): 103.

13. https://www.youtube.com/all_comments?v=ZR4sHDR-1XE.

14. Michael Kowalinski, "Ryan Trecartin's *Any Ever*," *Dazed Digital*, June 17, 2011.

15. Andrea Rosen announced in an email to the art community that she will close her gallery after twenty-seven years. Andrew Russeth, "Andrea Rosen Gallery, a Chelsea Stalwart, 'Will No Longer Have a Typical Permanent Public Space and Therefore No Longer Represent Living Artists,'" http://www.artnews.com/2017/02/21/andrea-rosen-gallery-a-chelsea-stalwart-will-no-longer-have-a-typical-permanent-public-space-and-therefore-no-longer-represent-living-artists/ (February 21, 2017).

16. Brian Droitcour, "Past and Future Camera: Lizzie Fitch and Ryan Trecartin's New Movies," http://www.artinamericamagazine.com/news-features/news/past-and-future-camera-lizzie-fitch-and-ryan-trecartins-new-movies/ (2016).

17. Michael Connor, "Post-Internet: What It Is and What It Was," in *You Are Here*: *Art after the Internet*, ed. Omar Kholeif (Manchester, U.K.: Cornerhouse, 2014), p. 61.

18. Lauren Cornell, "Beginnings + Ends," *Frieze Magazine* (November–December 2013).

19. Timothy Morton, *Hyperobjects*: *Philosophy and Ecology after the End of the World* (University of Minnesota Press, 2013).

20. Calvin Tomkins, "Experimental People," *New Yorker*, March 24, 2014.

Filmography

A Family Finds Entertainment. Video. Directed by Ryan Trecartin, 2004.

All My Churen. Video. Directed by Kalup Linzy, 2003.

All That Heaven Allows. Film. Directed by Douglas Sirk (Universal City, CA: Universal International Pictures), 1955.

Anémic Cinéma. Film. Directed by Marcel Duchamp, 1926.

The Blair Witch Project. Film. Directed by Daniel Myrick and Eduardo Sánchez (Orlando, FL: Haxan Films), 1999.

Boys Don't Cry. Film. Directed by Kimberly Peirce (Century City, CA: Fox Searchlight Pictures), 1999.

Center Jenny. Video. Directed by Ryan Trecartin, 2013.

Coma Boat. Video. Directed by Ryan Trecartin, 2013.

Country Ball 1989–2012. Video. Directed by Jacolby Satterwhite, 2012.

The Devil Wears Prada. Film. Directed by David Frankel (Los Angeles, CA: Twentieth Century Fox), 2006.

Eclipse of the Sun Virgin. Film. Directed by George Kuchar, 1967.

Ever Is Over All. Video. Directed by Pipilotti Rist, 1997.

Far from Heaven. Film. Directed by Todd Haynes (Universal City, CA: Focus Features), 2002.

Flaming Creatures. Film. Directed by Jack Smith, 1963.

Ghosts before Breakfast. Film. Directed by Hans Richter, 1928.

The Great Train Robbery. Film. Directed by Edwin S. Porter (New York: Edison Manufacturing Company), 1903.

The Hairflip! Video. Directed by Chris Crocker, 2008.

Hiatus. Video. Directed by Ericka Beckman, 1999.

Hold Me While I'm Naked. Film. Directed by George Kuchar, 1966.

I-BE Area. Video. Directed by Ryan Trecartin, 2007.

Item Falls. Video. Directed by Ryan Trecartin, 2013.

Jack Smith and the Destruction of Atlantis. Film. Directed by Mary Jordan (Brooklyn, NY: Tongue Press), 2006.

Junior War. Video. Directed by Ryan Trecartin, 2013.

K-CoreaINC.K (section a). Video. Directed by Ryan Trecartin, 2009.

Man with a Movie Camera. Film. Directed by Dziga Vertov (Kiev, Ukraine: VUFKU), 1929.

Mark Trade. Video. Directed by Ryan Trecartin, 2016.

Mildred Pierce. Film. Directed by Michael Curtiz (Hollywood, CA: Warner Bros.), 1945.

No President. Film. Directed by Jack Smith, 1967–70.

P.opular S.ky (section ish). Video. Directed by Ryan Trecartin, 2009.

Permission Streak. Video. Directed by Ryan Trecartin, 2016.

Ready (Re'Search Wait'S). Video. Directed by Ryan Trecartin, 2010.

The Re'Search (Re'Search Wait'S). Video. Directed by Ryan Trecartin, 2010.

Retour à la Raison. Film. Directed by Man Ray, 1923.

Roamie View History Enhancement (Re'Search Wait'S). Video. Directed by Ryan Trecartin, 2010.

Semiotics of the Kitchen. Video. Directed by Martha Rosler, 1975.

Sherlock Jr. Film. Directed by Buster Keaton (Hollywood, CA: Buster Keaton Productions), 1924.

Sibling Topics (section a). Video. Directed by Ryan Trecartin, 2009.

Stunt Tank. Video. Directed by Ryan Trecartin, 2016.

Super Mario Bros. Movie. Video. Directed by Paper Rad and Cory Arcangel, 2005.

Temp Stop (Re'Search Wait'S). Video. Directed by Ryan Trecartin, 2010.

Temple Time. Video. Directed by Ryan Trecartin, 2016.

(Tommy-Chat Just E-mailed Me.). Video. Directed by Ryan Trecartin, 2006.

Valentine's Day Girl. Video. Directed by Ryan Trecartin, 2001.

Wayne's World. Film. Directed by Penelope Spheeris (Los Angeles, CA: Paramount Pictures), 1992.

Wayne's World. Video. Directed by Ryan Trecartin, 2003.

What's The Love Making Babies For. Video. Directed by Ryan Trecartin, 2003.

Whispering Pines. Video. Directed by Shana Moulton, 2002–present.

Yo! A Romantic Comedy. Video. Directed by Ryan Trecartin, 2002.

Bibliography

Adorno, Theodor, and Max Horkheimer. "The Culture Industry: Enlightenment as Mass Deception." In Critical Visions in *Film Theory: Classic and Contemporary Readings.* Edited by Timothy Corrigan, Patricia White, and Meta Mazaj. Boston: Bedford/St. Martin's, 2011.

Alvarez, Ana Cecilia. "How to Hide from Big Brother," *Dazed Digital* (March 2014). http://www.dazeddigital.com/artsandculture/article/19131/1/artists-writers-show-how-to-hide-from-big-brother-government-surveillance.

Babuscio, Jack. "The Cinema of Camp." In *Camp: Queer Aesthetics and the Performing Subject: A Reader.* Edited by Fabio Cleto. Ann Arbor: University of Michigan Press, 1999.

Bakhtin, Mikhail. *Rabelais and His World.* Cambridge, Mass.: MIT Press, 1968.

Barthes, Roland, and Andy Stafford. *The Language of Fashion.* Oxford; New York: Berg, 2006.

Bess, Gabby. "DISown Blows Away the Boundaries between Art and Commerce." *Paper Magazine* (March 11, 2014). http://www.papermag.com/2014/03/disown_art_show.php.

Blumenstein, Ellen. *Lizzie Fitch/Ryan Trecartin: Site Visit.* Koenig Books, London, 2014.

Boellstorff, Tom. "Virtuality: Placing the Virtual Body: Avatar, Chora, Cypherg." In *A Companion to the Anthropology of the Body and Embodiment.* Edited by Frances E. Mascia-Lees. Chichester, West Sussex, U.K.; Malden, Mass.: Wiley-Blackwell, 2011.

Bonami, Francesco. "The Good, the Bad, and the Ugly." *Frieze* 141 (September 2011).

Bourriaud, Nicolas, and Tate Britain. *Altermodern: Tate Triennial.* London: Tate Publishing, 2009.

——. "Altermodern Manifesto: Postmodernism Is Dead." 2009.http://www.tate.org.uk/whats-on/tate-britain/exhibition/altermodern/explain-altermodern/altermodern-explainedmanifesto.

Bourriaud, Nicolas. *Relational Aesthetics.* Dijon: Les Presses du reel, 2002.

Bridle, James. "#Hackyourfuture: Hack the word!" (July 2013). http://www.dazeddigital.com/artsandculture/article/16298/1/hackyourfuture-hack-the-word.

Brooks, Karen. “Nothing Sells Like Teen Spirit: The Commodification of Youth Culture.” *Youth Cultures: Texts, Images, and Identities*. Edited by Kerry Mallan and Sharyn Pearce. Westport, Conn.: Praeger, 2003.

Butler, Jeremy G. *Television: Critical Methods and Applications*. 4th ed. New York: Routledge, 2012.

Butler, Judith. *Gender Trouble: Feminism and the Subversion of Identity*. New York: Routledge, 1999.

Burley, Isabella. “Say Hello to ‘Avant-Normcore’ ” (March 2, 2014). http://www.dazeddigital.com/fashion/article/19081/1/say-hello-to-avant-normcore.

Calefato, Patrizia. *The Clothed Body*. New York: Berg, 2004.

Christian, Aymar Jean. “Camp 2.0: A Queer Performance of the Personal.” *Communication, Culture, & Critique* 3, no. 3 (2010).

Cooper, Dennis. “First Take, Dennis Cooper on Ryan Trecartin.” *Artforum*, January 2006.

Cornell, Lauren. “Medium Living.” In *Any Ever: Ryan Trecartin*. New York: Skira Rizzoli Publications in association with Elizabeth Dee, 2011.

———. “New Age Thinking.” In *Younger Than Jesus: The Generation Book*. Edited by Lauren Cornell and New Museum of Contemporary Art (New York). New York; Göttingen: New Museum; Steidl, 2009, pp. 19–29.

———. “Techno-animism.” *Mousse* 37, February 2013.

Cornell, Lauren, and Ed Halter. *Mass Effect: Art and the Internet in the Twenty-First Century*. MIT Press, 2015.

Crane, Diana. *Fashion and Its Social Agendas: Class, Gender, and Identity in Clothing*. Chicago: University of Chicago Press, 2000.

Davis, Douglas. “The Work of Art in the Age of Digital Reproduction (An Evolving Thesis: 1991–1995),” in *Leonardo* 28, no. 5, Third Annual New York Digital Salon. (1995): 381–86.

Dent, Beau. “Reading Ryan Trecartin’s *SITE VISIT* @ KW,” http://www.aqnb.com/2014/09/19/ryan-trecartins-site-visit-kw-reviewed/.

Doty, Alexander. *Flaming Classics: Queering the Film Canon*. New York: Routledge, 2000.

Droitcour, Brian. “Past and Future Camera: Lizzie Fitch and Ryan Trecartin’s New Movies,” 2016. http://www.artinamericamagazine.com/

news-features/news/past-and-future-camera-lizzie-fitch-and-ryan-trecartins-new-movies/.

Drucker, Susan J., and Gary Gumpert. *Regulating Convergence*. New York: Peter Lang, 2010.

Duffy, Brooke E., Tara Liss-Marino, and Katherine Sender. "Reflexivity in Television Depictions of Media Industries: Peeking Behind the Gilt Curtain." *Communication, Culture & Critique* 4, no. 3 (September 2011).

Duggan, Ginger Gregg, and Judith Hoos Fox. "Characters on Parade: Contemporary Character Design Invades the Catwalk." In *Not a Toy: Radical Character Design in Fashion and Costume*. Berlin: Pictoplasma, 2011.

Dyer, Richard. *Now You See It: Studies on Lesbian and Gay Film*. 2nd ed. London; New York: Routledge, 2003.

Dyer, Richard. *Pastiche*. London; New York: Routledge, 2007.

Elsaesser, Thomas. "Tales of Sound and Fury: Observations on the Family Melodrama." In *Home Is Where the Heart Is: Studies in Melodrama and the Woman's Film*. Edited by C. Gledhill. London: British Film Institute, 1987.

Entwistle, Joanne. "Fashion and the Fleshy Body: Dress as Embodied Practice," in *Fashion Theory* 4, no. 3 (2000).

Falconer, Rachel. "Rebooting the Relationship between Art and Tech," January 29, 2014. http://www.theguardian.com/technology/2014/jan/29/rebooting-the-relationship-between-art-and-tech.

Fiske, John. *Television Culture*. London; New York: Methuen, 1987.

Flinn, Caryl. "The Deaths of Camp." In *Camp: Queer Aesthetics and the Performing Subject: A Reader*. Edited by Fabio Cleto, Ann Arbor: University of Michigan Press, 1999.

Ford, Whitney. "The Q&A: Ryan Trecartin, Video Artist, 2010.http://moreintelligentlife.com/blog/whitney-ford/qa-ryan-trecartin.

Freeman, Elizabeth. *Time Binds: Queer Temporalities, Queer Histories*. Perverse Modernities. Durham N.C.: Duke University Press, 2010.

Galloway, Alexander. "Origins of the First-Person Shooter." In *Critical Visions in Film Theory: Classic and Contemporary Readings*. Edited by Timothy Corrigan, Patricia White, and Meta Mazaj. Boston: Bedford/St. Martin's, 2011.

Gibson, Pamela Church. *Fashion and Celebrity Culture*. Oxford; New York: Berg Publishers, 2012.

Gioni, Massimiliano. "We Are Too Many." In *Younger Than Jesus: The Generation Book*. Edited by Lauren Cornell and New Museum of Contemporary Art (New York). New York; Göttingen: New Museum; Steidl, 2009, pp. 31–43.

Goldberg, RoseLee. *Performance Art: From Futurism to the Present*. Thames & Hudson World of Art. 3rd ed. New York: Thames & Hudson, 2011.

Granata, Francesca. "Decentering Fashion: Carnival Performance and the Grotesque Body." In *Not a Toy: Radical Character Design in Fashion and Costume*. Berlin: Pictoplasma, 2011.

Granata, Francesca. *Experimental Fashion: Performance Art, Carnival and the Grotesque Body*. I. B.Tauris, 2017.

Grosz, Elizabeth. "Bodies and Pleasures in Queer Theory." *Who Can Speak? Authority and Critical Identity*. Edited by Judith Roof and Robyn Wiegman. Urbana: University of Illinois Press, 1995.

Haig, John H., Andrew Nathaniel. *The New Nelson Japanese-English Character Dictionary*. Rutland, Vt. Tokyo: C. E. Tuttle Co., 1997.

Halberstam, Judith. *In a Queer Time and Place: Transgender Bodies, Subcultural Lives*. New York: New York University Press, 2005.

Handy, Bruce. "He Called Me Ellen Degenerate?" *Time* (April 13, 1997).

Helfand, Jessica. *Screen: Essays on Graphic Design, New Media, and Visual Culture*. New York: Princeton Architectural Press, 2001.

Hoberman, J. *Jack Smith and His Secret Flix*. Program Notes for the American Museum of the Moving Image, January 5, 1998.

Hoptman, Laura. "Them." In *Younger Than Jesus: The Generation Book*. Edited by Lauren Cornell and New Museum of Contemporary Art (New York). New York; Göttingen: New Museum; Steidl, 2009, pp. 45–54.

Hothi, Ajay RS, and Christabel Stewart. "Pop Eats Itself." In *Tank Magazine* 53, May 2011.

Howes, David. *Empire of the Senses: The Sensual Culture Reader*. Oxford: Berg, 2005.

Jones, Amelia. *Self/Image: Technology, Representation, and the Contemporary Subject*. London; New York: Routledge, 2006.

K-Hole. "Youth Mode: A Report on Freedom by K-Hole and Box 1824," 2015. http://khole.net/.

Kazanjian, Dodie. "The Body Eccentric." *Vogue*, February 2010.

Kennedy, Randy. "His Nonlinear Reality, and Welcome to It." *New York Times*, February 1, 2009, Arts and Entertainment, p. 1(L).

Kholeif, Omar. *Moving Image*. Cambridge, Mass.: MIT Press, 2015.

Kitamura, Katie, and Hari Kunzru. "Ryan Trecartin: In Conversation." *Frieze* 142 (October 2011).

Klinger, Barbara. *Melodrama and Meaning: History, Culture, and the Films of Douglas Sirk*. Bloomington: Indiana University Press, 1994.

Koestenbaum, Wayne. "Situation Hacker." *Artforum* 47, no. 10 (Summer 2009).

Kowalinski, Michael. "Ryan Trecartin's *Any Ever*." *Dazed Digital* (June 17, 2011). http://www.dazeddigital.com/artsandculture/article/10618/1/ryan-trecartins-any-ever.

Kramer, David Jacob. "Controlling the Chaos." *Paper*, June 17, 2011.Krause-Wahl, Antje. "Between Studio and Catwalk—Artists in Fashion Magazines," in *Fashion Theory* 13, no. 1 (2009).

Kristeva, Julia. *Powers of Horror: An Essay on Abjection*. New York: Columbia University Press, 1982.

Lange, Jennifer. "Interview with Director Ryan Trecartin" (May 20, 2008). http://wexarts.org/blog/interview-director-ryan-trecartin.

Lehrer-Graiwer, Sarah. "In the Studio: Ryan Trecartin." *Art in America*, June 2013.

Littleton, Darryl, and Tuezdae Littleton. *Comediennes: Laugh Be a Lady*. Milwaukee, Wis.: Applause Theatre & Cinema Books, 2012.

Lubow, Arthur. "Ryan's Web." *W* 11, 2010.

Manovich, Lev, "What Is Digital Cinema?" In *Critical Visions in Film Theory: Classic and Contemporary Readings*. Edited by Timothy Corrigan, Patricia White, and Meta Mazaj. Boston: Bedford/St. Martin's, 2011.

McGarry, Kevin. "Ryan." *V Magazine*, February 2015.

——. *Ryan Trecartin*, Hammer Projects Catalogue. Los Angeles: Hammer Museum, 2008.

——. "The Video: Center Jenny," 2013. http://www.vmagazine.com/site/content/1845/the-video-center-jenny.

———. "Worlds Apart." In *Any Ever: Ryan Trecartin*. New York: Skira Rizzoli Publications in association with Elizabeth Dee, 2011.

Meigh-Andrews, Chris. *A History of Video Art: The Development of Form and Function*. Oxford; New York: Berg, 2006.

Mercer, John, and Martin Shingler. *Melodrama: Genre, Style, Sensibility*. London; New York: Wallflower, 2004.

Morton, Timothy. *Hyperobjects: Philosophy and Ecology after the End of the World*. University of Minnesota Press, 2013.

Muñoz, José Esteban. *Disidentifications: Queers of Color and the Performance of Politics*. Minneapolis: University of Minnesota Press, 1999.

Murray, Janet Horowitz. *Hamlet on the Holodeck: The Future of Narrative in Cyberspace*. New York: Free Press, 1997.

Nakamura, Lisa. *Cybertypes: Race, Ethnicity, and Identity on the Internet*. New York: Routledge, 2002.

Nayar, Pramod K. *An Introduction to New Media and Cybercultures*. Chichester, West Sussex, U.K.; Malden, MA: Wiley-Blackwell, 2010.

Neale, Steve. "Melodrama and Tears," in *Screen* 27, no. 6 (1986): 6–22.

Niedzviecki, Hal. *The Peep Diaries: How We're Learning to Love Watching Ourselves and Our Neighbors*. San Francisco, CA: City Lights Books, 2009.

Norden, Linda. "When the Rainbow Is an Option." In *Any Ever: Ryan Trecartin*. New York: Skira Rizzoli Publications in association with Elizabeth Dee, 2011.

Nowell-Smith, Geoffrey. "Minelli and Melodrama," *Screen* 18, no. 2 (Summer 1977): 113–19.

Oswell, David. "A Question of Belonging: Television, Youth and the Domestic." In *Cool Places: Geographies of Youth Cultures*. Edited by Tracey Skelton and Gill Valentine. London: Routledge, 1998.

Petrella, Ivan. "Queer Eye for the Straight Guy: The Making Over of Liberation Theology, A Queer Discursive Approach." In *Liberation Theology and Sexuality*. Edited by Marcella Althaus-Reid. England; Burlington, Vt.: Ashgate, 2006.

Perrin, Ellen C. *Sexual Orientation in Child and Adolescent Health Care*. New York: Kluwer Academic, 2002.

Phillips, Lisa. "Director's Foreword." In *Younger Than Jesus: The Generation*

Book. Edited by Lauren Cornell and New Museum of Contemporary Art (New York). New York; Göttingen: New Museum; Steidl, 2009.

Psarra, Sophia. *Architecture and Narrative: The Formation of Space and Cultural Meaning*. Milton Park, Abingdon, Oxon; New York: Routledge, 2009.

Pulitzer, Sam. "Ryan Trecartin." *Artforum* (September 2011).

Rees, A. L. *A History of Experimental Film and Video: From the Canonical Avant-Garde to Contemporary British Practice*. London: BFI Publishing, 1999.

———. *Expanded Cinema: Art, Performance, Film*. London New York: Tate Publisher. Distributed in the United States and Canada by Abrams, 2011.

Roberts, John. *The Intangibilities of Form: Skill and Deskilling in Art after the Readymade*. London; New York: Verso, 2007.

Robertson, Adi. "Inside *High Fidelity*, the Virtual Reality Successor to '*Second Life*'" (May 19, 2014). http://www.theverge.com/2014/5/19/5732386/high-fidelity-philip-rosendale-telepresence-second-life-hands-on.

Ruberg, Bonnie, Adrienne Shaw, and Project Muse. *Queer Game Studies*. Minneapolis: University of Minnesota Press, 2017.

Russeth, Andrew. "Andrea Rosen Gallery, a Chelsea Stalwart, 'Will No Longer Have a Typical Permanent Public Space and Therefore No Longer Represent Living Artists'" (February, 21, 2017). http://www.artnews.com/2017/02/21 andrea-rosen-gallery-a-chelsea-stalwart-will-no-longer-have-a-typical-permanent-public-space-and-therefore-no-longer-represent-living-artists/.

Sanchez, Michael. "2011," in *Artforum*, Summer 2013, 295–301.

Shattuc, Jane. *Television, Tabloids, and Tears Fassbinder and Popular Culture*. Minneapolis: University of Minnesota Press, 1994.

Schatz, Thomas. *Hollywood Genres: Formulas, Filmmaking, and the Studio System*. Philadelphia: Temple University Press, 1981.

Schjeldahl, Peter. "Party On: Ryan Trecartin at P.S. 1." *New Yorker*, June 27, 2011, p. 84.

Sedgwick, Eve Kosofsky. *Tendencies*. Durham, N.C.: Duke University Press, 1993.

Silber, Jon. "Interview with Ryan Trecartin, Video Artist, 'Any Ever,'" 2011. http://www.creativeplanetnetwork.com/dv/feature/interview-ryan-trecartin-video-artist-any-ever/16738.

Silberman, Steve. "We're Teen, We're Queer, and We've Got E-mail." In *The Columbia Reader on Lesbians and Gay Men in Media, Society, and Politics*. Edited by Larry P. Gross and James D. Woods. New York: Columbia University Press, 1999.

Sitney, P. Adams. *Visionary Film: The American Avant-Garde, 1943–2000*. 3rd ed. Oxford; New York: Oxford University Press, 2002.

Smith, Terry. *What Is Contemporary Art?* Chicago: University of Chicago Press, 2009.

Smith, Roberta. "Like Living, Only More So." *New York Times*, June 24, 2011, Arts and Entertainment, C25.

Sontag, Susan. "Notes on 'Camp.'" In *Camp: Queer Aesthetics and the Performing Subject: A Reader*. Edited by Fabio Cleto. Triangulations. Ann Arbor: University of Michigan Press, 1999.

Sonvilla-Weiss, Stefan. *Mashup Cultures*. Vienna; New York: Springer-Verlag, 2010.

Stam, Robert. *Reflexivity in Film and Literature: From Don Quixote to Jean-Luc Godard*. Ann Arbor, MI: UMI Research Press, 1985.

———. *Subversive Pleasures: Bakhtin, Cultural Criticism, and Film*. Parallax. Baltimore, Md.: Johns Hopkins University Press, 1989.

Steele, Bruce C. "Justifying Our Love: Pedro Zamora." *Advocate*, November 12, 2012.

Stein, Joel. "Millennials: The Me Me Me Generation" (May 20, 2013). http://time.com/247/millennials-the-me-me-me-generation/.

Stoschek, Julia, and Julia Stoschek Foundation. *Collection Number Six: Flaming Creatures* [in Parallel text in English and German], vol. 1. Deutschland: Hatje Cantz, 2013.

Swanberg, Joe. "*A Family Finds Entertainment*: An Ongoing Discussion with Ryan Trecartin," 2007. http://www.filmbrats.com/editorials/ryantrecartin.html.

Taylor, Jodie. *Playing It Queer: Popular Music, Identity and Queer World-Making*. Bern: Peter Lang, 2012.

Tenhaaf, Nell. "Mysteries of the Bioapparatus." In Immersed in *Technology: Art and Virtual Environments*. Edited by Mary Anne Moser and Douglas MacLeod. Cambridge, Mass.: MIT Press, 1996.

Tomkins, Calvin. "Experimental People." *New Yorker*, March 24, 2014.

Trecartin, Ryan. "Ryan's Web 1.0," 2010. http://dismagazine.com/dysmorphia/9844/ryan-trecartin-w-magazine/.

Trecartin, Ryan, and James Franco. "All-American Golden Boy." *Another Man*. November 2010.

Trecartin, Ryan, Kevin McGarry, Lauren Cornell, Lizzie Fitch, Linda Norden, Cindy Sherman, and Jeffrey Deitch. *Any Ever: Ryan Trecartin*. New York: Skira Rizzoli Publications in association with Elizabeth Dee, 2011.

Trecartin, Ryan and Kristina Lee Podesva. "When the Time Comes You Won't Understand the Battlefield." *Fillip* 13 (Spring 2011).

Tudor, Matilda. *Cyberqueer Techno-Practices: Digital Space-Making and Networking among Swedish Gay Men*. MA thesis, Stockholm University, 2012.

Turner, Victor. "Carnival in Rio: Dionysian Drama in an Industrialized Society." In *The Anthropology of Performance*. New York: PAJ Publications, 1986.

Vernallis, Carol. *Experiencing Music Video: Aesthetics and Cultural Context*. Columbia University Press, 2004.

Wakeford, Nina. "Cyberqueer." In *Sexualities: Critical Concepts in Sociology*. Edited by Kenneth Plummer. Routledge, 2002.

Wara, Agatha. "What Does Nike Want?" (May 24, 2012). http://dismagazine.com/dystopia/evolved-lifestyles/32718/what-does-nike-want/.

Warr, Tracey, and Amelia Jones. *The Artist's Body*. New York: Phaidon, 2012.

Werner, Anna-Lena. "Ryan Trecartin: *SITE VISIT*," 2014. http: //www.artfridge.de/2014/10/ryan-trecartin-site-visit.html.

Wiley, Chris. "We Have a Situation." *Frieze* 142 (October 2011).

Zimmermann, Patricia R. "An Amateurized Media Universe." *Jump Cut* 55 (Fall 2013).

Zittrain, Jonathan. *The Future of the Internet and How to Stop It*. New Haven, Conn.: Yale University Press, 2008.

Index